THE ASYLUM
OF
HOWARD HUGHES

THE ASYLUM
OF
HOWARD HUGHES

Jack G. Real

with

Bill Yenne

To order additional copies of this book, contact:
Xlibris Corporation
1-888-795-4274
www.Xlibris.com
Orders@Xlibris.com
19043

CONTENTS

This book is dedicated to my wife, Janeth,
whose love endured a lifetime. During the last three years
of Howard's life, I was living with him and was away
from her much of the time. She visited me twice in England
during 1973 and during the winter of 1975-1976,
she spent four months in the Bahamas with me.

She was a serious diabetic with most of her arteries gone,
and when Howard and I moved to Mexico in February 1976,
I put her in the Jackson Memorial Hospital in Miami.
Later, my son drove her home to California from Miami.
She died in 1994.

It was her hope that someday I would write a book
about my life with Howard. She wanted the truth to be told.

Janeth, this book is for you!

FRONTISPIECE

The eight-year period that Jack and I were so closely associated, beginning with Howard Hughes' death in 1976 and ending with the sale by the Hughes estate of Hughes Helicopters to McDonnell Douglas in 1984, was a time of continuous crisis in the Hughes estate, a time of numerous crises which I will not elaborate on but will say threatened the very survival of the estate and the Hughes business empire.

These crises at the estate level ran parallel to and were greatly magnified by crises at Hughes Helicopters. In the fall of 1979, when Jack was brought in to take charge of this faltering company, he tore into our problems with unbelievable force and energy, performing radical surgery on the vital organs of the company with remarkable tact, skill, and deftness and in very short order. In four short years, he addressed and worked through the myriad of problems throughout the company, facing them and finding solutions to problems that I thought were impossible.

It is not nearly as widely known as it should be, but Jack Real presided over one of the most remarkable major corporate turnarounds in the annals of American business. For this, Jack earned the lasting gratitude of all of us who were responsible for the Hughes Estate and its survival.

Finally, Jack is a particularly appropriate recipient of the Howard Hughes Memorial Award because of his close personal relationship with Hughes himself, particularly during the last three years of his life.

Indeed Jack Real was Howard Hughes' last best friend.

—William Rice "Will" Lummis, the first cousin of Howard Robard

Hughes (and the administrator of his estate) speaking at the presentation of the Howard Hughes Memorial Award to Jack Real on January 24, 1991 at the Hughes Flying Boat, Long Beach, California.

FOREWORD

By Hal Klopper

Manager of Communications
The Boeing Company, Mesa, Arizona
Rotorcraft Unit, formerly Hughes Helicopters, Inc.

In 1971, Howard Hughes offered Jack Garrett Real the opportunity to run his entire aviation empire, which included the Hughes Aircraft Company and Hughes AirWest. By doing so, the reclusive billionaire once again demonstrated his trust, faith and unconditional backing of his best friend and confidant. Jack Real didn't take this offer lightly and it is one of the many yet untold stories about Howard Hughes that Real recalls in this book with remarkable detail and clarity.

Many of the stories that follow have never been published before. Amazingly, being Howard Hughes' closest confidant was only a full-time "second job" for Jack Real. Jack's own accomplishments through 60 years in the aviation industry have earned him the respect and admiration of his peers and co-workers, and the right to tell his own story.

From 1939 to 1971, Jack Real helped build the fortunes of the Lockheed Aircraft Company. He had served the aviation giant for 32 years before joining Howard as Vice President of the Hughes Tool Company's Aviation Division.

Over the years, Real found himself building a career with Lockheed during the day and spending his nights flying with Hughes in one of his planes or chatting endlessly about everything under the sun. When Hughes became reclusive, Real continued to communicate with him by phone or by hand-written memos, frequently on a daily basis. The billionaire often turned to his trusted friend to bail him out of a financial jam or get him to a new safe haven without anyone knowing.

Jack Real had a unique perspective on the life of Howard Hughes and the closed world in which he lived. Now, more than a quarter century after the death of Howard Hughes, Jack Real is ready to tell his story.

ACKNOWLEDGEMENTS

Jack Real and Bill Yenne would like to thank the following people who have been extremely helpful in providing aid and encouragement in the process of telling this story.

Hal Klopper, Manager of Communications for the Boeing Company's Rotorcraft unit in Mesa, Arizona (formerly Hughes Helicopters, Inc.): Hal spent four years helping to develop many of the stories for this project, interviewing Jack on frequent occasions, and researching the details about Howard Hughes that Jack kept stored in his head and on paper. We owe a great deal to Hal for his tireless efforts and his belief that this book should be published.

Ben Schemmer, former publisher of *The Armed Forces Journal*:
A friend of Jack's since 1965, Ben was the early supporter of this project. As Jack puts it, "he taught me how to use commas. He was a great supporter."

George Francom, a former aide to Howard Hughes:
Jack recalls that George was "the best of Howard's aides. He would always get me to Howard." He was Jack's loyal friend for the last 10 years of Howard's life.

Tony Blackman:
Tony was the British pilot who brought life back to Howard in London, and he has continued to be a friend to Jack ever since. He is not only a great pilot, but also a great writer.

In addition, Gordon Margulis and Mell Stewart provided valuable support to Howard and to Jack.

Azia Yenne and Melody Lee for their help in transcribing the many hours of taped conversations that form the basis for this book.

Finally, we are indebted to Bob Maheu for his support through the years, and for tirelessly encouraging the completion of this project.

PROLOGUE

By Jack Real

There was a 20-year window in my six-decade involvement with aviation that was unbelievably exciting and challenging, and Howard Hughes made it so! In those 20 years, I believe I was as close to him as any man. He was interesting, imaginative, highly intelligent, different, and uncompromising—the ever indomitable Howard Hughes.

CHAPTER 1

OUR EARLY YEARS

THE PARALLEL LIVES OF
HOWARD HUGHES AND JACK REAL

I was born in the Upper Peninsula of Michigan on May 31, 1915, nearly a decade after Howard Robard Hughes was born in Texas on Christmas Eve in 1905. By the time that I had reached my teens, Howard's was not yet a household name, but he was already establishing himself in the first industry upon which he would make his mark, the movies. I was just an impressionable high school kid when I saw *Hell's Angels*, which Howard produced, and which was released in 1930. I was already impressed with the wonders of aviation, and I especially remember this film for the great World War I flying scenes, laboriously recreated using actual World War I aircraft.

Little did I know at the time, that aviation would bring the two of us together, and that I would become Howard's closest advisor on aviation matters for the last two decades of his life.

My family had lived in Michigan for two generations, Howard's roots were in Texas, but just barely. Howard's father, Howard Robard Hughes, Sr., moved to the Lone Star State in 1901, hoping to strike it rich in the Texas oil boom. Using the skills he had picked up working as a hard rock miner in Missouri, the senior Hughes worked his way from one oil patch to the next, and he had amassed a modest nest egg by the time he married Allene Gano in Dallas in 1904. The turning point in his business career came in 1908, when he invented a particularly effective drilling bit. In

August 1909, the Hughes empire was born when Howard's father patented his amazing drilling tool.

Later that year, the Hughes family moved to Houston, where Howard's father established the factory which still manufactures the Hughes' patented bits. Howard Robard Hughes, Sr. discovered that he was a much better salesman than he was a hands-on oil man, so he spent most of his time on the road, promoting his drill bit, while Allene raised their young son, Howard.

Houston and the Texas Gulf Coast teemed with disease-carrying insects, and in those years before antibiotics, the fear of illness was a common preoccupation, especially for an overprotective mother with a somewhat sickly only child. This was almost certainly the origin of Howard's later obsession with germs for which he is repeatedly caricatured.

On the other hand, Howard had a brilliant analytical mind. Even without formal training, he was intuitively, an extraordinary engineer. Like his father, he had an exceptional ability to understand machines and how they work. Just as his father had designed the famous drilling bit, Howard would play an important role in designing a series of airplanes.

Howard's mother passed away in 1922, and his father died in 1924, leaving him an orphan at 17, and suddenly a very rich young man. His share of the estate was worth more than half a million dollars, a considerable sum for 1924, and the equivalent of what would be *six million* in turn of the century dollars.

His next move was very out of character for the average orphaned rich kid, but very much in keeping with the business instinct that Howard would display during the coming years. Instead of cashing out and taking the money, Howard raised additional cash to buy out the other heirs, the members of his father's family.

The fight with his own family for control of the Hughes Tool Company helped to define Howard as a businessman, just as the resulting alienation between him and the rest of his family helped to define Howard as a man. By the time that he turned 19, Howard was a millionaire and the owner of the Hughes Tool Company, although he had to petition the court to treat him as an adult.

By the time he was 20, Howard had written the only known will that he ever signed. By this time he had also, like his aunt Annette, married Ella Rice, the 22-year-old grand-niece of Rice Institute founder William Marsh Rice. A few months after their June 1925 wedding, Howard and Ella left Houston for California. Though he would later, for income tax purposes, insist that he was always a Texas resident, Howard never lived in the state again. In fact, during the rest of his life, he made only one single, 24-hour visit to Texas.

The Hughes Tool Company, meanwhile, would continue to grow and flourish for nearly half a century with minimal involvement on his part.

Howard's big dream when he moved to California in 1925 was to go into the movies, not as an actor, although he was classically tall, dark and handsome, but as a producer. The Hollywood scene was just then getting going, and Howard would be part of it during its golden age. He started a film company and hired an accountant named Noah Dietrich, who would remain as his right-hand man until 1957, shortly before I started working closely with him.

Nearly everyone in Howard's family insisted that he was crazy. They were sure that he was going to lose the family fortune producing movies, but this made Howard all the more determined to succeed. After one low-budget flop, his company produced a series of hits that culminated in *Hell's Angels*.

In the meantime, Howard's preoccupation with his movies and his new love of flying left little time for his wife, and Ella left him. Though the divorce was not final until the end of 1929, Howard was already on the way to developing the image and the swinging lifestyle of the rich, young and desirable Hollywood bachelor. Howard "discovered" screen goddess Jean Harlow and gave her the first significant acting role of her career in *Hell's Angels*.

For all of his reputation as a dashing man-about-town, Howard was truly a very shy person. He had a natural inclination to avoid the Hollywood party circuit and did not plunge into social entanglements. This inaccessibility certainly must have added to his reputation and his mystique. In later years, as he withdrew from society completely, his image as a man of mystery was certainly magnified to the extreme by this trait.

On the last day of June 1930, on the same day that *Hell's Angels* premiered, Howard acquired a building at 7000 Romaine Street in Hollywood. This was to remain the center of his empire for three decades. While Noah Dietrich maintained his office at Romaine Street until Howard fired him in 1957, Howard himself never actually kept regular office hours there, or anywhere. Howard did not even set foot in this building during the last two decades of his life, but the Romaine Street communications center would become virtually the only conduit between Howard and the outside world. This was especially true during the sixties, when he was in Las Vegas, and after he chose to permanently live outside the United States in 1970. The building on Romaine Street was the important repository of his private papers, and master prints of his films.

IN THE AIR

The thirties saw Howard's interests moving more toward aviation. Charles Lindbergh's solo conquest of the Atlantic in May 1927 had sparked a great deal of popular interest in flying, and it was certainly on the minds of many young men, Howard and I included. Howard was so anxious to become involved, that, in 1933, he actually signed on as a pilot with American Airways under an assumed name! After he made one transcontinental flight, his secret was discovered and he was forced to quit.

Howard turned to air racing and won first place in the 1934 All-American Air Meet in Florida. It would not be long before his proclivity for engineering led him to build a racing airplane of his own design. He leased some space in a hangar at the Grand Central Air Terminal in Glendale, California and created the "Aircraft Development Group" of the Hughes Tool Company. This later officially became the "Aircraft Division" of the Hughes Tool Company Built under a cloak of complete secrecy was the remarkable Hughes H-1, an all-metal monoplane that was one of the most advanced aircraft of its day.

When the H-1 was ready to fly, there was only one choice of a test pilot, Howard, himself. Howard achieved speeds in excess of 300 mph on his first flight in the H-1 on August 18, 1935. This was amazing given that the world speed record at the time was only 314 mph. Less than a month later, on September 13, he took his new airplane down to Santa Ana for an assault on the world speed record. With an average of 352.38 mph on several passes over the closed course, Howard and his silver bird shattered the record. However, the day ended rather ignominiously for Howard when he ran out of gas and had to make a wheels-up crash landing in a beet field.

Four months later, Howard Hughes was back in the headlines for yet another aviation milestone. Flying a Northrop Gamma that he leased from Jacqueline Cochran, another ambitious young air racer, Howard succeeded in setting a transcontinental speed record of 259 mph, flying non-stop from Burbank, California to Newark, New Jersey in nine hours, 26 minutes and 10 seconds. He broke his radio antenna on takeoff, so he was out of touch with the ground for the entire flight, a situation that certainly kept the media guessing. Of course, this was an omen of things to come, because as the years went by, speculating about the whereabouts of Howard Hughes would become the favorite media pastime.

The next goal for Howard would be what was for that era, the crowning achievement in aviation, a record-breaking flight around the world. He elected to use a twin-engine airliner, the Super Electra for this undertaking. It was one of the fastest airplanes in the world, and it had sufficient range.

On the evening of July 10, 1938, Howard took off from New York City's Floyd Bennett Field with a four-man crew, bound, he said, for Paris. Charles Lindbergh's flight 11 years before still stood as the record time between the two cities, and Howard claimed that he planned to beat it. He did. His time of 16 hours and 38 minutes cut Lucky Lindy's by half. Of course, Howard had 11 years of the leaps and bounds in aviation technology on his side.

On the afternoon of July 14, Howard brought the ship down at Floyd Bennett Field. After a record flight of three days, 19 hours, and 17 minutes, Howard was greeted by a huge throng of well-wishers. The following day, he got a ticker tape parade in New York City, and took a well-earned place in the pantheon of aviation history. On July 30, Howard flew the Super Electra on to a triumphal return to Houston. After less than a day in the town where he grew up, and where he had lost both his parents, Howard headed back to Burbank, California. He would never lay his eyes on Houston or the Hughes Tool Company factory again.

By this time, I was well aware of Howard Hughes and his successes. Little did I realize that two decades later, he and I would be sharing a cockpit several times a week in the skies over Southern California.

MY OWN ROAD TO BURBANK

I graduated from Michigan Tech in 1937 with a bachelor's degree in mechanical engineering. This was the depths of the Great Depression, and I was fortunate to get a job right away. This first job was with Western Electric in Chicago, but it was really just a training program. In the spring of 1939, the Lockheed Aircraft Company ran a classified advertisement in *The Chicago Tribune*, soliciting engineers. I passed the test that they gave to the applicants and headed west. Within a year of reaching California in the summer of 1939, Lockheed had promoted me to senior design engineer on the Model 18 Lodestar, which was similar to the Super Electra that Howard had used for his round-the-world flight.

In 1945, Lockheed assigned me to work for the company's chief of research and development, Clarence "Kelly" Johnson. He was the legendary engineer who would later head up the Lockheed Advanced Products Division. Kelly had a straightforward, no-nonsense approach to aircraft design, which resulted in some of the most technologically advanced aircraft in the world at the time, including the revolutionary P-38 Lightning and America's first operational jet fighter, the P-80 Shooting Star. Kelly Johnson and a hand-picked team were virtually sealed into a canvas-roofed building next to the Lockheed wind tunnel and told to design and build a prototype jet fighter in 180 days, and they did. This was the beginning of the Lockheed Advanced Development Projects (ADP) office, which continues to be known as the "Skunk Works."

HOWARD'S AVIATION TRIUMPHS AND TRAGEDIES

Having returned to California in triumph from his flight around the world in 1938, Howard set about to expand his business empire. In May 1939, he began buying stock in an airline called Transcontinental & Western Air (TWA), which would later become world famous as TransWorld Airlines, or by its initials. Though he never had any management role at TWA, Howard would wield tremendous power for the next two decades by virtue of his being the airline's majority shareholder. Though the management sometimes had a hard time grasping it, TWA was *his* airline.

Howard also returned briefly to movie-making with *The Outlaw*, a film best remembered as the first movie to star sex goddess Jane Russell. Meanwhile, trivia buffs remember Howard's involvement best because of the bra that he designed for Jane to wear in the movie.

By the time that World War II began, Howard's interests had definitely turned away from Hollywood movies and back to aviation. The Hughes Tool Company Aircraft Division in Culver City, near what is now the Los Angeles International Airport, was the center of his life. For the sake of clarity, it should be pointed out that Howard actually owned two aircraft companies. In 1934, he had formed the Aircraft Development Group as a subsidiary of the Hughes Tool Company. This soon became the Aircraft Division of the tool company. In 1935, he formed the Hughes Aircraft Company, which was never associated with the Hughes Tool Company. The Aircraft *Division* built Howard's airplanes and eventually became a successful manufacturer of helicopters. In 1972, it would become the Hughes Helicopter Division (although it was known as the Hughes Helicopter Company). In 1953, ownership of the Hughes Aircraft *Company* passed to the Howard Hughes Medical Institute, after which it became an extraordinarily successful manufacturer of missiles and electronics, and eventually of communications satellites. After Howard passed away, the Hughes Helicopter Company was sold to McDonnell Douglas, and the Hughes Aircraft Company was sold to General Motors.

During World War II, Howard conceived the idea for his second airplane, which he hoped to sell to the US Army Air Corps (US Army Air Forces, USAAF, after June 1941). Originally, it was to have been designated H-2, but he changed it to D-2 to reflect a revolutionary new construction process called Duramold that involved molding resin-impregnated plywood into large aircraft parts. Howard and the Hughes Tool Company Aircraft Division were unable to interest the government in the idea of a wooden airplane, so he undertook, paying the D-2 out of his own pocket. In May 1942, partially because of the respect that President Roosevelt himself had for Howard's accomplishments in aviation, the USAAF ordered a Hughes Duramold airplane.

Two of the D-2 were completed, and Howard took one of them up on its first flight on June 20, 1943 from a secret test center located at Harper's Dry Lake in the Mojave Desert. The short-lived story of the D-2 ended on November 11, when lightning struck the hangar that contained the two wooden aircraft, starting a fire that destroyed them both. In the meantime, USAAF Commanding General Henry Harley "Hap" Arnold ordered General Oliver Echols, the USAAF Materiel Command procurement chief, to order Hughes Duramold aircraft for photoreconnaissance duties under the designation XF-11.

World War II ended before the engines were available for the aircraft. By the spring of 1946 the first XF-11 was ready for tests. The first flight was scheduled for July 7. Howard took off from Culver City at 5:20 pm, and the flight went so well that Howard let the planned 45-minute flight stretch out to 75 minutes. Suddenly, he experienced strong drag on the right wing. He was rapidly losing altitude as he tried to compensate for the problem and diagnose the cause. He said later that it felt as though "some giant had the right wing of the airplane in his hand and was pushing it back and down."

Howard initially assumed that some portion of the airplane had broken off and was causing the drag, so he tried to compensate for the problem by throttling back the left engine to balance the two. In fact, a loss of hydraulic fluid had caused the rear part of the right propeller to reverse pitch, resulting in the severe drag and loss of lift on the right side.

He attempted an emergency landing on the Los Angeles Country Club golf course, but the XF-11 went down 300 feet short, crashing into the Beverly Hills home of Lieutenant Colonel Charles Meyer, who was away in Nuremberg, Germany serving as an interpreter at the War Crimes Trials. Both house and airplane were completely destroyed in the ensuing fire.

Howard was pulled from the wreckage by a Marine Corps sergeant named William Durkin, who was at a house nearby. He had saved Howard's life, but Howard was severely injured. Howard was taken to Good Samaritan Hospital. He arrived conscious, although he was given only a 50-50 chance of survival. He reportedly hovered near death for several days before improving rather rapidly. Howard would live for another 30 years, but he never fully recovered.

He had burns on his left chest wall, his left ear, his left buttocks, and his left hand. There were multiple lacerations, as well as bruises and abrasions over his entire body, and his internal injuries were much more serious. He had suffered a contusion to his heart. His first three right ribs were broken, including damage to the first costochondral junction. Also fractured were his left clavicle and his seventh cervical vertebra, involving the right transverse and right articular facets between his sixth and seventh vertebrae, with an anterior displacement of the sixth on the seventh. He suffered hemorrhaging into his superior mediastinum and around his esophagus, which caused esophageal obstruction for four days. He suffered subcutaneous emphysema in his right and left chest walls. He had also received a scar on his upper lip that he would cover with a mustache for the rest of his life.

From the first hours that he was admitted, and through his entire hospital stay, the physicians in charge of Howard's care were

Dr. Lawrence Chaffin and Dr. Verne Mason. Dr. Chaffin had been Howard's doctor since 1932 and, three decades later, he would be the last doctor to attend him during the last hours before he died. Dr. Mason was an internist who was popular with personalities in the entertainment industry, and who had seen Howard periodically since 1937.

To ease Howard's pain and to prevent shock, Dr. Mason initially prescribed morphine. Howard left the hospital on August 11, 1946, without going through a thorough drug withdrawal program. He went to a Beverly Hills Hotel bungalow at 9966 Beverly Grove Drive, where Dr. Mason would have full charge of all of his medical needs. He was taken off of morphine and given codeine in the form of Empirin Compound 4, which was eventually self-administered by Howard himself through needle injection. Although morphine and codeine are both opium derivatives, codeine is less habit forming. Theoretically, once he stepped down from morphine to codeine, Howard could have been easily weaned off of an addiction to codeine. This did not occur and he remained addicted to increasing dosages of codeine for the rest of his life.

When the Howard Hughes Medical Institute was organized in late 1953, Dr. Mason was given a lead position with the Institute in Miami. Dr. Norman Crane, who had shared office space with Dr. Mason in Beverly Hills, tended some of Dr. Mason's patients after he moved to Miami, and he eventually became one of the physicians in Howard's entourage.

On September 9, 1946, two months and two days after the XF-11 crash, Howard was back in the cockpit of one of his personal planes for a flight back east. Even though he was still in pain and under doctors' care, he wanted to show the world that he was back on his feet and able to fly.

In the meantime, the USAAF was anxious to cancel the XF-11 program. World War II had been over for a year and they were anxious to close out all the ongoing experimental programs involving aircraft that they could not afford to put into production. By now the second XF-11 aircraft had been completed, with conventional propellers, and was ready for its first flight, but the USAAF insisted that it be test flown by someone other than Howard. He considered this an insult, and on April 5, 1947, he took the aircraft up from Culver City for its debut. After 90 uneventful minutes, Howard brought the aircraft back to a perfect landing, and to the applause of the Hughes Tool Company Aircraft Division employees who had built it.

The XF-11 was one of the great "might have been" aircraft of World War II. If the USAAF had taken it seriously when it was first proposed, and if reliable engines would have been available on time, it could have played an important operational role in helping win the war.

However, the XF-11 was not the biggest project undertaken by the Hughes Tool Company Aircraft Division during the war. That distinction lay with the airplane that was, coincidently, the largest airplane ever built. Like the XF-11, this remarkable aircraft would be constructed using the Duramold process.

The idea for the world's largest airplane began in the dark days of 1942, when Allied shipping in the North Atlantic was being blasted with merciless efficiency by German U-Boats. In discussing the situation, Howard and shipbuilder Henry J. Kaiser conceived the idea of a fleet of enormous flying boats that could obviate the U-Boat threat by simply flying over them!

Kaiser commanded considerable confidence in Washington at the time because his West Coast shipyards were efficiently and economically turning out transport ships by the dozen to support the American war effort. Entrusting Henry J. Kaiser to get a job done was considered a sure thing. A prototype was ordered under the designation HK-1 (Hughes-Kaiser, first). The only problem was that the funding was contingent on finding a way to build the airplanes without the use of "strategic materials." In layman's terms, no aluminum. Because of the Duramold process, this was not a problem, the aircraft could be built of wood. Though she would come to wear the nickname *Spruce Goose*, which Howard despised, the big prototype was to be constructed primarily of birch (a hardwood), with very little spruce (a softwood) present among her components. Officially, the HK-1 would be named "Hercules" after the son of Zeus in Greek legend, who had unparalleled strength and lifting capacity.

By the end of 1942, the worst of the U-Boat threat had passed, but the HK-1 project had only just begun. Meanwhile, relations between Hughes and Kaiser became strained, and Howard carried on alone. The aircraft was officially redesignated H-4 because Kaiser was no longer involved, but it continued to be referred to internally as the HK-1, or simply as the "Hughes Flying Boat." The project stretched through 1943, and by March 1944, the government decided that completion of the project was no longer necessary to the war effort. The prototype could be built under terms of the original contract, but the additional aircraft were cancelled.

In June 1946, nearly a year after the end of the war, the one and only Hughes Flying Boat was completed at Culver City, California and moved to a specially constructed hangar on the edge of Long Beach Harbor. Everything about the Hughes Flying Boat was gargantuan. It was 218.5 feet long, as much as two B-29s and only 13 feet shorter than the Boeing 747 jumbo jet of today. Its wingspan was 320.5 feet, more than that of *three* B-17 Flying Fortresses, and more than half again greater than that of a 747. The Hughes Flying Boat is listed in *The Guinness Book of World Records* as having a larger wingspan than any other aircraft ever constructed.

The Hughes Flying Boat had been sitting in its Long Beach hangar for a little more than a year when Senator Owen Brewster called Howard before the Senate War Investigating Committee in August 1947 to accuse him of fraud. He called the HK-1 a "flying lumberyard," a "white elephant" and worse. Howard managed to successfully survive the hearings by winning public support with his admonishment to the senators that "During the war, I got less than one percent of the aircraft contracts, and now I'm getting 99 percent of the investigations."

The Senate backed off, and Howard returned to California. On Sunday, November 2, 1947 he went down to Long Beach, ostensibly to take the Hughes Flying Boat out for taxi trials. With 50,000 people watching, he taxied the birchwood behemoth onto the choppy waters of Long Beach Harbor. He ran up the engines and made several turns across the harbor, telling the 30 reporters who were aboard that the first flight would come in 1948. Then he dropped off the reporters and taxied out for one more test.

Howard opened the engine throttles and the Hughes Flying Boat was airborne. He lifted the big ship 70 feet off the water, and flew for one mile in less than a minute at a top speed of 80 mph before making a perfect landing. The world's largest airplane had finally flown. The detractors of the program were silenced as the Hughes Flying Boat became an icon of American aviation history.

I still vividly remember the radio reports on the day that the Hughes Flying Boat made her first flight, and I always have wished that I had made that one hour drive from Burbank to Long Beach to watch it happen. Many years later, through the twists and turns that take place in a person's life, I would end up as the caretaker of Hughes Flying Boat in her final resting place, and that story is told on the last page of this book.

NADINE AND BILL

As Howard had become immersed in the details of his aircraft projects, his attention gradually shifted away from his Romaine Street headquarters. Where once he had not kept regular office hours, he had now abandoned even the pretense of having an office. He spent a great deal of time in Washington during the late 1940s because of the Senate hearings concerning his aircraft projects, and it can be said that he figuratively—if not literally—never went back to the office after that. He conducted all of his business at his bungalow at the Beverly Hills Hotel or at other locations.

This did not mean, however, that Romaine Street diminished in importance as the center of Hughes Tool Company activities in California. Indeed, it was just the opposite. Because Howard was no longer reachable at a fixed location, the switchboard at Romaine Street was the essential link in his business affairs. This communications center was not only the sole conduit of Howard's personal and business messages, it would become the central crossroads of power within the empire of Howard Hughes.

It can be said, and it often has been said, that whoever was in control at Romaine Street was in control of Howard Hughes. As I saw personally, this would be especially true during the last quarter century of Howard's life, as he gradually withdrew from contact with the outside world. It was during the period of Howard's preoccupation with the XF-11, the Hughes Flying Boat and the Senate investigations, that two key people came to work at Romaine Street. During the last quarter century of Howard's life, these two, Nadine Henley and Frank William "Bill" Gay, would come to exercise power that I perceived as being virtually absolute.

Nadine Henley was first hired as an administrative assistant at the Hughes Tool Company Aircraft Division at Culver City in 1939. Howard met her during one of his after-hours visits to the factory. As the story goes, Nadine had stayed late and was finishing putting on her lipstick before she left for the night. Howard asked her if she could type, she said she could, and he had her type something for him that he needed that night to take to a meeting in Washington. He was a perfectionist, and the typing wasn't right, so he made her type it over and over. They were up most of the night, so he told her she didn't have to come in till noon the next day.

Gradually, her role expanded, and, when she didn't get a promotion that she wanted at the Hughes Tool Company Aircraft Division, Howard simply hired her as his personal secretary. He probably felt comfortable with her because they were almost exactly the same age. She started spending a great deal of time at Howard's Beverly Hills Hotel bungalow, but the relationship was purely business. Nadine had a long-time relationship with a handsome insurance salesman named Wendell Thain, and Howard was involved off and on with a number of young Hollywood starlets, especially Jean Peters, who he first met in 1946 when she was 19, and who would become Howard's second wife in 1957.

Probably the most important document that Nadine Henley ever typed for Howard was his last known will. She began working on it during the winter of 1943 and 1944, and she retyped it numerous times over the coming years as Howard changed his mind about the various provisions. In 1950, when he announced that he was ready to sign it, she retrieved it from the safety deposit box in a Los Angeles bank where she kept it. After looking through it for an hour, he returned it to her unsigned and instructed her to put it back in the box. He never touched this will again, and none of us found a copy of his later will, which I am certain he wrote sometime during the 1960s.

In 1947, the second of the two key people in the story of Romaine Street came into the picture. As the story was related to me, one day there was a knock on the door of the two-bedroom apartment that Wendell Thain occupied in Hollywood Hills. There stood a rosy cheeked young woman, obviously pregnant, and a tall, slender young man.

"Uncle Wendell," the girl announced. "You don't remember me, but I'm Mary Thain, your niece from Utah, and this is my husband, Bill Gay. We're married. He needs a job. We need someplace to stay."

She went on to explain that they had come to California to seek their fortune, and that, as Wendell was well aware, the housing market in the Los Angeles area was tight.

"You can stay here tonight, and I'll see what I can do about a job," he told her.

Wendell then picked up the phone and called Nadine. "We can't be at my place tonight, I've got company."

"I'll get him a job in the morning," Nadine reassured Wendell. "I'll hire him as my driver."

The following morning, Frank William Gay went to work at the Hughes Tool Company, and with the arrival of the first paycheck, Wendell Thain had his apartment back to himself—and Nadine.

In later years, I heard Bill Gay tell people that he had earned his master's degree from Columbia University in New York City but apparently his college career consisted of a short stay at Brigham Young University in Provo, Utah.

Nadine took a liking to the clean, efficient young Mormon

man from Utah, and, under her wing, he was given greater and greater responsibility and authority. In December 1947, at Nadine's urging, Bill Gay had his first audience with Howard Hughes. Again, with a nudge from Nadine, Howard made Gay his administrative assistant.

This post put Gay in charge of scheduling Howard's meetings, and it gave him authority over the all-important Romaine Street switchboard, which was known internally as "Operations." Over the next few years, Gay proceeded to staff operations with people, mostly fellow Mormons, whom he met through contacts at his church. As I saw it, Operations gradually came to be staffed with people who had been hired by, and who owed their allegiance to, Bill Gay. I could see that people who demonstrated disloyalty to Gay were likewise fired or transferred to the outer fringes of Howard's empire.

By the early 1950s, by virtue of their positions, Nadine Henley and Bill Gay had solidified a power base that was at least as solid of a footing as that of any of the highest executives of the various Hughes companies.

THE MEDICAL INSTITUTE

One of the most important elements in Howard's network of companies was not a company at all, but rather a charity—the Howard Hughes Medical Institute. As with many charity organizations, the Institute was part philanthropy and part tax shelter. On the philanthropy side, the Institute had grown out of Howard's memory of his disease-plagued childhood on the Gulf Coast of Texas, and his long-held desire to provide a place for research into the causes and cures of such diseases.

Created in December 1953, the Howard Hughes Medical Institute was assigned 100 percent of the stock in the Hughes Aircraft Company, over which Howard would exercise little, if any, control. From its offices in Miami, the Institute would dispense grant money to medical researchers.

Critics often sneer at the Howard Hughes Medical Institute as merely a tax dodge, and many of his detractors portray Howard as ruthless and uncaring when it comes to the goals of medical research. In fact, the Howard Hughes that I knew had a heart of gold which he demonstrated on many occasions. These are generally forgotten by people who would rather focus on the more outrageous aspects of his life.

For example, I recall an incident that occurred in 1960, when Howard cancelled a meeting with his bankers to help someone. A Lockheed employee involved in the meeting was delayed while trying to help an elderly neighbor into a local hospital. The woman, Mrs. Jane Daniels, was 95 years old and she had broken her hip in a fall. Howard asked me to arrange to get her into the Good Samaritan Hospital in downtown Los Angeles.

Howard then decided that he wanted an eminent orthopedic surgeon named Dr. Francis McKeever to perform the surgery on her hip. We located him at a medical convention in New Orleans, and Howard ordered an airplane to fly him to Los Angeles immediately. Dr. McKeever repaired the break with a pin, and for the next several days, Howard phoned me every few hours to check on her welfare. When I had to tell him that the woman was dying, he couldn't accept that, saying he believed she was over-sedated. Howard then flew in another specialist who confirmed that Howard was right, and her medication was adjusted.

During the ensuing weeks, her hospital bills were paid from an unknown source, which her family assumed to be me. Actually, Howard had paid them all. Mrs. Daniels lived to be 100 years old because Howard Hughes would not give up on her.

CHAPTER 2

OUR PATHS CROSS

THE STAGE IS SET

My life changed most significantly in 1957 when my area of responsibility at Lockheed shifted to the L-188 Electra. This new turboprop airliner would fly for the first time in December 1957, and it had been the job of my organization, the Engineering Flight Test Division, to certify it. Little did I know at the time that I would also be pressed into service to sell the Electra to the airline that had once been Lockheed's best customer.

By the mid-1950s, the airlines and the flying public had been convinced that jets and turboprops were the way of the future. Among the airlines that had been interested in the Electra was TWA, in which Howard Hughes held a 78 percent share. Ever since he had used a Lockheed aircraft for his 1938 round-the-world flight, Howard had always liked Lockheed equipment. He had been the inspiration for Lockheed's previous airliner, the Constellation, and had even been active in helping to design it. During the 1940s and early 1950s, TWA had ordered more Constellations than any other airline. However, TWA had not placed an order for the new Electra, and therein lies a tale.

Cyrus Rowlett "C.R." Smith, president of American Airlines, ordered 35 Electras, in September, Eddie Rickenbacker, president of Eastern Air Lines, followed suit with an order for 40. By the time of the first flight, six United States airlines had ordered a total of 129 Electras, but that did not include TWA. Bob Gross, the chairman of the board at Lockheed, had every reason to believe that an order from TWA was just a routine matter. Howard was a personal friend, and TWA had been the best non-military customer in Lockheed history.

Bob phoned Howard in September 1957, and said with a chuckle, "I've sold 40 Electras to Eddie Rickenbacker, and I've sold 35 to C.R. Smith. Maybe I could find *one* for you."

Bob Gross was joking of course. They both knew that TWA could have as many as Howard wanted, but Howard never had a sense of humor. Howard was so angry that he hung up and quit speaking to Bob, permanently. At the time, of course, Bob assumed that it would be just a matter of a few weeks before the two old friends would be back to normal, but he was terribly wrong. Except for one brief exchange a few years later, Bob Gross and Howard Hughes never spoke to one another again.

In the meantime, Bob wanted to get past what he thought was a temporary setback, and to sell a fleet of Electras to TWA. Someone had to speak to Howard and pick up the pieces. Because Howard was so particular, that someone would have to be able to speak Howard's language when it came to airplanes. Because I was involved in the experimental testing of the Electra, it would become my job to bring him back into the fold.

Two months after the incident, when it was obvious that Howard was not going to return any calls from Bob Gross, the chairman called me into his office and instructed me to meet Howard, get him interested in the Electra, encourage him to fly in the aircraft, and, ultimately, sell him at least 40 Electras.

I had figured that working with Howard Hughes was going to be just one more interesting assignment. I was only half right. I hadn't counted on it turning into a full-time job that kept me busy around the clock for many, many years. And for the next four years, I would be on the phone with Howard Hughes nearly every day. From November 1957, until his death on April 5, 1976, Howard Hughes and I shared a friendship that would endure time and distance.

HOW I FINALLY MET
THE ENIGMATIC HOWARD HUGHES

Our first meeting would set the tone for our relationship. By this point in his career, Howard had no office, so meeting him was never a matter of going to one of the many buildings that his various companies and their subsidiaries maintained in Southern California. As was typical of Howard Hughes' style, we would always meet in secrecy, at odd hours of the day and at previously undisclosed locations.

Through an intermediary, I received word that Howard had agreed to meet with a representative of Lockheed, but that I would not be told the exact place of the meeting until the last minute. After the call came, I went to a designated meeting spot, arriving at 9:00 pm as instructed, and waited.

It was well after 11:00 pm when a car slowly pulled up behind me and blinked its lights. I walked to the car and saw Howard Hughes sitting in the back seat.

After we had spoken for a couple of minutes, Howard asked me to drive him home and quickly dismissed his own driver. We then went to my car, a beat-up 1949 Plymouth. We talked—like the two aeronautical engineers that we were—until 4:00 am. I then drove him to the Beverly Hills Hotel, and headed for home with just enough time to shower, eat breakfast and get to work by 7:30 am.

The day after our evening meeting, I got a call from the Lockheed corporate office saying that they had heard from Howard's office that I had been deemed acceptable as an intermediary. The lines of communication were now open. Howard would usually initiate the calls, but he gave me a couple of what he called "very sensitive numbers" that would get to him directly. If I had to get to him immediately, I would just call one of those numbers, but most of the time I would go through the switchboard at the Beverly Hills Hotel.

At Lockheed, Bob Gross and Carl Haddon, the president of the Lockheed-California Company, were delighted that the relationship had proceeded so quickly. I soon had pressure on me from the company to keep the dialogue up, because they could see some Electra sales at the end of the line.

The approach I took to get Howard interested was to just tell him all about the airplane, because he was a real devotee of aviation technology. For example, I sent him a crew operating manual, which we had given to the airlines. He called me up and said that he had spent 12 hours reading it, and I believe he did. He said that he had found four basic mathematical errors in the book, and that he had corrected them. He was right, and Lockheed was wrong. I was very embarrassed, because the manual section of all the airplanes came under my department. This serves to show how devoted Howard was, and that he knew the engineering business very well.

Over the coming months, I became totally engrossed in the problems that he had at TWA. In addition to the Electras that we were discussing his buying from Lockheed, Howard had also committed TWA to buy 30 Convair 880 jetliners, and a large number of Boeing 707 jetliners.

He wanted to involve me and in turn, Lockheed itself, in trying to obtain enough financing to satisfy the needs of TWA for new equipment. He had already contracted for the purchase of the aircraft from Convair and Boeing, and he told me that he was willing to buy the Electras if Lockheed would somehow help him with the financing. His long-term financing had fallen out of bed, and he asked me to get Lockheed to take the lead role to bring the New York bankers together to finance TWA's new fleet of jets and turboprops.

Howard had short-term paper with the Bank of America in Los Angeles, but this was not renewable. He was planning to buy a tremendous assortment of airplanes, and this was going to require a consortium bank loan. He had lined up Irving Trust Company, which was the leading bank in a group of seven banks, and he had Equitable and Prudential, two groups of insurance companies that would take a lead position in the consortium. He had gotten the Dillon Read investment house to try to put the program together, but they had failed on two occasions.

Meanwhile, I had convinced Charles Barker, who had retired from Lockheed's finance department, to come out of retirement to work with the people in the Hughes organization to help put together a plan.

As for Howard and I, our personal conversations were more likely to be about aviation than financial matters. He just loved to talk aviation. By now, we were talking for two or three hours every day—about flying characteristics, fan engines, jet engines, split compressors, split turbines, and turboprops.

We usually spoke on the phone, but he came out to my office several times between 1958 and early 1960. He would arrive in the evening, and we would take a tour through the factory, or part of the factory. Sometimes he would sit in the Electra and do some paperwork, and then have couriers come and pick it up to be delivered somewhere. Then, late at night, or maybe early in the morning, I would drive him home to the Beverly Hills Hotel.

On four or five occasions, Howard asked to use the phone in my office to call his wife, Jean Peters. I recall that the calls were placed between 11:00 pm and midnight, and that he talked to her for about an hour each time. He did not mind me listening, and he always said that I could keep the door to my office open. I remember thinking that it was like listening to two teenagers talking. They were definitely a couple that was very much in love.

As I got to know Howard during his visits to Burbank, I gradually got a taste for his idiosyncrasies. On one of his nocturnal visits to the Lockheed Engineering Flight Test building, Howard had used my office to sign some papers that were to be sent to New York, and one of his drivers had picked up the packet so it would catch the TWA red-eye flight to the East Coast. He said he was tired and that he wanted to take a short nap. I offered him my couch, or a bed or couch in the pilots' room. He chose the pilots' room and slept for more than two hours.

When Howard awoke, he asked if he could use the pilots' room in the future as a regular place to take naps. I told him that the room was always undisturbed from 8:00 pm until 6:00 am, and that he was welcome to use it. True to his fastidious form, he requested changes in the room, and specified Pequoit linen by name. I promised that these additions and changes would be done, and I told him that we would make up the beds when he arrived the next time. On his next visit, I showed him how we had rearranged the room and where we had stored his linen. He seemed to be pleased, but he never used the room again.

Howard and I had quickly developed a very straightforward relationship. Aviation and aeronautical engineering were subjects that we both knew and understood, and we respected one another's opinions and ideas. During our conversations, and in the long memos that we passed back and forth, we shared a great many ideas. He loved to discuss aviation, but he was very opinionated, and it was unusual for him to change his mind. One of these rare occasions occurred in August 1961, when Howard wrote to me about the advantages and disadvantages of pure jet engines versus turboprop engines, in which the torque power from a jet engine is used to drive the propeller through a speed-reduction gearbox. "Now, as you know, Jack," Howard wrote, "When we first moved into the jet era I was inclined to favor the pure jet and I expressed my doubt that there would be a permanent place for the turboprop. As you remember, Jack, I even discussed with you on many occasions the conversion of the [turboprop] Electra into a low mach number pure jet. I have given this entire situation a great deal of study since that time and I have revised my opinions completely. I feel there is very definitely a permanent place for the turboprop in the future air transport picture—a very important place indeed. I will not get into the technicalities of this reasoning, but I assure you, Jack, I can now make a hell of an argument that there is an area of the future air transport system pattern which can be filled only by the turboprop. And it is a very large and important area indeed."

Howard was right, of course. Today, turboprop aircraft are heavily used as transport aircraft around the world. One of the most famous is the Lockheed C-130 that I had helped to develop in the 1950s. It was still in production at the turn of the century, and it was in service with the US Air Force and with more than 30 other air forces and civilian operators around the world.

FLYING WITH HOWARD

Howard piloted the Lockheed Electra himself many times between 1958 and 1960, and I always went with him. I remember one occasion when we flew down to San Diego in late 1960. Ironically, the purpose of the trip was for Howard to fly a rival company's airliner. He had ordered 30 of the new Convair 880 jetliners, and he wanted to visit the Convair factory to take the controls for his first flight in one of them. The 880 had been in flight test only since January 1959, and none had yet been delivered.

As we were departing Lindbergh Field in the Electra after a day spent flying the 880, Howard mentioned the large, California-style home that he and Jean Peters had recently leased in the exclusive community of Rancho Santa Fe, about 20 miles north of San Diego. He said that he wanted to show it to me, and I agreed. Howard flew low over the house and asked me if I had seen it.

I mistakenly said, "No."

He looked at me with a mischievous grin and said, "You will this time."

Banking hard to the left, he circled for another up-close-and-personal look at the house. On the second pass, I could see the nails in the roof shingles. We were so low that the neighbors could easily read the tail number on the Electra, and we were reported to the police. In turn, the police reported us to the Civil Aeronautics Administration for making a tree-top pass over a residential area in a huge four-engine airliner.

By the time we returned to Burbank, the Federal Aviation Agency had determined that the airplane was owned by the Lockheed-California Company, and Lockheed had been notified. As soon as I stepped out of the Electra, I was summoned to the president's office. As head of flight test, flights by the company-owned Electra were my responsibility. Carl Haddon was irate.

"What idiot pilot of yours pulled that foolish stunt?" he thundered.

"It wasn't a Lockheed pilot," I replied. "The 'idiot pilot' was Howard Hughes."

"Was Mr. Hughes happy with his flight?" Carl asked meekly, after a brief, awkward silence.

When I told him that Howard was pleased, Carl became elated. I think he forgot why he had called me to his office.

THE BLOODY DIVORCE OF HOWARD HUGHES AND TWA

Ultimately, Howard Hughes and TWA never did get the financing necessary to buy the Electras. It came down to being a personnel problem. Howard was unhappy with Charles Thomas, who was the president of TWA, and Thomas was determined to show his independence by not allowing himself to be bullied by the airliner's majority shareholder. Despite the fact that Thomas had been a member of the Lockheed board of directors, he was very vehement in his desire *not* to buy the Electra. This was his way of showing his independence, and it made Howard very angry, because Howard wanted the Electras. At the same time, Thomas wanted to buy a total of 30 Convair 880s, and Howard wanted no more than 20 of them for TWA.

Meanwhile, the financing that TWA needed for its fleet expansion, particularly the short-term money with the banks and the Equitable Insurance Company, was contingent on a continuation of management. When Howard refused to extend the employment contract that TWA had with Charles Thomas, the banks became disenchanted with Howard. The necessary financing package collapsed, and there was no deal on the Electras. TWA would never operate this aircraft.

The Electra issue and the firing of Charles Thomas were the straws that broke the camel's back for Howard's relationship with TWA. The banks and debt-holders were tired of his hands-on meddling in the operations of TWA.

Little did it matter that he had a better understanding of aviation and the airline business than they did. Little did it matter that his creation of the Lockheed Constellation had turned TWA from a regional airline into an international force in the industry. They wanted him out, and his sacking of Thomas was just what they needed to force the TWA stock that was held by the Hughes Tool Company out of Howard's control and into a trusteeship.

In December 1960, after an eight-month court battle, the banks and the other TWA creditors succeeded in forcing Howard to place his stock into a 10-year trust under the control of three trustees, in return for their granting $165 million in financing that the airline desperately needed to stay afloat. Howard resigned as a director and officer of Hughes Tool Company on December 21, and 10 days later, the Tool Company, still entirely owned by Howard, finalized the deal with TWA's bankers and financiers.

This was a major turning point in Howard's life. Robbed of his role in "his" airline, and of his direct involvement in his own company, he would spend the ensuing years dodging the media and subpoenas promulgated by frivolous litigants, and becoming the recluse that the media would love to ridicule and caricature.

CHAPTER 3

THE TURBULENT SIXTIES

BUYING JETSTARS

Even though he had just lost control of TWA, his being forced to cancel the Electra order made Howard feel as though he had let Lockheed down. His association with the company had spanned more than two decades. He had made his trip around the world with a Lockheed Model 14 in 1938, and he had developed the Constellation, Lockheed's most successful commercial product. Lockheed was nearly broke in the 1930s. He provided Lockheed with the money to do it and, in turn, Lockheed gave him a beautiful airplane in the Constellation.

Howard also felt like he had let me down *personally*—I was the one who had "sold" him the Electras that the banks would not let him pay for.

I remember a conversation early in 1961, when I found myself pleading with him. I said, "Howard, please, we'll get you another time. Let it go. You're trying too hard. Let it go. There will be other battles to be won."

The TWA case would go on for 12 years, and in order to settle it, Howard would be forced to sell the Hughes Tool Company, his birthright. Strangely, in early 1976, six months before he died, Howard told me that he blamed three men for causing him to lose control of TWA. These three men were Bob Gross, Jack Real, and Howard Robard Hughes.

In the spring of 1961, as the dust settled, the Lockheed management now asked me to sell Howard some JetStars. The

Lockheed JetStar was a small executive jet that originated in the mid-1950s as Lockheed's response to a United States government request for a military utility aircraft. The prototype had first flown at Burbank in September 1957, but, because of cuts in the US Defense Department budget, no military orders were forthcoming. Lockheed then decided to take a chance on the commercial market for the JetStar, and an assembly line was established at our Marietta, Georgia, facility. Now Lockheed wanted Howard Hughes to buy some. He had actually flown a JetStar in 1960 on one of his visits to the Lockheed facility at Palmdale, California, and Lockheed felt that, if he wasn't going to buy any more Lockheed airplanes for TWA, the richest man in America might want to buy a few JetStars for his own fleet.

Personally, I felt the man didn't *need* any JetStars, but I was working for, and getting paid by, Lockheed, so I started to tell him the virtues of the JetStar. I sold him one, and then another one. When it was all over, I had sold him 12 JetStars, but he never even took the first one that I sold him out of Georgia. Lockheed just kept it in storage for him, and later we resold it.

The nice part of the story of the 12 we sold him, is that I was able to resell five for him later. It was a seller's market, and I think he made about $250,000 profit on each of the five, but he would just take the money and we would move it into a later serial number JetStar. I finally sold him the last three just before I left Lockheed, a package deal. He never used any of the JetStars—the one flight that he'd made in 1960 was the only time that he'd ever flown in a JetStar.

SELLING TWA

During the early 1960s, I kept in touch with Howard regularly, but we had relatively less contact than we'd had between 1957 and 1961. This changed in 1966. It was Easter week, and I was in the Michigan copper country attending the funeral of an elderly aunt. On the day before Good Friday, I received a call from Howard with some great news. Less than 10 minutes before his call to me, he had sold his 78 percent interest in TWA.

I was the first person to know of the sale—other than Raymond Cook, his Houston attorney, who handled the paperwork. Raymond later told me that Merrill Lynch had given Howard a deadline to sign the papers confirming the sale by 3:00 that afternoon. Howard had decided to take a nap, and he woke up at 2:50 pm, signed the papers and the deal was done.

The closing price of TWA stock was $78 that day, but Howard told me that the sale price would be whatever the market price was on May 13, 1966. For the next month, Howard would call nearly every day to tell me what his check would be based on that day. TWA closed on May 13 at $89. The all-time high had been $91. The sale yielded $565 million, a staggering sum for the middle 1960s, but worth *three billion* in turn of the century dollars. He was now the richest man in the United States, and possibly the richest man in the world, discounting the various royal families.

Howard read me an article from the financial page of *The New York Times* which was entitled "Yes, Virginia, There Is a Santa Claus." It was a parody of the famous 1897 Francis Church editorial in *The New York Sun* with the same title. The article went on to say that Howard was not selling at the top of the market—and Virginia should be assured that airline stocks had a long way to go—up. I thought of that article in 1975 when he showed some interest in again acquiring TWA. I told him that the stock price was $6 a share. He dropped the subject.

In 1962, TWA president Charles C. Tillinghast and his attorney, John Sonnett, realized that the TWA legal case provided Hughes an option that if he ever got enough money, he could regain his position of control of TWA again, holding approximately 78 percent of the company and relieving himself of the three trustees. Sonnett and his fellow conspirators could tell that TWA was beginning to feel better in the airline market, so they came up with another plan. They told the Civil Aeronautics Board that Howard was senile and not capable of running any airline—due to his "senility." Howard responded with a unique ploy. His friend Floyd Odlum was a major shareholder in Northeast, and he also held a majority position in Atlas Corporation—which controlled large holdings of uranium—while Howard had a smaller holding in Atlas.

In the days of the Civil Aeronautics Board, they did not like to see a United States airline in bankruptcy, and at the moment, Northeast Airlines was close to bankruptcy. Howard gave Odlum his Atlas holding for a better position in Northeast. With that arrangement, the Civil Aeronautics Board found themselves in a dilemma. Odlum's wife and Howard's old friend Jacqueline Cochran continued on the board. Odlum proposed to place Howard's New York attorney, Chester Davis, on the board of the new Northeast. On one side, if Howard infused enough money (equity) in Northeast, the airline would forego bankruptcy. The Civil Aeronautics Board did not want any repeat of the hectic days when Howard had his run-in with TWA. The Civil Aeronautics Board decided against bankruptcy, but chose Louis Hector, an attorney who previously had been the head of the Civil Aeronautics Board. The Civil Aeronautics Board asked Hector to serve as the trustee of Northeast Airlines. Jim Austin, the former president of Northeast, still functioned as a president but under the control of a group of attorneys and the trustee, Louis Hector.

When Howard first attempted to buy Northeast in 1962, the CAB would not approve his controlling two airlines, TWA plus Northeast. Furthermore, they would not allow him to get back control of TWA, even if he could raise the money without a hearing. He would avoid anything involving his appearing in public, such as would be necessary if there was a hearing.

Anticipating the sale of his TWA stock, Howard placed his interest in Northeast into a trust controlled by Louis Hector, who sold Northeast to Storer Broadcasting. Howard used the money that he got from the sale of Northeast to buy AirWest, later Hughes AirWest, in 1968.

When the sale of his TWA shares went through, Howard was faced with the tax implications of his huge windfall. One way around the tax problem was to reinvest the money. With this in mind, he phoned me to say that he wanted me to help him reinvest

$400 million of his new fortune to acquire 20 Lockheed C-5A Galaxy military transports. The Galaxy would be the largest production aircraft in the world, with a gross weight of 837,000 pounds and a range of over 7,600 miles.

His plan was a visionary use for the C-5A. He wanted to use the big airplanes to transport three levels of foreign-built luxury cars from Europe to various inland United States cities such as Chicago, Omaha, Dallas, and Minneapolis. He reasoned that part of the cost of transporting cars from Europe was the ground shipment costs after the cars reached various harbors in the United States such as New York City, Galveston, Los Angeles, Seattle, San Francisco or Boston. His idea predated and anticipated the huge air freight business that would be brought about by the Boeing 747 freighters that would go into service a decade later.

I moved a team of sales personnel and engineers to Burbank from the Lockheed-Georgia Company plant where the Galaxies would be built, to discuss the matter. The meetings took almost two weeks, and unbelievably, Lockheed quoted a cost of $18 million each, which turned out to be way below the actual cost.

The marketing folks left Burbank with their planning numbers, and I presented the deal to Howard. I could tell that he had already lost interest in the Galaxies, but I sensed he was going to do something, that he was going to move someplace with his money.

Meanwhile, though, the state of California, wanting to have their share of the fortune of America's richest man, wanted to bill him for state income taxes. Howard had lived in California for more than 40 years, but he maintained that his official residence was in Texas. This was, after all, home to the Hughes Tool Company, the principal source of his on-going income.

Since he considered himself a Texas resident, and he had never actually owned a home in California, Howard felt that he should not be subject to California income tax. The state naturally disagreed.

To underscore his point, Howard was prepared to leave the state that had been his home for four decades, *forever*.

GOING INTO EXILE

Howard and Jean Peters had continued to live in their leased home in Rancho Santa Fe until Thanksgiving of 1961, when plumbing problems had forced them to leave. They moved back to Los Angeles, where they would live in another leased home at 1001 Bel Air Road until 1966, when the state income tax situation became oppressive. Howard had decided to resolve the residency issue once and for all by simply leaving the state permanently. Though nobody realized it at the time, he would never again set foot in California, even to visit. He would remain essentially in exile, living in hotel suites—a man on the run—for the rest of his life.

By this time, Dr. Norman Crane, who had once shared an office with Howard's former internist, Dr. Verne Mason, had become Howard's personal physician. Though he actually saw Howard only occasionally, he had gradually taken over Dr. Mason's role in writing prescriptions for the medications that Howard sought, and he had become part of Howard's entourage.

As he told me later, Dr. Crane had asked Howard in the early summer of 1966 for a two-week vacation to visit his elderly father in Maine, who he had not seen in many years.

"We'll all go," Howard said, anxious for any excuse to leave California. "We'll stop off in Boston, and you can go to Maine from there."

This is how Howard's decision to relocate to Boston came about. He confided to me shortly after he made the decision, and he told me that he had decided not to fly, but rather to make a railroad trip.

Howard had not been seen in public for several years and there was a great deal of constant media speculation about him. The rumors about his personal eccentricities had begun to circulate, and a great deal of money was being offered by the supermarket tabloids for information about him or, better still, pictures of the elusive Howard Hughes. When the media found out that he was leaving California, there would be a crush of reporters and curiosity seekers following him.

I offered to help in whatever way that I could, and he asked me to arrange for the two Beechcraft Queen Air airplanes that Lockheed owned to fly him and his party up to Barstow, California, which is a major railroad junction. He would board the train there, rather than in Los Angeles, in order to throw the reporters off his trail. Meanwhile, he had one of his aides, Robert Maheu, book two private rail cars, one for his staff, and a second, originally built for newspaper tycoon William Randolph Hearst, for himself.

At the last minute, he decided to board the train at Pasadena. On July 18, 1966, leaving Jean Peters behind in Bel Air, Howard took the train east to Boston. There was, of course, no public announcement about Howard's leaving California, and nothing was told to the media about the mysterious party that would be travelling across the United States in a private train.

The train arrived in Boston at 5:00 pm, but as Howard started to get off, he was told by his staff that the press had formed at the train to greet him as he left the station. Not wanting to be harassed, he called his security chief, former Los Angeles police officer Jack Hooper, and asked him to do something. Hooper arranged to have the train and its two private cars moved to the railroad yard. Here, Howard was bundled into a flower truck and the driver took them to the Ritz Carlton Hotel, where he and his entourage had booked the entire fifth floor.

During the first week that he was at the Ritz, Howard phoned me every day to tell me how he was fooling the press. For example, one day, a painter in uniform arrived to do some work, but Howard's aides uncovered a Graflex camera in his painter's kit. By now, the media had set up a prize of $10,000 for the individual who could get a picture of Howard Hughes.

A few weeks later, I was planning to take a long postponed family vacation to my home on Lake Superior. Howard's switchboard managed to track me down in Rhinelander, Wisconsin, which was an overnight stop en route to the Michigan Upper Peninsula. I was told that Howard had lost track of me for a few days and I was to call him immediately.

I phoned him at one o'clock in the morning, and we talked for more than an hour. The walls in the motel were so thin that the people next to us were pounding on the wall yelling for me to shut up. I wonder what they would have said if they had known that the guy in the next room was on the phone with the elusive and enigmatic Howard Hughes!

The gist of the call was that Howard wanted me to come to Boston. He said that he had a great deal to talk to me about, but I told him that I would have some difficulty getting away because of my job. I had been a vice president at Lockheed for about a year, and I had many of my own problems. We argued about it. He insisted I come back, and I said I just couldn't. Then, he told me that he wanted to go down to Georgia, where he had three of his fleet of JetStars in storage, and start to do some flying again.

"Why don't we buy a place down there?" he asked. "I'll live there for awhile, and you can get a month or two off to come down and fly with me."

I tried to explain that this flexible part of my life was gone. I was now in management, and I had different responsibilities now. I just did not have the time to go flying like I'd had back in 1957-1960 when we were junketing around in the Electras.

When my family and I arrived at my relatives' home on Lake Superior, Howard caught up with me again, and I had to spend the next five days acquiring a place for him to live in Georgia. Chuck DeBedts, my friend and co-worker at the Lockheed-Georgia Company in Marietta, was a wonderful help, and by Friday, we had found Howard a penthouse atop an Atlanta condominium building. However, they required us to put up a $10,000 deposit to hold it. Chuck talked the realtor out of the deposit, saying that the banks were closed for the weekend, but we agreed to deliver the $10,000 to them on Monday morning to secure a long-term lease.

On Monday, however, Howard called me to say that he had

changed his mind—so I had to tell the owners that the $10,000 wouldn't be there that day.

Though he would later tell people that he was planning all along to go to the Bahamas from Boston, Howard had no idea where he wanted to go, or where he really wanted to live.

He also seemed to have no idea whether he wanted to see Jean Peters again. In fact, he never would. She had not been part of the transcontinental train trip, and when she came back to Boston to visit him in early August, he refused to even see her. They talked, but only through a closed door. Nevertheless, he was persuasive in making her believe that they would, once again, have a normal life together. He told her to look for a home in Connecticut. He said that he was thinking that they should move there permanently. She was delighted with this news and started looking for property through a realtor.

Of course, he and Jean never did move to Connecticut, and I don't believe that he ever really intended to live there. By then, Jean had probably realized that their marriage was over. She never saw him again.

By the end of August, after Jean had returned to California, Howard decided that he would go to Montreal. He asked me to arrange transportation, so I prevailed on Lockheed to transfer their Convair 240 aircraft and crew to Boston. I put the crew up at a small hotel outside of town to avoid the press finding out about them, and about Howard's impending move. When everything was in place, he decided to postpone the flight until the next day, and then the next. Every morning, we would discuss whether it was time to go.

I also had the crew file for a clearance to Montpelier, Vermont every night. The plan was that once we were in the air, we would then refile for Montreal. This was done to prevent the media from finding out where our final destination would be. During the time that the flight crew was in Boston, they were cared for by two ex-Boston policemen, who would drive them on sightseeing tours around the city every day. The Convair remained parked at the corner of the airfield, so that it would not attract any attention, but so that it would be ready at a moment's notice.

After a month of this, Dick Pulver, the president of Lockheed-Georgia, demanded that I return the Convair 240 to Marietta. Howard countered by offering to *buy* the Convair. He also offered to put the crew on a retainer. Pulver would not allow it. I finally called the chairman of Lockheed, Dan Haughton, and he agreed that Howard could have the aircraft for three more weeks.

Finally, in October, I had to return the airplane to Georgia. When I sent it back, Howard became very distressed. He had wanted to go to Montreal, but his aides wouldn't let him. I was starting to get a sense of the growing influence that the aides were having over him. He wanted to go to Atlanta. He wanted to go to Montreal. They didn't.

Howard would never go to Atlanta or Montreal, and Dr. Norman Crane, who'd been the catalyst for the decision to go to Boston, was never able to get away from the Howard Hughes entourage to see his father in Maine.

The weather was getting cold in Boston and Montreal, so the aides had decided that Howard should go someplace where it would be warm. The entourage was on the move again.

PICKING LAS VEGAS

As Howard and I were planning for the move to Montreal, the New England winter was rapidly approaching. The nights had started to grow longer, and, even though Howard never went outdoors, he was aware that the cold winds were beginning to blow. John Holmes, as the spokesman for Howard's aides, had been telling Howard how cold Montreal would be in the winter, and how great Las Vegas could be.

"Let's go to Las Vegas," Holmes had told Howard. "While they've got 12-foot snow drifts in Montreal, the two of us can get up every morning in Las Vegas and play nine holes of golf."

Even though they both realized that Howard would never set foot on a fairway, he was finally swayed by John's lobbying efforts.

Six years later, when he gave his famous 1972 telephone interview, Howard said that he had intended his stay in Las Vegas to be a brief one. He said that he had been planning to go to the Bahamas, but I had never heard him mention this at the time.

All the time that I had the airplane standing by, we had never discussed the Bahamas—or Las Vegas. As far as I could tell, the decisions for the moves to Boston and Las Vegas were made on the spur of the moment, and when he moved to Las Vegas, no timetable existed for a move from Las Vegas to anywhere else. As it turned out, he *would* go to the Bahamas after Las Vegas—but not for *four years*.

Once again, Howard's long-time aide, Bob Maheu was called upon to move the group. As Bob recalls, Howard originally had wanted to move to the Cal-Neva Lodge on the north shore of Lake Tahoe, but that he had changed his mind several weeks before the move. Howard Hughes left Boston as he had arrived, under tight security and aboard a private rail car. Remembering the tense situation with the curious on his arrival in Boston, Howard decided that he wanted to reach Las Vegas in the dead of night, when the fewest people would be on the streets of "the city that never sleeps."

Bob Maheu handled the planning, and scheduled the transcontinental rail trip so that Howard would arrive in Las Vegas at night. However, the Union Pacific locomotive pulling the private cars broke down near Salt Lake City. Maheu had to rent another locomotive immediately, and at great cost, to assure that Howard reached Las Vegas in darkness. The operation turned out to be successful, and Howard crossed the threshold of the Desert Inn Hotel & Casino at 4:00 am on November 27, 1966. As Bob recalls, the first choice of a hotel was the Dunes, but the top floor was unavailable, so Howard and Bob had agreed on the Desert Inn.

During the next four years, Howard would never set foot on a golf course. Indeed, he would never set foot outside his darkened suite on the top floor of the Desert Inn.

FRIDAY THE 13TH

Although I never saw Howard during those four years that he

lived at the Desert Inn, I did speak with him by telephone on an almost weekly, and sometimes daily, basis.

While he was in Las Vegas, we had numerous business deals going. Howard had the half-billion dollars from the TWA stock sale burning a hole in his pocket, and we talked about a great many ideas for investing it. Of course one of his first investments was his $13.2 million purchase of the Desert Inn itself, which was finalized on April 1, 1967. This was only the first of many Las Vegas properties that Howard would acquire over the ensuing four years, but he also had other investment ideas, many of which would involve me.

One of our major topics of discussion during those years was a merger of the Lockheed Aircraft Company with his Hughes Aircraft Company (the Hughes Tool Company was never involved). He had a love of aviation and he always felt that he should own Lockheed. He pictured himself as having been Lockheed's "angel" ever since 1938, when he flew around the world in a Lockheed Model 14.

Once again, as I had been in 1957, I became the contact man between Lockheed and Howard Hughes. This time, however, Howard had a great deal more money and the stakes were much bigger. Around the beginning of 1967, I was having lunch with Dan Haughton, Lockheed's chairman, and he asked me, "Do you know what Hughes is going to do with his money?"

I told Dan that I thought Howard was going to invest $300 million in Lockheed stock because he felt that Lockheed needed the infusion of capital.

Haughton was obviously excited about the prospect. "Look at how much money $300 million really is," he said with amazement. "He'll have a billion dollars in three years."

"But, Dan," I replied, "What are your 25,000 shares going to be worth? What about my 5,000 shares? It's where you sit on the totem pole."

Dan thought it was almost unfair to say that in two years Howard's $300 million would grow to $1 billion. I wish I still had my 5,000 shares today.

In the meantime, Howard told me that he had decided to not only take over Lockheed, but to also buy the Douglas Aircraft Company from Don Douglas and merge it with Lockheed. Douglas was on the verge of bankruptcy, even though they were one of the three largest aircraft companies in America. They had a great backlog of orders for new aircraft, but they had very little cash to run the business.

Because of the way that Boeing had treated him during his final days as the operating power at TWA, he wanted to be in a position to beat them—and he felt that if he could engineer a merger of Douglas and Lockheed, such a company would be unbeatable.

Howard had a great deal of respect for Douglas' middle management, particularly the engineering management, and their products were highly respected within the industry. The Douglas DC-9 series had just entered service in 1965, and there was a strong demand for the new Douglas T-tailed twin-jet in the marketplace. It was on its way to becoming a very attractive and successful production program. The stretched DC-8-70 series aircraft also had a great market, because Boeing's competitive aircraft, the 707, could not be stretched or enlarged.

In 1967, however, the early success of the DC-9 program had meant that the resources of the Douglas Aircraft Company, in terms of both money and manpower, were being pushed to the limit. Because of the Vietnam War, there was a high demand for military aircraft, and this translated into a shortage of skilled aircraft workers. On the money side, as deliveries of the DC-9 slipped or were delayed because of shortages, so did customer payments. This put the Douglas Aircraft Company in a cash flow crunch.

As I understood it at the time, the Douglas treasurer, John Leslie, had obtained some short-term financing, but the money was coming due, and the banks were not interested in extending the loans. Douglas needed a long-term loan and it was not available. The only way out for Douglas would be a merger with a financially healthier company. Howard had been led to believe that there were two bidders other than himself and Lockheed. One was

Garrett, a Los Angeles aerospace systems company (which had merged with the Signal Oil Company in 1964), and the McDonnell Aircraft Company of St. Louis. However, the other Southern California aerospace giants, North American Aviation and General Dynamics' Convair Division, were also interested, as were Chrysler and Martin Marietta.

Howard had been talking to Keath Carver, the number one man in the Bank of America office in Los Angeles, who told him that Bank of America would settle their Douglas loans on very attractive terms, perhaps as much as 50 percent, if Howard Hughes took over the Douglas Aircraft Company. The Bank of America knew that Howard still had essentially all the money from the TWA sale, and they were anxious to do business with him. Carver had been told that Howard was prepared to put $300 million into Douglas to cover work in process, such as new tooling for the DC-9 series, and this prospect had gotten the bank's attention.

There was a two-week period when Howard and I talked for hours every day about his purchase and merger of Lockheed and Douglas. He asked me to keep the Lockheed management up to date with our conversations, and Dan Haughton clearly shared our enthusiasm.

A few days before what Howard called "the day of decision," Keath Carver called me to be certain that I was also talking to Lockheed regarding the merger. The conversation was very brief but I did assure him that Lockheed was aware of Howard's plans.

I never told Lockheed, nor do I think that Howard ever told the Bank of America, of his long-term plans to combine the merged Lockheed/Douglas entity with the Hughes Aircraft Company and to take the latter out from under the control of the Howard Hughes Medical Institute. Howard had never been happy about how the Institute was financially organized. As I recall, he blamed it on Tom Slack, a member of his Houston law firm, and who was also a member of the TWA board of directors. During the early 1960s, while Howard was trying to keep TWA afloat, he could not borrow any money through either the Howard Hughes Medical Institute or the Hughes Aircraft Company, even though he was the sole trustee of the Howard Hughes Medical Institute and the president and sole owner of Hughes Aircraft Company. To do this, he would have to go back to the United States Treasury Department and reconstitute the Howard Hughes Medical Institute as a charity. He would bind himself to a guaranteed payment each quarter forever. It probably would be very difficult to accomplish if not impossible.

With the Lockheed/Douglas merger, he could convert his debentures or reinvest them in a new issue that would pay much more than Hughes Aircraft Company was paying the Howard Hughes Medical Institute. He thought he would then have the flexibility to borrow against the assets of the Hughes Aircraft Company if the need ever arose. His rationale was that with this plan, the Howard Hughes Medical Institute would be better off financially, and in addition, the goals of the Howard Hughes Medical Institute would still be intact. With the merger, he would be in the catbird's seat. If the United States Treasury went along with his plan, he then could merge the Hughes Aircraft Company into the new merged Lockheed/Douglas entity. But, of course, this could happen only after the proposed Lockheed/Douglas merger was completed.

The long-awaited "day of decision" came on the second Friday in January in 1967—Friday the 13th. I received a hurried call from Howard at 8:00 that morning saying that he had word from Carver that "today was the day" to make his commitment.

"Get in touch with Haughton *now!*" Howard told me. "If Haughton says '*Yes*,' I'll take his word and go, so please tell him to decide now if Lockheed will go. I have to make a commitment in 30 minutes."

I phoned Haughton, who was in Seattle with his staff attending a meeting, and told him of my conversation with Howard. Obviously caught up in the urgency of the moment, he told me to stand by for a minute while he phoned Felix Rohatyn, the investment genius at the Lazard-Freres firm in New York.

I was on hold for more than a minute, but not long. When Dan Haughton came back on the line, he was much more relaxed.

"Jack, I told Rohatyn what you said, and he said not to worry," Dan explained. "He told me that Bank of America is just putting a little pressure on Howard. We know how he likes to procrastinate. Felix said he's sure that the real deadline is *next* Friday. It can't possibly be *this* Friday. Don't tell Hughes that Lockheed will be going for the merger. Come into my office in Burbank over the weekend, tomorrow or Sunday, and we'll write up a proper commitment to give him next week."

It was about 8:20 am when I hung up. Howard had told me that he needed Lockheed's commitment by 8:30. But then, he *did* like to procrastinate. I phoned Howard back at the Desert Inn, but he was on another phone call. I left him a message, a not too intelligent message, as it turned out, telling him that Dan Haughton and I thought the date for the decision would be the following week, and that we would be working out the details with the corporate folks over the weekend.

I avoided Howard's calls for the rest of the day, not wanting to talk about it further, since there was nothing more that could be done until I met with Haughton and the Lockheed management over the weekend.

Late in the afternoon, the company's JetStar landed at Lockheed Air Terminal at Burbank and Dan Haughton returned to his office. At about 5:00, I received a call from Dan.

"Jack, I just got the news," he said, his voice quavering. "They made an announcement. Douglas and McDonnell formally announced their merger at 3:30 this afternoon."

The McDonnell Douglas Corporation was a reality. Felix Rohatyn had guessed wrong. Howard had been right.

I found out later that the McDonnell family, namely John McDonnell, who was the founder's son, had been buying up Douglas stock for the two weeks previous to the merger announcement. By Friday the 13th, the McDonnell family owned 300,000 shares of Douglas stock, compared to 9,000 shares owned by the Douglas family, and they were ready to pay $43 a share for 1.5 million shares that were outstanding. They wound up paying

$45.80 per share, or $68.7 million. Howard had earmarked more than four times that much to make the deal.

Haughton was deeply depressed by the McDonnell Douglas merger. After he retired as chairman of the board, he was asked whether he had made any mistakes when he was running Lockheed. He said, "Yes, I had the chance to merge with Douglas and I blew it."

I felt even more sorrow for Dan than I felt for Howard. Howard must have been upset, because he did not call me for a week, nor did I receive any messages from him. In our relationship, a week was a long absence.

We never talked about the Douglas/Lockheed merger again, but we never stopped talking about reconstituting the Howard Hughes Medical Institute by a straight merger of the Hughes Aircraft Company and Lockheed, with him being paid in debentures, with most of the earnings being turned over to Howard Hughes Medical Institute.

In 1970, and again in 1971, Howard's New York attorney, Chester Davis, and I met with Lockheed management to attempt to accomplish such a merger. However, by 1971, the affairs of Lockheed were on a downward slide, and the advantages of a merger were not nearly as attractive to Hughes as they had been in 1966 and 1967. Our efforts in this direction remained on hold until we were living in London in 1973.

After the Douglas deal fell apart in January 1967, Howard would turn his attention to Las Vegas. Eventually, he would become the biggest casino owner in the state. Within a year, he had spent $65 million and he owned 20 percent of the hotel space on Las Vegas Boulevard South—the fabled "Strip." After he finalized the acquisition of the Desert Inn on April Fool's Day in 1967, he went on to buy the Sands Hotel & Casino, the Castaways Hotel & Casino across the Strip from the Sands, and the Frontier Hotel & Casino. He also bought North Las Vegas Airport and Alamo Airways, a charter operator located at McCarran Airport, the main Las Vegas airport. He even bought KLAS-TV so that he would be assured of always being able to watch televised movies in the middle of the night.

Another acquisition that Howard made during his years at the Desert Inn was that of an airline known as AirWest. I became involved helping Howard buy AirWest almost by accident when I got pulled into my "second career" at Lockheed, selling airliners to Howard Hughes.

JACK REAL, AIRPLANE SALESMAN

For nearly two decades, I quietly reigned as one of the world's best airplane salesmen. Granted, almost all of my sales involved Howard Hughes in one way or another, but they were sales none-the-less. I sold dozens of airplanes to Howard, and after he died, I sold 31 of those aircraft once again when we liquidated Howard's estate. But no one else has ever done what I did in 1968, to sell 100 wide body jets to a single customer at one time. Few people know that without that historic sale, Lockheed's L-1011 TriStar jetliner program might never have gotten off the ground. That's an achievement I'll always cherish. It's an interesting story as well.

In late 1964, Frank Kolk of American Airlines had tried to interest United States aircraft manufacturers in the idea of designing and producing a large twin-engine wide body aircraft powered by a turbofan engine.

Kolk did an aggressive job of selling this concept, but at the time, both Douglas and Boeing had a full plate and only Lockheed would answer the request for proposals. Boeing was then involved with the United States supersonic aircraft program, having won the competition against Lockheed for the American entry into this field. Meanwhile, Boeing was doing preliminary work on the Model 747 jetliner, a wide body aircraft that would be larger than the aircraft envisioned by Kolk. Douglas was in the throes of the serious financial problems that would drive them into the merger with McDonnell in 1967.

After Lockheed accepted American's concept, both parties agreed to accept Eastern Air Lines as a third partner, and soon thereafter, at the insistence of Eastern, the aircraft, now designated as the L-1011, incorporated a third engine, added at the base of the vertical fin.

Meanwhile, Lockheed had struck a deal with the British government in which they would buy at least 50 L-1011s for their national flag carrier, British Overseas Airways Company (BOAC), if Lockheed would install the British-made Rolls Royce RB211 engine in *all* L-1011 aircraft that were to be built. Years later, after he retired, Dan Haughton, admitted that initially offering the L-1011 with only one engine choice was second only to the failed merger with Douglas as one of the biggest mistakes of his career.

Even as Lockheed was diligently developing the L-1011, however, Douglas had also looked at the market, and had started to design a three-engine jetliner in the same size and weight class under the designation DC-10. After the McDonnell Douglas merger in 1967, the new corporation devoted a great deal of effort and resources to the DC-10 program.

In February 1968, after weekly telephone and personal conferences between Lockheed and American Airlines, the contract was ready to be signed for the initial order of L-1011 aircraft. Dan Haughton and his staff arrived in New York for a meeting and a signing ceremony with C.R. Smith, the American CEO and Chairman. Their timing was bad. Just a few hours earlier, President Lyndon Johnson had appointed C.R. Smith to be on his cabinet as the new Secretary of Commerce, and Smith had made a quick trip to Washington.

George Spater had been picked as American's new CEO, but when Haughton and company arrived, Spater was not available. He was in his office with the door closed. He had guests. The Lockheed party would have to wait.

Finally, Spater came out of his office, arm in arm with James Smith "Mr. Mac" McDonnell, chairman of McDonnell Douglas. Things didn't look good. Spater stunned Haughton with the news that American had chosen the DC-10 over the L-1011. Mr. Mac had offered him the DC-10s for $14.3 million each—a million dollars less than the Lockheed price for the L-1011.

The Lockheed team returned to California over the weekend very disappointed with the loss of the kick-off order from American. It was especially disappointing since Lockheed had initially been the only manufacturer to respond to the call from American. Frank Carlin, the CFO of the Lockheed-California Company, met with Dan Haughton in the hall of Building 63 at 6:30 am that Sunday, and suggested to Dan that he should cut the L-1011 price to $13.5 million and offer it for sale for 30 days.

"If you can't sell 200 aircraft in 30 days," Carlin said, "Just fold the program."

Dan called me a few minutes later and asked me to stop in to his office to discuss his conversation with Carlin. Dan stared at me in a way that only he could. There was fear in his eyes, a sense of impending doom. He didn't have to say much. The lines on his face told the whole story. Finally, he asked me to call Howard Hughes and sell him some L-1011s. He wanted me to sell a lot of them, and quickly.

I stepped out of Dan's office and immediately placed a call to Howard at the Desert Inn in Las Vegas.

I'd like to say that it was tough, and that it took a super sales job on my part, but the truth is that it was easy. Howard liked the idea, and, even though he didn't own an airline at the time, he didn't hesitate long before telling me to consummate the deal. In just a few minutes, I had sold Howard Hughes 100 L-1011 aircraft for a total price of about $1.35 billion. It was arguably the largest commercial airplane deal that had ever been made up to that time.

I told Howard that he need not take any of the first 25 L-1011s that were built, because the British already had committed to most of these, but that he would need to take every one from number 26 through number 125. The next morning, the Lockheed Board approved the plan. A few days later, Dan called me. His deep sense of gloom had been replaced by cheery enthusiasm. In fact, he was in such a good mood that he actually wanted me to "unsell" some of the aircraft that I had already sold.

"Jack, we're really optimistic about the L-1011." He said happily. "The marketing group feels that it will be easy to sell at least 400, but you've tied up all the good positions. We can only let Mr. Hughes buy 50 aircraft."

Based on what they perceived as my ease in selling 100 aircraft with one phone call, Dan's sales force thought it would be a piece of cake. In the next 15 years Lockheed would actually sell only 250 L-1011 aircraft. Coincidently, one of the major domestic customers would be TWA, the airline that Howard had molded for almost three decades before allowing it to slip through his fingers.

I reminded Dan about the history of failure for overly eager salesmen, and we had a big argument before finally settling on 75. Strangely enough, Lockheed agreed to go back to the original order for 100 by the time that the Hughes Tool Company signed the contract and made the down payment on the Thursday before Good Friday in April 1968.

BUY ME AN AIRLINE!

By the middle of 1968, I was holding down three jobs. In addition to my "regular" job as head of Lockheed's helicopter division, I was selling airplanes for Dan Haughton and undertaking an almost impossible task for Howard Hughes.

When Howard's litigation attorneys heard about his signing the deal with Lockheed to buy 100 L-1011s from Lockheed, they were nervous. They feared that they would now lose the TWA lawsuit against Howard, which continued even after Howard sold his controlling interest in the airline. TWA alleged that Howard always bought the aircraft he wanted and forced them on TWA. They said that the case would be weaker now as he was buying aircraft without an airline.

Howard's solution was simple. He called Jack Real to help him.

"Buy me an airline," he told me. "Find us a home for my L-1011s."

I was working long hours those days on the Lockheed AH-56 Cheyenne helicopter program, and I really did not have the time to devote to helping Howard Hughes acquire another airline, but

I had long since learned that I could never say "no" to Howard Hughes.

Through Dudley Swim, a Stanford classmate of Lockheed's Carl Kotchian who owned 19 percent of National Airlines, we came close to putting a deal together. However, every time I tried to set up a meeting with Dudley at his home in Carmel, California, it seemed like I would have to cancel it in order to rush off to Washington or St. Louis to be with the US Army to discuss our helicopter program. I also tried to get Western Airlines for Howard, but I was bidding against Las Vegas casino-owner Kirk Kerkorian who was putting a great deal of pressure on Terry Drinkwater, the Western Airlines CEO to sell him the airline.

The blame for not getting Western really belongs with me, because I really did not apply my best efforts to the task. I needed to do something quickly.

I knew that *something* could be done quickly, but that this something was not necessarily in Howard's best interest. I knew that AirWest, or "AirWorst" as it was known, was a target that could be grabbed instantly, but like most things that can be had easily, it was not really worth having. AirWest had been formed in July 1968 through a merger of Bonanza Air Lines, Pacific Air Lines and West Coast Airlines. When the new carrier ran into a morass of scheduling problems soon after it was created, it afforded an opportunity for a bargain hunter, or a man especially anxious to buy an airline.

Being as busy as I was, I would try to dodge most of Howard's daytime calls, but about a month after signing the L-1011 contract, I got a call from him late in the day just before I went home. He was complaining about my lack of success in buying an airline.

"You promised me," Howard said, almost as if he were reading from a checklist of goals I needed to achieve. "You promised me that you'd get me an airline, but you haven't delivered."

"If it's an airline you want and if time is an issue," I said jokingly, making a reference to Airworst, "I can get you one tonight, although I think we should wait until the end of the year and buy it at the bankruptcy sale."

Howard took the bait, even though it was offered in jest. "Then it's settled," he said. "Report back with good news."

That was a challenge I wasn't really expecting.

"I'll get right on it in the morning," I said.

"You said you could do it tonight," Howard reminded me. "Do it tonight."

I went right to work, but it took a bit longer than I has expected. I called Russ Ray at Lockheed, a classy L-1011 salesman who would aid me for the next week in getting the information regarding AirWest. Russ went on to have a great career in aviation, but I don't think his involvement with me helped his meteoric rise. We spent the next six days and nights working out the details and then he had Howard's lawyers buy the airline. After lengthy negotiations, the stockholders finally approved the sale of the company to Howard on December 27, 1968. Until the company's sale to Republic Airlines in 1980, four years after Howard's death, it would be known as "Hughes AirWest." It was, however, a short haul domestic carrier that had no use for Howard's L-1011s, and we never found a use for them.

Lockheed had given him a bargain price for the L-1011s, so when two years of searching for an airline partner that could use them proved fruitless, Lockheed was more than willing to return Howard's down payment. My fabulous billion-dollar airplane sale faded away. It was like hitting a home run but failing to touch home plate. Nevertheless, no one could deny that I had launched a zinger that would have impressed even Mark McGwire and Sammy Sosa. Seventy home runs in one season. One hundred wide-body airplanes at one time. I think they're both in the same league.

In 1974, Howard again would have me on a chase for a major airline. At that time, National Airlines was being shopped around by Bud Maytag, then National's president, for a potential merger with either Delta or Northwest. At that time, National's stock was selling for $9 a share. It probably could have been acquired for $12 a share on a tender offer since the stock would sell in large blocks to the three major shareholders: Maytag, Bob Truax, and the heirs of the estate of Dudley Swim. In truth, Howard didn't have enough money by that time to swing that deal, but it didn't really matter. I knew by Howard's mannerisms that he had lost interest in National. Even if the money had been there, his thoughts had clearly turned elsewhere.

"Howard, I don't think your heart's really interested in National Airlines," I said bluntly. "You want another airline."

Howard nodded.

"Can I guess?" I said.

Hughes nodded. I didn't need to look at his face for a clue. I already knew the answer and quickly jotted down the name on a piece of paper and handed it to Howard.

"This one?" I said.

Howard nodded again.

The note contained just three letters: TWA. (What else could I have written?)

I told Howard that it would be a disaster. He ignored me. He didn't care.

"Forget it," I said more firmly. "Besides, TWA stock now sells for $6 a share and you sold your shares in May 1966 for $88 a share. What's the point?"

Howard didn't respond. He didn't need to. We both understood the point all too well.

OUR HELICOPTER CAREERS

Howard's years at the Desert Inn coincided with a time when both of us were deeply involved in helicopter programs. For me, it was to be the period in which Lockheed developed the AH-56 Cheyenne, and for him, it was seeing the Aircraft Division of the Hughes Tool Company evolve into one of the most important helicopter companies in the world. The helicopter that did that for him was the Model 500, which would get its start as the Army's OH-6A. Lockheed was initially involved in the Army program that led to the OH-6A, but dropped out to pursue the Cheyenne project before the Hughes Tool Company Aircraft Division won its production contract for the OH-6A.

In the early 1960s, when the US Army had announced that it was soliciting proposals for its Light Observation Helicopter (LOH) program, Lockheed and the Aircraft Division of the Hughes Tool Company were two of the nine firms that entered the competition. The initial Hughes proposal was rejected because their aircraft was 600 pounds lighter than the average of the other proposed helicopters. However, due to an aggressive marketing effort, Hughes was allowed to enter the competition. After an initial evaluation of proposals, the US Army chose Bell, Hiller, and Hughes to each build five helicopters and enter a fly-off competition.

The Bell entry turned out to be too heavy, so it came down to a choice between Hiller and Hughes, with the winner to be selected on the basis of the best unit price. The price was to be based on 1,071 helicopters, although, at the time, the Army intended to order just 714 and leave open an "option" on the rest.

Howard very much wanted to get the Hughes Tool Company Aircraft Division into the helicopter business, and he was willing to take a loss in order to accomplish this goal. The estimated cost of each helicopter would be $30,200, so Howard, determined to get the contract at any cost, bid $19,860. He was willing to take a loss of more than $10,000 per helicopter in order to win. The Hiller company's bid, meanwhile, was $29,450. On May 26, 1965, the US Army went with the Hughes Tool Company Aircraft Division bid, and placed an order for 714 Light Observation Helicopters under the designation OH-6A.

Howard, who was still living in Bel Air at the time, was still physically close to the Culver City factory where the helicopters would be built, but he would never set foot on the assembly line, and he would leave California before the production was fully under way.

In January 1966, as the conflict in Vietnam was heating up, the Army went back to the Hughes Tool Company Aircraft Division for 121 more helicopters. Since the Hughes Tool Company Aircraft Division was the Army's only source for LOHs, the Army decided to rebid the subsequent orders. Hiller decided not to reenter the competition, but Bell did. During the competitive fly-off, the

Hughes helicopter easily out-performed the Bell entry because of its lighter weight.

After the fly-off, there was a sealed bidding procedure to determine who would get the contract. On the Friday afternoon before the Monday deadline for the sealed bids, Howard called me to discuss his dilemma. He asked me to recommend a price for the Hughes OH-6A entry.

"You've had a dozen people working four months on this price quote," I reminded him, "So why should you ask me?"

At that time I was working 12 hours a day, six days a week at Lockheed on the AH-56 Cheyenne, and I was really exhausted. But he insisted. Finally, I agreed to do it, but I challenged him by saying, "I'll work all weekend on this, but with one provision. That is, whatever my number is, in spite of the fact that your team has worked for months on it, on Monday, you'll use it."

I knew full well that he could not accept the challenge, but he said it was a deal.

I went home and worked all Saturday and all Sunday on it. On Sunday night, I called him in Las Vegas. He was asleep, so I left a message. My price was $53,400.

The following day, I was in a staff meeting when he called at 11:00 in the morning—an hour before the Army was scheduled to open the sealed bids. A phone message that read "Howard Hughes is on hold for you," always got me out of a staff meeting.

He repeated my number and told me: "You must be kidding!"

I discussed it with him and reminded him of our gentlemen's agreement.

"You aren't going to hold me to that agreement, are you?"

I said "yes," and told him I'd have to get back to my meeting.

Half an hour later, he called me again

"Close your eyes for two minutes," he demanded. "Next to me, you have the best powers of ESP [extrasensory perception] in the world. Close your eyes for two minutes and then give me the number that it will take to win."

I waited two minutes and told him the number was *$53,400.*

Fifteen minutes before the envelopes were to be opened, he got me out of the meeting again and asked me if I would be mad if he added anything to my number in spite of our original agreement. Like a fool, I said, "I don't get mad with anybody, but I'll be terribly, terribly disappointed if you do this to me."

"Let's restate this," he said. "You won't be mad, but you'll be terribly, terribly disappointed? That's the deal?"

I hung up the phone.

They opened the envelopes in St. Louis a few minutes later with a large crowd in attendance. Against my advice, Howard had upped the number I gave him to $59,700. He lost. Bell won with a bid of *$53,450* per ship.

The Army saw only the $59,700 from Hughes and the $53,450 number from Bell. Nobody other than Howard and I knew about "our" price of $53,400. If he had not raised the number that I'd given him, he would have had the best price by $50. He had promised me that he would use my number, but it was his company and he could use any number he wanted.

Bell would receive an order for 2,200 of its aircraft under the designation OH-58, and Hughes would ultimately build 1,438 OH-6s. Of these, the first 1,000 had to be built at the original price—$19,700, with the engine supplied (GFE). Howard lost over $100 million, or $400 million in today's dollars. He always told me that this was his contribution to the American war effort during the Vietnam War.

CHAPTER 4

GOING ABROAD

THE CENTERS OF POWER

Shortly after Howard had arrived in Las Vegas in November 1966, Robert Maheu had become chief executive officer of the newly-created Hughes Nevada Operations, and he would be in charge of managing Howard's growing number of holdings in the state for the next four years. Bob had first entered the Hughes organization in 1954, when he was retained by Howard's Washington tax attorneys. A former FBI counter-intelligence agent turned private investigator, one of Bob's earliest assignments was to ascertain whether Jean Peters' first husband, Stuart W. Cramer, III, was an employee of the Central Intelligence Agency. Bob determined that Cramer's involvement with the agency was not a formal one.

Through the years, Howard came to depend on Bob for various tasks, and his connections in the intelligence community were quite valuable. Gradually, he took on a greater importance within the organization, although he was an outside consultant and never an employee of the Hughes Tool Company. His company, Robert A. Maheu & Associates, was founded in 1954, and it still exists.

When Howard moved to Las Vegas, Bob Maheu was in the right place at the right time. He knew Las Vegas and he knew the people who ran it. He was the perfect man to handle negotiations for the Desert Inn purchase, as well as for all the subsequent casino deals that would take place over the ensuing four years.

For all of the power that appeared to be centered around

Howard in Las Vegas, the oasis in the desert that had become his home was never the center of power within the empire.

Appearances were deceiving. During those four years of Howard's residence in Las Vegas, Bob Maheu was the most visible embodiment of the Howard Hughes organization. Howard was in Las Vegas. Maheu was in Las Vegas. Maheu headed Hughes Nevada Operations, so it was readily assumed by the media, and indeed by everyone, that Howard Hughes and Bob Maheu met regularly and had a close relationship. However, during their entire working relationship, Bob Maheu saw Howard Hughes on only two occasions, once in the Bahamas during Howard and Jean's 1957 honeymoon stay, and once on the early morning of November 27, 1966 when Howard arrived in Las Vegas from Boston.

All of the communication between Bob and Howard during Howard's stay in Las Vegas was by phone, telecopier or by notes that Howard wrote on his always-present yellow legal pads.

The fact that they never met had nothing to do with any ill feelings that Howard had for Bob at the time. In fact, Howard had more contact with Maheu than with any other executive in his organization, including Raymond Holliday, who was the chief executive of the Hughes Tool Company in Houston. The reason that Howard never saw Bob was that, during his Las Vegas years, Howard cut himself off from nearly everybody. All access to his darkened room on the top floor of the Desert Inn was controlled by his aides, who were the only ones with access to his room, which was located behind a series of locked doors. Even the guards who maintained a 24-hour vigil outside the outer door never laid eyes on Howard. He never went out and only the aides went in.

When the corps of aides first began to form in Bel Air in the early 1960s, Howard was clearly in control, but by the time he had moved to Las Vegas, the tables had turned.

All of the aides worked under the umbrella of the communications center at the Hughes offices at 7000 Romaine Street in Los Angeles. The man who headed that center, and the man to whom the aides owed their loyalty, was Frank William "Bill" Gay.

As noted in the first chapter, Bill Gay came to work for the Hughes Tool Company in 1947 as an aide to Howard's personal secretary, Nadine Henley. Her friend, Wendell Thain, was the uncle of Bill Gay's wife, Mary Elizabeth Thain Gay. Later in 1947, Howard had personally picked Gay to establish a message center for him at his headquarters at 7000 Romaine Street. This gave Gay a great deal of power because he would have access to most of Howard's personal and business messages. In 1973, the family ties would grow yet stronger, as Mary Elizabeth's brother, Dr. Wilbur Thain, came into Howard's life as one of a coterie of "attending physicians" that cared for Howard during the last years of his life.

Gay had been one of Howard's closest personal aides during the 1950s, especially with regard to communications, but the two had a curious falling out in 1958. Howard had found out that Mary Elizabeth was in bed with the flu, and he feared catching it so he ordered Bill Gay to stay away from the Romaine Street office.

Gay then rented new offices—paid for by the Hughes Tool Company—at 17000 Ventura Boulevard in Encino. Located about a half-hour north of 7000 Romaine Street, the new offices were just a few blocks from Bill Gay's home. After 1958, Gay would not lay eyes on Howard again until 1973, and I don't believe that they met face to face again after that for the rest of Howard's life.

The loyalty of the corps of aides to their direct boss, Bill Gay, meant that he was gradually becoming one of the most powerful men in Howard's organization. Even many messages from important executives at the Hughes Aircraft Company or the Hughes Tool Company did not get delivered to Howard without Bill Gay's approval.

Because of Howard's reclusivity and his yearning for absolute privacy, it got to the point where months, or even years, slipped by without anyone else actually seeing him, and vice versa. The aides came to control all aspects of his private life. Working in two-week shifts, they surrounded him 24 hours a day and monitored everything he read, heard, or saw. They set up a switchboard to screen all of his phone calls, and they hand-carried all of his mail and memorandums. They saw to it that nobody other than, occasionally, one of Howard's doctors, ever got through the maze of locked doors that separated Howard from the rest of the Desert Inn and the world beyond.

The aides, these men who guarded Howard's privacy like he was a set of crown jewels in a vault, had all started with the Hughes companies in extremely mundane positions. They had apparently become part of Howard's inner circle through a combination of being at the right place at the right time and by demonstrating their loyalty to Bill Gay.

During the Las Vegas years, and, indeed for the rest of Howard's life, five core aides answering directly to Bill Gay controlled everything having to do with his day to day existence. These five were Clarence "Chuck" Waldron, Howard Eckersley, George Francom, John Holmes and Levar Myler. Two other aides, Roy Crawford and Charles "Chuck" Woodcock, were part of the entourage in the early days, but they would be banished from the inner circle after Howard left Las Vegas because of their perceived disloyalty to Bill Gay. A sixth aide, James Rickard, would join the inner circle in 1972.

The aides worked in shifts, with two weeks on duty, then two weeks off, living and sleeping just outside Howard's bedroom door. This would be the case from 1961 until the day that Howard died. They were paid as much as, or more than, the executives at the Hughes companies and, of course, all of their expenses—from their meals while on duty to the education of their children—were paid in full.

Levar Myler was a former car wash attendant who became a Hughes Tool Company chauffeur in 1950 and worked his way into the inner circle by cultivating his relationship with Gay.

Howard Eckersley started as one of Howard's motion picture projectionists while he was living in Bel Air in the 1950s, and moved to the inner circle in 1964 when Levar Myler was sidetracked with a heart attack.

John Holmes had been a salesman for Johnson Wax before he joined Howard's film company, Hughes Productions, in 1949. Like Eckersley and Francom, he moved to the inner circle while

Howard was living in Bel Air, and his specialty became looking after Howard's meals.

George Francom started with the Hughes Tool Company in 1954 as a chauffeur, and became one of the personal aides while Howard was living in Bel Air. George was probably the most honest of Howard's aide corps, and he was always the most cordial to me. Although both John Holmes and Eckersley were generally fair with me, George was my only true friend within Howard's inner circle, and he was one of the most trusted. He was very tall and a very physical individual who loved to scuba dive. He was soft-spoken but used his physical presence to make his point known. I was glad he was my friend. I wouldn't have wanted him as an enemy.

Chuck Waldron, like Myler and Francom, had been hired as a driver, but he did not come into the company until 1957. His promotion to the inner circle came at the end of the Las Vegas period, when he was brought in to replace the exiled Roy Crawford. All of the five core aides, except John Holmes, were, like Bill Gay, members of the Mormon Church.

The sixth aide, Jim Rickard, was also a member of the church. Although he would not become part of the inner circle until 1972, he had started as a Hughes Tool Company driver in 1953. Like most of the others, he was fiercely loyal to Bill Gay, and it was this loyalty that almost certainly led to his being posted to the inner circle.

I had met Gay in passing a few times, but much of what I knew about him prior to my joining the company in 1971 was colored by what Howard had told me of the "Hughes Dynamics" affair, which occurred back in 1962. Gay had apparently conceived a plan to create a business organization called Hughes Dynamics, that would be a subsidiary of the Hughes Tool Company and would direct the management side of Howard's businesses that were based in the Los Angeles area, and to provide management expertise to low capitalized companies. The key man in the organization was Gay's friend, Jack Pettit, a man who, as I understood it, had earned a degree for study of tides.

I was later told that while Pettit was a student at Brigham

Young University in Utah, he brought Gay to the Mormon Church when Gay was ill, and that they had prayed together for three days and nights for a cure.

The mystery of Hughes Dynamics is how these two men came to create and attempt to manage such an enterprise. Neither man had any managerial experience. Gay's experience with the Hughes Tool Company had been limited to coordinating the aides and the drivers, and serving on the Hughes Tool Company board. He had attended Brigham Young University for less than one year, although he told Evelyn Rothschild, the leader of the Rothschild Bank in London, that he had earned his master's degree from Columbia University. To impress visitors, he always kept the current issue of *The Harvard Business Review* on his conference table.

Created without Howard's knowledge or approval, Hughes Dynamics was located in a suite of luxurious offices in Westwood at the Kirkeby Building, located between Wilshire Boulevard and the campus of the University of California at Los Angeles. These offices were extremely ostentatious. For instance, the carpeting was so thick that it could not be carried upstairs. It had to be lifted to the roof by a helicopter and then let down to the desired floor.

Russ Rourke, a former engineer with TWA, and later an owner of an airline consulting company known as Westwood Associates, once took me to see the sumptuous offices that Gay had built for Hughes Dynamics in the Kirkeby Building. Westwood Associates was the new tenant that assumed the offices of Hughes Dynamics after Howard had ordered it put out of business. The building is now known as the Occidental Petroleum Cultural Center Building, which houses the UCLA Armand Hammer Museum of Art and Cultural Center.

The Hughes Dynamics subsidiary, whose existence was concealed from Howard, lost several million dollars in less than a year. Apparently, Howard found out about it by accident when he was reviewing the profit and loss statements of his various enterprises with Raymond Cook, his long-time attorney and confidant.

Howard came across an entity identified as "Hughes Dynamics," and he pushed Cook for an explanation. Cook knew that this would put Gay in a serious dilemma, but he finally explained to Howard what Hughes Dynamics was. As I understood it, Howard became livid. He ordered Gay to be fired.

A few days after this had happened, I had spoken to Howard, who was still living at Rancho Santa Fe at the time. I was going to send some drawings of the Electra to him, and he said that he would have Gay send someone to visit me and pick them up. He told me then that he had fired Gay, but he quickly added that he would keep him on the payroll because he thought Gay had too much inside knowledge of Howard's businesses. As Howard put it, "He can play tennis to his heart's content, but he'll never again have a work assignment. I just want to keep my eye on him."

Things didn't work out that way. Gay would spend his time doing much more than playing tennis, and it would be Gay keeping an eye on Howard, rather than vice versa. After being forced to vacate his "palace" at the Kirkeby Building, Gay returned to Encino, where he continued to pull the strings at Romaine Street and quietly, but effectively, to consolidate his power within the empire of Howard Hughes.

In retrospect, I believe that Howard also kept Gay around because he knew too much about Howard's drug problem. I was able to see that, from 1962 until he died in 1976, Howard had a driving passion against Gay. While Howard was living at the Desert Inn, he had ordered Gay never to visit him in Las Vegas, and it would be the same while Howard was in the Bahamas. The Hughes Dynamics incident, coupled with Howard's deep feeling that Gay had destroyed his marriage with Jean Peters, severely hurt Gay's influence with Howard.

Nevertheless, Bill Gay would continue to wield a great deal of power within the Hughes empire because of his access to most of Howard's messages, his close friendship with Nadine Henley, and the control that he continued to maintain over the aides that formed Howard's inner circle. Indeed, Raymond Cook would ultimately be one of those who would fall by the wayside of Gay's road back into a position of control over Howard's affairs.

Cook was a very talented, well educated man, and a devotee of

Howard, especially in the ongoing TWA situation. After this case was resolved, he served Howard with his many other legal problems. In August 1975, Cook and his wife were both killed in a car crash that was ruled as accidental. Cook's death deeply upset Howard for a very long time.

The power that Bill Gay had within the Hughes empire was amazing for a man who had been fired in 1962. Though, like Maheu, he never actually saw Howard during the Las Vegas years, Gay seemed to hold as much power over Howard personally as Bob Maheu had over Howard's business affairs in Nevada. Gay had access to Howard's communications and he had control over Eckersley, Francom, Holmes, Myler, and Waldron, the only people who had physical access to Howard's inner sanctum.

By 1970, Gay was ready to make his power play to oust Bob Maheu. Gradually, the aides started feeding Howard negative information, some, not all, of it true, about Bob and his handling of Howard's affairs. At the same time, they stopped putting Bob's phone calls through to Howard, cutting off his access to his boss.

In November 1970, when Maheu attempted to have Chester Davis removed from representing Howard in the long-running TWA litigation, Davis and Bill Gay prepared a proxy for Howard's signature that would give them, along with Hughes Tool Company boss Raymond Holliday, complete control of all Howard's operations in Nevada. Because Hughes Nevada Operations was never a formally constituted subsidiary of Hughes Tool Company, and because Maheu had never officially been an employee or executive of the Hughes Tool Company, this was easy to do.

Meanwhile, Howard had come down with pneumonia in October. He was very ill, and unable to deal with all of the intrigues that were being played out in his name in the world beyond the locked doors.

On November 14, having been convinced that Maheu had turned on him, an ailing Howard Hughes signed the proxy that gave control of his Nevada empire to the triumvirate of Davis, Gay and Holliday. Bob Maheu did not yet know it, but he had just lost his job.

LEAVING LAS VEGAS

Where did Howard get that thought that Bob Maheu had become his enemy? I had seen Howard respond to suggestions many times over the years, so it required no leap of faith to assume that Howard's sudden emotional response was the result of repeated and focused efforts by one or more individuals to discredit Bob Maheu in Howard's eyes. A barrage of negative comments had swayed Howard's opinion of Maheu and caused his fall from grace. A similar attack would later almost cost me my own friendship with Howard.

Howard's plans to leave the gaming mecca were never discussed with Bob Maheu, and when he did leave, 11 days after he signed the proxy in November 1970, it came as a complete surprise to Bob.

Beginning in about September of 1969, I was made aware through my conversations with Howard that he intended to leave Las Vegas eventually, and go to the Bahamas for a very long stay. However, this was a closely guarded secret that almost nobody shared. In retrospect, the move is seen by many as being part of Howard's effort to sever his relationship with Robert Maheu, but in the 14 months that we discussed the move, he never inferred that the trip was an attempt to leave Bob Maheu. Indeed, most of Howard's references to him were complimentary. In 1969, I was not fully aware of the power struggle that was ensuing between Maheu on one side, and Bill Gay and Chester Davis on the other.

Just as Bob Maheu had made Howard's travel arrangements for his trips in and out of Boston in 1966, my role in Howard's leaving Las Vegas was to arrange transportation. He wanted me to get two JetStars, one for him and his staff, and one for his security forces, which were still headed by Jack Hooper.

In July 1970, after I had assured him that I could get the loan of two JetStars from Lockheed, Howard told me that he wanted to start flying again himself. He suggested that he would like to stop over in Florida for awhile before he moved to the Bahamas, and he asked me to find a suitable location in the state that we could use as a base for his getting back into the pilots' seat. After considering the various factors involved in the planned move, I recommended St. Augustine. He concurred with my selection, so I sent some personnel from Lockheed's Marietta, Georgia plant to temporarily tie up some accommodations in the city and at the airport.

In October, when Howard became seriously ill with pneumonia, I cancelled the plans for an intermediate stop in Florida. At the end of the month, he informed me that he needed only one JetStar, and he advised me that he was not going to bring his security group to the Bahamas. There was the usual instruction to me regarding absolute secrecy about the move, but he also warned me not to tell Maheu or Hooper—or any of his California staff people, including Bill Gay.

The issue of the timing of the move was also keyed to the weather. Howard was concerned about leaving the hotel to board the aircraft when the wind was more than 10 miles per hour, because he feared coming in contact with dust that had been contaminated by radiation from the nuclear tests that were conducted at the United States government's Nevada Test Site, 40 miles northwest of Las Vegas.

This was one of the reasons that he had never ventured outside his suite at the Desert Inn during the four years that he had lived there. When his fear of atomic dust was made known in the 1970s, Howard was ridiculed as paranoid, but subsequent revelations about the danger from these tests indicate that Howard's fears were not without justification.

Nearly every day of the 14-month period that we discussed the move, I would, at Howard's request, obtain a weather report for the Las Vegas area. Finally, in mid-November, I received word that the time was near. I alerted Bob Fuhrman, who had succeeded Dick Pulver as the president of the Lockheed-Georgia Company, and he ordered a new JetStar to be ready to move Howard and his entourage to their destination. In the interest of providing Howard with absolute security, I arranged for the JetStar to land at Nellis AFB rather than at McCarran Airport.

The date was set for November 20, less than a week after the signing of the proxy. Howard requested that fresh milk and sandwiches—chicken with the crust removed from the bread—be put aboard, and this was done. Then came word that Howard had postponed his move until the following day, and the crew in Georgia was ordered to stand down. The same thing happened again the next day, and the next.

For five days, the trip was postponed, but early in the morning of Wednesday, November 25, Thanksgiving eve, I was assured by Howard that the trip was really a go, and again, I told the Georgia folks to prepare new chicken sandwiches, get some fresh milk and stand by to make the flight.

The JetStar arrived at Nellis AFB, a few miles north of Las Vegas, about 30 minutes before Howard's aides took him out of the Desert Inn for the last time. Two days short of four years after he had arrived under the wraps of total secrecy, Howard Robard Hughes was leaving Las Vegas under total secrecy. He was confined to a stretcher because the pneumonia had exhausted him, but he was in good spirits. He enjoyed the flight, his first since long before he left California in 1966, immensely.

The day after Howard arrived in Nassau, I received a long call from him, thanking me profusely for arranging his exit from Las Vegas. He asked me to keep the airplane at Nassau, but it was up for sale, and without telling him, I moved it out of the Bahamas on the day before Christmas. It had been there for almost a month, and Lockheed was putting pressure on me to get their airplane back.

There was a very aggressive salesman at Lockheed, and he used the publicity about Howard leaving Las Vegas on this JetStar to sell it to a rich Mexican businessman, and he got the full list price. At that time, getting the full list price for a JetStar was unique.

Howard called me in Burbank after Christmas and said, "I want to buy the JetStar."

"I can't sell it to you because Lockheed already sold it to the Mexican guy."

"Tell the Mexican he can't have it."

"It's too late," I told Howard. "We've consummated the deal and it's down at Love Field in Fort Worth getting additional avionics installed. I'll tell you what we'll do, though. We have another one down there that we're building on spec. Lockheed has the Emery Brothers do the interiors for most of their airplanes. Whenever the Lockheed-Georgia Company needs an interior in a JetStar, they located the Emerys. They're at Love Field. Why don't I give you this airplane? I can give it to you at a discount."

"Okay," he said, "Providing that we push the crew, the people at Emery's that are working on it, so that it'll be done in first-class shape. Then we'll move it to California, but not right away. In the meantime, I want you to find a place to put it."

The JetStar was finished as he requested, and it went into storage as he requested, but he would never see it. As it would always be with Howard, most of the times that he bought an airplane, he never actually picked it up. When he died, he had airplanes he had never seen parked in hangars all over the world.

CHAPTER 5

THE VIEW FROM INSIDE

COMING ABOARD

In February 1971, less that three months after Howard left Las Vegas, I received a call from Hughes Tool Company chief executive Raymond Holliday inviting me to be his guest at the tool company factory in Houston. I flew down, and spent two days reviewing all the phases of the oil drill bit manufacturing operation. He also took me to lunch at the Petroleum Club, where he introduced me to his friends in the oil business.

On the way to the airport to catch my flight back to Los Angeles, I finally asked Raymond why he had invited me to visit the Hughes Tool Company. He replied that it was at Howard's request, and he then added: "Someday the whole operation will be yours to operate. Howard wants *you* to look after the whole Hughes organization."

I was stunned. I was flattered, of course, but I was stunned at such a proposition. I didn't want the whole responsibility of Howard's entire operation, and I told Raymond that I felt there were people well entrenched in the companies who were doing a good job. At that stage of my life, I just wasn't willing to come in and take such a job.

In late April 1971, however, Raymond paid me a visit in Los Angeles and took me to lunch at the Century Plaza Hotel. He told me that the offer was still on the table, and that Howard also still wanted me to take a lead position in completing a merger of Hughes Aircraft Company and Lockheed. I had been on that project for years with no success and told him about how we had almost merged the two companies with Douglas in 1967.

Essentially, I told Raymond that I was rejecting the offer. I was very blunt. I said that I did not feel that I could do everything that Howard wanted me to do. I just said no.

Raymond pleaded with me and told me that Howard had said that Raymond could not go back to Houston until I agreed to join the Hughes Tool Company.

"Please tell Mr. Hughes that you're coming," he begged, "So he'll be happy, and so I can go home."

I always liked Raymond, so I said I would let him know. This went on for four or five days, while Raymond remained in Los Angeles. Then he made me an amazing offer. He proposed to make me the number two man at Hughes Tool Company immediately. He pointed out all the advantages such a position could have, adding that in two years, he would retire and I would take his place. He offered me an annual salary of $100,000—which was a huge salary for 1971—but I refused. I told him that I'd accept $60,000, which was $10,000 more than I was getting at Lockheed.

He urged me to take at least $80,000, insisting that I get more than Bill Gay, who was receiving $75,000, but I got my way and settled for $60,000. Holliday then asked me to tell Howard that I had accepted his offer, and to get back to him as soon as possible.

Before I contacted Howard, I went to see Dan Haughton, the Lockheed chairman. I told him that I had received a better offer from the Hughes Tool Company. When he insisted that I was already being well paid, I told him that I had been offered $100,000. I didn't tell him about the negotiation, but in any event, I did not lie—I was offered $100,000. Haughton didn't try to negotiate with me. He just said that he was reluctant to have me leave. I think he liked having me with Lockheed because of the personal relationship that I had developed with Howard Hughes.

By this time, I had received several messages from Howard, inviting me to run all of his businesses. One memo, that I never saw until after Howard's death, was written in April 1971. In it, he had told me:

> "You would have complete control of the Culver City Plant [Hughes Tool Company Aircraft Division, later Hughes Helicopters], the Tucson plant, all of our operations in the San Fernando Valley, including the plant just acquired from Ramo Woolrich [actually Woolridge]—All the facilities of both H.T.Co. and H.A.C. at or near the Los Angeles Airport, plus all our facilities at or near Newport Beach. In short, Jack, what I am offering you is the management and control of all the plants, offices, laboratories, and other facilities of both Hughes Tool Company on the entire West Coast of the U.S. and in addition all the facilities and activities of Hughes Aircraft Company, including the operations and facilities at Tucson, plus all others, even those abroad.
>
> "I am most serious about this and would appreciate a reply. Many thanks, Howard."

When I discovered this memo after Howard's death, I noticed that one other paragraph had been bracketed and marked with the word "Omit." This paragraph read:

> "Incidently, I neglected to mention that this would include the presidency of AirWest as of immediately."

The word "Omit" was printed. Howard always wrote in cursive. He never printed, but Bill Gay did.

Raymond Holliday obviously knew about at least some of the messages that were going back and forth between Howard and me, but I don't know whether he ever saw this particular memo.

I sent my message of acceptance to Howard, who congratulated me for coming aboard, and said emphatically: "I'm not offering you the number two job. You've got it all. I accept your resignation from Lockheed with pleasure."

He insisted that I run *everything* and said that I could have an office wherever I wished—in Los Angeles or New York—except Houston.

That week, I announced my retirement from Lockheed, and we had a farewell party at the executive dining room at the Lockheed Air Terminal in Burbank.

The following night at 8:00 pm, Bill Gay asked to come and see me at my office in the Lockheed facility at Van Nuys. Prior to this, I had known Gay only in passing, and had not thought of him as a person with a great deal of power and authority within the Hughes organization.

I could not have been more wrong.

AT THE MERCY OF A SCOUNDREL

Bill Gay would quickly become the villain in my life. He had a long history with the Hughes Tool Company, and he had carefully "stacked" Howard's inner circle with aides that were loyal to him at Howard's expense. Gay apparently had no intention of sharing any of the power he had shrewdly acquired through the preceding quarter century.

When Gay came to see me that night in May 1971, I was not prepared for his having such detailed knowledge of all my dealings with Howard and other members of Howard's organization. Knowing about his role in the communications center at Romaine Street, I should have realized that he had access to copies of all the messages between Howard and myself that had passed through Howard's aides.

He chided me for accepting Raymond Holliday's offer to be his number two man, blasting Raymond as a drunk, and saying that the offer was just a means for Raymond to get to Howard through me.

While he was in my office that night, Gay showed me a new organization chart that he had recently conceived. It showed Howard at the top, and the Hughes Tool Company over to one side. In the main part of the chart was the "Howard Hughes Corporation," with two executive vice presidents in the same box—

Gay and myself. I was to have the title of vice president of aviation, and I would have everything that had to do with aviation, including the Aircraft Division of the Hughes Tool Company (Hughes Helicopters), the fixed base operation at McCarran Airport in Las Vegas, and, I assumed, Hughes AirWest. Under this plan, Bill Gay would have control of the Las Vegas hotels.

I made one of the major mistakes in my life. I accepted Gay's proposal. Gay was delighted and said he would start building me a suite of offices in the morning. I got an office a year later.

On my farewell tour of the Lockheed Corporate offices, I dropped by the office of Tom Morrow, the executive VP of Lockheed Corporation. Tom called me a "sucker" for falling into such a trap.

He was right. Just as I was naively unprepared for the depth of Gay's knowledge of my past dealings with Howard, I was unprepared for his bitter animosity toward me. This was the result of his jealousy of my long-standing friendship with Howard, and his fear that whatever authority I might take on would only diminish his power. At first, to placate me, Gay had assured me that I would go on the board of directors of Hughes AirWest and the Hughes Tool Company immediately. It took 18 months before I went on the airline board, and I never went on the board of the Hughes Tool Company.

I went to work for the Hughes Tool Company on May 31, 1971—my birthday—but when I arrived at the Hughes offices in Encino, I discovered that I had no office, nor even a chair. I had to sit at whatever empty desk I could find. When I mentioned this to Gay, he flippantly said, "I'll get you a desk next to Bob Caverly, so the two of you can sit around and tell each other what a poor manager I am."

Caverly had been hired by Gay in 1970 to run the Las Vegas hotels and casinos. He had been with a major hotel chain and came with a good reputation, but Gay fired him soon after he was hired. A few months after being dismissed, he became an oil company executive.

I soon realized that, in spite of my salary and my position, I now headed an organization filled with people who were, for all practical purposes, unemployed. They had no responsibility, and, like me, had nothing to do. They were all individuals who had a labor contract or an understanding of a work contract, and they all drew salaries. But they had nothing to do, and they did nothing. This group included Jim Austin, the former chairman of Northeast Airlines; Fran Fox, the former Los Angeles Airport commissioner and later a vice president of aviation affairs working for Bob Maheu in Las Vegas; Bruce Stedman, former vice president of finance of Northeast Airlines; and John Seymour, the former manager of the "Howard Hughes" Airport (actually North Las Vegas Airport); as well as two of Howard's former aides, Roy Crawford and Chuck Woodcock. It was very depressing to see such talented men sitting around with nothing to do.

All of these men had, at some time or other, fallen into Bill Gay's bad graces, and, over the coming months, other candidates would be put into this group—which came to be known informally as "Jack Real's Group."

Since the ouster of Robert Maheu in November 1970, a five-member board of directors had been formed for the Hughes Tool Company. These five included Bill Gay, Nadine Henley, Chester Davis, John Holmes and Levar Myler. Holmes and Myler were two of Howard's aides who were loyal to him only as long as they did not receive any conflicting instructions from Gay. How Gay got on the board is a matter of speculation, since Howard told me he had never authorized it—and I knew that he had officially fired Gay in 1962. I raised this issue on several occasions with Howard but I never received a satisfactory answer. I knew that once Howard dismissed a subject, there was little or no chance of bringing it up again.

Without any direction from anyone, I kept busy putting together the Hughes AirWest expansion plans. I would visit Irving Tague, the general manager of Hughes AirWest, about twice a month, but he always reminded me that Gay did not want me to make any decisions. I had not, at this time, seen the April 1971 memo from Howard which gave me "the presidency of AirWest as of immediately," but Bill Gay had seen it, and he had it.

Another player in this act was Chester Davis, who had been Howard's lead attorney for the TWA case, and who had been the attorney involved in settling the uranium claims for multimillionaire financier Floyd Odlum in the early 1960s. Odlum had recommended Davis to Howard as the kind of rough, tough fighter that he would need in the TWA federal case in the Second Circuit Court in New York City. Howard agreed with Odlum and added Davis to the TWA case, although for many years before that, Howard had been represented by Raymond Cook.

Born in Italy as Caesar Simon, Chester was a gregarious man who stood nearly six feet tall and weighed about 190 pounds. His mother had been Italian, and his father Algerian, but he was adopted by his stepfather, a man named Chester Davis, so he changed his own name to Chester Davis, Jr. He graduated from Princeton and Harvard Law School and spent most of his career on Wall Street before he started his own firm and became general counsel of the Hughes Tool Company during the course of the TWA case. I always felt that his toughness and ethnic background gave him a distinctive look. Chester had been a chain-smoker and a heavy drinker until his doctor forced him to quit both habits.

In July 1971, two months after I had joined the group, Chester called and invited me to come with Gay and spend four or five days in Miami.

"Howard looks to you on aviation matters," Chester told me. "I think we all ought to talk about what we want to do in your area."

There was a Hughes Tool Company JetStar—one of the fleet that I'd sold to Howard—that flew between Los Angeles and Miami on a weekly basis, so I contacted Rand Clark, one of Gay's aides, and asked him when the JetStar was going to leave for Miami. He said he would check and get back to me. Finally he called and told me it would be leaving on Saturday from Van Nuys at 10:00 am.

I reached the airport at 9:00, only to learn that the aircraft had left at 8:00. The next Monday, I told Rand what I thought about him for tricking me.

"I work for Bill Gay," he shrugged. "I have to follow orders."

When Gay returned, I faced him and told him what I thought of his keeping me away from Miami, and how I felt about the way I'd been treated since joining the group. I also complained to Gay about not having gotten any messages from Howard since I had joined the company.

"There are no messages for you from Howard, and there won't be any," Gay told me proudly. "And there is no point for you to send Howard any messages, because they won't be delivered to him."

I reminded Gay what he had said at my office at Lockheed the night before I resigned, that I would be put on the board of Hughes AirWest and the Hughes Tool Company. He told me that, regardless of what I thought when I was hired, there would be nothing for me at the Hughes Tool Company.

"I suggest that you just go home," he smiled. "I would just as soon see you leave. You'll have a check mailed to your house each Thursday as long as Howard Hughes is alive, but there is no further need for your services here. Just go home and cash the paychecks. There is no job."

Howard expected to hear from me, and he wanted to get messages to me, but his efforts, like mine, were blocked. Two years later, John Holmes told me that Gay had instructed the aides to tell Howard that I had quit. They told Howard that I had left my wife and was living in Europe. Howard had instructed them to hire a private detective company to find me. They never did. They didn't need to. I was at the Encino office every day.

EVEN JEAN PETERS

The extent to which Bill Gay exercised his control over Howard's business affairs was remarkable, but it also extended deeply into Howard's private life. This even included Howard's marriage to Jean Peters. Clearly, their's was not an ideal marriage, but it also seemed to me that Gay exploited a bad situation and engineered events that led up to their divorce.

I really don't know whether Howard's hatred of Bill Gay was

because of what Gay did to his marriage, but I can testify that Gay hated Jean, and that Howard blamed Gay for sabotaging their relationship. I think Gay saw her as an obstacle in his campaign to control all that was Howard's. If Howard had died without a will while still married—even if he hadn't seen his wife in years—then Jean would have inherited his estate. I think Gay was frightened by such a prospect. She was not a person, she was an obstacle to be overcome, and Gay controlled the communications—even between them.

After they moved back to Bel Air from Rancho Santa Fe in November 1961, Howard and Jean lived apart, even though they were in the same building. For a time, they saw one another regularly, but soon, like everyone else, Jean's communications with her husband had to go through the switchboard. When Howard had moved to Boston in 1966, Jean visited. When Howard moved to Las Vegas, Jean talked about coming, but she never did. She could not share him with a darkened room, and continue to communicate by memo when he was 10 feet away. They did communicate, but across a state line and under the watchful eye of Bill Gay.

Finally, in January 1970, while Howard was still in Las Vegas, she made the announcement that they were getting a divorce.

Just as their wedding in January 1957 had been held quickly and abruptly in a small town in Nevada, so too was their divorce. This time, however, Howard did not appear. He arranged for a car and driver to take Jean from Los Angeles to Henderson, Nevada and back. It was my understanding that Bill Gay had arranged with the driver that he should be notified immediately when the divorce decree was issued.

I happened to be with a group of people in Bill Gay's suite on the top floor of the Century Plaza Hotel in Los Angeles on June 18, 1971 when the call came in. It was a true eye-opener for someone like me, who had been with the company for less than three weeks. I recall that after he hung up the phone, Gay leapt up and went berserk. He literally danced around the room, hugging everyone, even me. He kept saying: "I'm so happy! I'm so happy!"

A few years later, I spoke with Jean's driver about her lonely drive to Nevada that day. He told me that she hoped, and half expected, that Howard would make contact with her before the car reached Henderson. He told me emphatically that all Howard would have had to say was "Don't," and there would have been no divorce.

I guess she was still in love with the man.

THE TEXAS INTERNATIONAL AFFAIR

Without any direction from anyone on Bill Gay's side of the company, and without any significant communication from Howard himself during most of 1971, I kept busy, working with Bruce Stedman and Irving Tague to develop ways that Hughes AirWest could extend its route structure through a merger or an acquisition. I knew that I could have access to the Lockheed computers, and having just left Lockheed, I knew that they were using a software system in their effort to sell L-1011 jetliners that was capable of looking at specific airline profiles. I had access to this system and used it to look for possible merger partners.

Nat Simat, an aviation consultant, had done some work on the same subject earlier that year, so I talked with him. Nat was an old friend of Chester Davis, having worked with Chester for years on the TWA litigation. Nat, Irv Tague, and myself had a few meetings at which we discussed possible merger candidates, including Alaska Airlines, Frontier Airlines, Braniff Airlines, and Texas International Airlines.

All of these candidates were "played" on the Lockheed L-1011 computer, and Texas International worked out to be the best candidate for many reasons. First, it had an operation which, when merged with AirWest, would yield a synergistic system. The two lines both fed into common cities, particularly Salt Lake City and Los Angeles. The second reason was that it could be bought fairly cheaply. The third and most important reason was that it was on the verge of bankruptcy.

One stumbling block to the acquisition was that, at that time, government regulatory agencies such as the Interstate Commerce Commission and Civil Aeronautics Board made every effort to assure that public transportation, be it railroads, buses, or airlines, were widely held by the public. This mitigated against a one-man ownership, such as would be the case if Howard owned it. In spite of this, the government would not want to see a public transportation system go bankrupt, even though the alternative was to allow its purchase by a single individual.

I knew that the key player at Texas International Airlines was a man named Francisco "Frank" Lorenzo. I had known him when I was at Lockheed, and he knew that I was now with the Hughes organization. I also knew that he was deeply involved as a financial advisor to an entity known as Minnesota Enterprises, Inc., which owned 48 percent of Texas International. In September 1971, at the annual Conquistadors del Cielo meeting in Wyoming, I met with Frank Lorenzo, who was a guest of someone at the event. I knew that he had an interest in taking over the airline, but I didn't want him to know that I was interested in Texas International, so I was careful not to make any inquiries about his interest in Texas International Airlines.

At our meeting, however, he told me that he was financially involved in an airline called British West Indies Airlines (BWIA), and he would like someone to buy him out of that position.

During the next month, Bruce Stedman and I canvassed all of the creditors of Texas International Airlines and had an informal agreement with all of them except Texaco that they would write down the sums that were owed to them. This included amounts owed for aircraft. We met with the McDonnell Douglas Finance Company and the General American Transportation Corporation (GATX), and determined that they would accept a 50 percent write-down of their loans if Hughes Tool Company would assume the remainder.

Armed with these commitments, and knowing how precipitously close Texas International was to bankruptcy, I told Bill Gay that now was the time to strike a deal with Lorenzo or its major creditor, the Chase Manhattan Bank. He agreed and suggested that I should get Lorenzo to join us as an employee, and I was authorized to offer him $25,000 a year as salary.

On November, 16, 1971 I had a meeting with Lorenzo in his office on Park Avenue in New York City. He was anxious to see me, thinking that I had come to respond to his offer for BWIA. When I sprung it on him that we wanted to take over Texas International, his face dropped. He became very nervous and left the meeting to make telephone calls.

During the meeting, I received a call from Bill Gay in Miami allowing me to increase the salary offer to Lorenzo to $30,000 per year. Needless to say, I did not embarrass myself by making him any offer. I sensed that Lorenzo was within three or four weeks of acquiring the airline, and the last people he wanted around was us.

"Please leave the airline alone," he begged. "Maybe a year from now, after I get it on its feet, maybe then we can consolidate."

I sensed that he was in bed with Chase Manhattan Bank, so Nat Simat and I went to visit the bank that afternoon. We met with a young Chase vice president named Al Marple. When I told him that we were interested in taking over the airline, and doing it quickly, he became very hostile to me.

"Why are you trying to butt into this affair at the last minute?" He said. "You're trying to prevent Frank Lorenzo from taking a position with an airline that he has worked so hard to save from bankruptcy. Let Frank have the airline, and in a year or two, then we'll merge the Lorenzo Texas International Airlines with Hughes AirWest."

He echoed what Lorenzo had said. It was almost as if they had planned it that way.

I told Marple and the Chase Manhattan bankers that, as a bank, they were taking the position without hearing our case, and we left the meeting. I next flew to Miami where Raymond Holliday, Chester Davis, Bill Gay and Nadine Henley were conferring with one another. I recounted my meetings in New York to them, particularly to Chester, who was not fully aware of the situation with Texas International, but who knew about it in a general sense.

"Don't bother with Lorenzo," he lectured me. "You should know that if three men own 48 percent of the company, you should be dealing with them—and nobody else."

I quickly made an appointment with the Minneapolis bankers/investors in Texas International Airlines—including Carl Polhad, who was the chairman of the board; John Christian, who was the president; and Donald Benson, who was their financial officer. I left Miami the same day and flew up to Minneapolis, where I was met at the airport by Bruce Stedman. In the cab from the airport to their offices, Bruce and I sketched out what we thought would be an interesting offer.

We proposed that the stock of Texas International would be paid off at the rate of $3.50 per share as debentures, and these debentures would pay five percent interest immediately and would be redeemed after 1978.

Other specific provisions were that McDonnell Douglas Finance Company and GATX both would accept a 50 percent write-down of their debt on aircraft and Hughes Tool Company would meet with the other suppliers and propose a 50 percent write-down of this debt. There would be a two-year moratorium of debt payback to the Chase Manhattan Bank, but in this period, the Hughes Tool Company would make interest payments.

They accepted, but told us that we had to move quickly because of the financial condition of the airline, and the pressure they were getting from Frank Lorenzo. I told them that we would have to submit this proposal that we had offered to them to our board for approval. I agreed to remain in contact with them, and said that I would be in Houston for the next board meeting, which was set for December 2, 1971.

I returned to New York City to brief Chester of the proposal, and then returned to Los Angeles to meet with the Bank of America, our major bankers, who agreed to the plan. Chester Davis wrote the proposal in proper legal fashion, and there was a board meeting at Chester's hotel in Century City on November 30 with Holliday in attendance, during which the Hughes Tool Company board bought the proposal. It was finally retyped on the morning of

December 1 in Los Angeles, and signed off as a firm offer by Harry Swenson, the director of Hughes AirWest. That afternoon, I flew to Houston with it.

That night, I met with Polhad, Christian, and Benson in Houston, and showed them our offer. It was essentially as we had conceived it in Minneapolis, and we broke up that night with a handshake. They happily told us that we had "bought ourselves an airline," but they would have to go through the ritual of submitting it to other interested parties in the morning.

The other parties were LaMarr Muse, who was then the president of Southwest Airlines, and Frank Lorenzo, who was representing himself, as well as Jet Capital, a small financial company that he owned. They would vote on our proposal, and they felt they would accept our proposal by late afternoon.

Having received such an enthusiastic response from the management of Texas International, we, indeed, felt that we had "bought ourselves an airline." I was certainly feeling confident enough to send Nat Simat to Washington to break the news to the Civil Aeronautics Board, so that they would not hear the news through a press release.

Nat left Houston at 8:00 on the morning of December 2. Meanwhile, Chase Manhattan Bank had called a meeting in Houston on the afternoon of December 3 that was intended to be a reconciliation meeting with the creditors. I met with the Minneapolis group for lunch, and they told me everything was on track, but they still had to reconvene in the afternoon. They asked me to call Chester Davis to ask Chase Manhattan to take a conciliatory attitude in the meeting. Chester's response was a little bit more profane than "Go to hell," but that was the essence of it. I reported back to the bankers that Chester Davis would love to do it, but he found it difficult to proceed.

At 3:00 that afternoon, all three of the Minneapolis group came into my hotel room, led by Polhad, and followed by Benson and Christian, who was smiling. He gave me the OK sign with his thumb and right forefinger.

"Before we tell you the outcome of the meeting," Polhad said,

"I want to ask if your company would loan us $300,000 to tide us over until we can reach Civil Aeronautics Board approval. We can collateralize the loan with our ground support equipment."

My first mistake that week had been sending Nat Simat to Washington. I now made my second mistake.

I excused myself to go to the bathroom, and frantically tried to phone Bill Gay. I reached his aide, George Vaughn, who told me "Mr. Gay is at a luncheon with Dick Hannah [one of his public relations men] at Perino's. He has left instructions that, under no conditions, is he to be disturbed."

I pleaded with Vaughn, but to no avail.

Next, I made the third mistake of calling Chester. I told him what the three men had asked.

"Hell no!" He scolded. "Tell them that they're hanging on the ropes, and if they don't take our offer 'as is,' we're walking away. Then kick them out of your room."

I went back to face the men from Minnesota.

"Mr. Davis would love to do something for you," I lied sheepishly, "but he feels constrained at this time."

Carl Polhad's face reddened and they left the room.

At 8:00 that evening, Christian and Benson returned to the room. They told me that, after our denial of the $300,000 loan, they had gone back to Frank Lorenzo, and that he now owned the airline.

If I had not sent Nat Simat to Washington, I am sure he would have had more success in making the appeal to Chester, because the two were old, dear friends. If I would have called nobody, and had just come out of the bathroom and said, "Gentlemen, you have the money," all that Davis and Gay could have done was to fire me. In retrospect, Howard would never have let them do that.

When I flew back to Encino the following day, I went in and told Gay how upset I was that he would not be disturbed when he was having lunch.

"I heard about your conversation with Mr. Davis," he said without looking up, "and I'm in total accord with the position he took. Count the days. In less than 90 days, Frank Lorenzo will come crawling in on his hands and knees, asking us to take him out of his dire predicament."

That day never came.

THE LAS VEGAS LEGACY

It was while he was at the Britannia in the Bahamas that Howard would have his only direct contact with the media after 1958. Late in 1971, the McGraw Hill publishing company announced that it was about to publish an "autobiography" of Howard Hughes. The author, Clifford Irving, claimed to have had access to Howard for many years and to have based the book on numerous personal interviews. Because Howard had not been seen in public for more than a decade, and nothing was known about him in the world outside his penthouses, the book was eagerly awaited by the public. *Life* magazine would be publishing excerpts and the book world was referring to the Howard Hughes/Clifford Irving book as the publishing event of the year.

The only problem with the book was that Howard had never even heard of Irving, nor had I, nor any of Howard's aides. The book had been written by Irving as a complete hoax. Irving had done such an extraordinary job of fabricating the "autobiography" that it was impossible for anyone outside Howard's inner circle, which consisted of barely a dozen people, to tell that it was really a hoax. Indeed, when the Hughes Tool Company issued a press release calling it a hoax, nobody believed the press release! The press release was assumed to be a deliberate falsehood to distance the company from whatever revelations that Howard had made in "his" book.

Only one man could confirm that Irving's book was a hoax, and Howard Hughes hadn't talked to anybody outside the inner circle for years. Irving knew this, and he knew that Howard had cut himself off from the outside world to the extreme. He gambled that Howard would not risk appearing in public to denounce it.

However, Howard took the unprecedented step of agreeing to a telephone interview with seven respected journalists that included

Jim Bacon of the Hearst newspapers, Marvin Miles of *The Los Angeles Times*, Vernon Scott of United Press International, Roy Neal of NBC News, Gene Handsaker of the Associated Press, Wayne Thomis of *The Chicago Tribune* and Gladwin Hill of *The New York Times*. The interview was nationally televised, but the object of the interview appeared only as a disembodied voice. The cameras and the reporters were at the Sheraton Universal Hotel in Los Angeles, but Howard was at the Britannia Beach Hotel, 3,500 miles away in the Bahamas—and, of course, he never appeared on camera.

Howard was interviewed for two and a half hours, during which time he emphatically denied that he had ever worked with Clifford Irving on the book. Irving, in turn, admitted that the "autobiography" was a hoax and eventually served jail time for defrauding the publishers.

The other thing that Howard succeeded in doing in the interview was insulting Bob Maheu. He called Bob "dishonest," and said that he "stole me blind." A month later, on February 10, Maheu sued the Hughes Tool Company for libel, asking for $17.5 million. In July 1974, a jury found in Bob Maheu's favor, and in December of that year, the court awarded him $2.8 million. This judgement was later dismissed on appeal and reset for trial.

Bob Maheu realized when he sued Howard that he was suing the company and not the man. Sadly, he knew that Howard's belief in his dishonesty had been planted in Howard's mind by others, but, as Bob observed many years later, he "had to make a move."

"It was a very difficult thing for me to do." Bob recalled. "I knew that it was not Howard. I had always felt, and he felt the same, that as long as we could talk, we could straighten out our differences. I never imagined the day when I *couldn't* talk to him. At that point, the Machiavellian group took over. The aides had more power than Howard did because they controlled all the communications."

On May 30, 1977, the case was finally settled in Bob's favor for an undisclosed sum. The presiding judge, Hon. Harry Pregerson issued the following statement: "I think all of us are very pleased that this torturous litigation is ended. I think it is in order for me to remind all of us here that the jury believed that Robert Maheu had been defamed and it would seem to me that this settlement between Mr. Maheu and the Summa Corporation [when Howard sold the Hughes Tool Company in 1972, his remaining holdings were combined under this new name] should vindicate him of any cloud that hovered over his head. I know that this litigation has been very troublesome for him and I'm sure that he is pleased that it is concluded, as we all are."

The suit was just another one of those things that nagged at Howard in his final years. At one point, Howard told me that he wanted to enlist the aid of multimillionaire developer and casino owner Del Webb to get Maheu to drop the suit. Webb, who had previously owned the New York Yankees, and whose construction company had built the Hughes Tool Company Aircraft Division factory in Culver City, would be given control of all Howard's hotels and casinos in Las Vegas if he could pull it off. Webb owned and operated, among other properties, the Mint and the Sahara in Las Vegas, as well as the Sahara Tahoe, and he was widely respected as a competent, no-nonsense operator.

There were legal barriers preventing me from making a direct offer. I knew that, clearly, such action could be judged as a bribe. Howard, however, devised a unique way around the problem of offering the bribe. I was to meet with Del Webb, and Howard suggested that I should get the message to him through extrasensory perception (ESP). Howard was a big believer in ESP, one of the fashionable parlor tricks of the 1970s, and he imagined that both he and I were especially gifted when it came to reading minds and projecting thoughts. I disagreed, but I went along with him.

I asked Lawrence A. "Pat" Hyland, the chief executive of the Hughes Aircraft Company, to set up the meeting just after New Year's Day in 1975. Pat was a mutual friend, and it was at his home in Holmby Hills, near Beverly Hills, that I met with Del Webb. It was a pleasant visit and the meetings lasted for two days. I did everything but come out and ask Del directly to help solve the problem. He did not respond to the bait. As Howard had said he feared, Del Webb was not a good "ESP receiver."

Yet Del was still a very perceptive and shrewd businessman. He told me bluntly that Howard was in deep trouble with his Las Vegas properties. Del considered Bill Gay to be less than capable of running Howard's Las Vegas interests—and that is perhaps a charitable assessment.

"It's a mystery to us other Vegas operators," Del told me, "Why Howard keeps Bill Gay in power. If he wants somebody from his home shop, he'd be better off with Nadine Henley."

This may have been the opening that I was looking for, so I asked him whether he would be interested in running the hotels.

"I sure would," he said. When we started discussing his running the Nevada properties, Del beamed and started asking about Howard and his health.

Del suggested I stay over in Los Angeles for another night while he obtained a pro forma of the 1973 earnings of the Hughes properties from the Nevada State Gaming Committee. Del had good connections in the state capital regarding the gaming records.

"I'll find out how much money all of Howard's hotels made last year," he said. I accepted Del's offer, especially since it gave me a rare opportunity to visit my wife, Janeth.

In the morning, Del gave me the Hughes income earnings for 1971. It was very close to $7.6 million.

"I'm surprised you made that much money," he said. "No one knows this man you've got running things for you in that town. him. He's a man of mysticism. I can't believe that Howard, who's always been a tough guy, would ever have him running his hotels. Why don't you tell Howard that?"

Del looked over the numbers for awhile, and finally he said, "Tell Howard that the hotels would earn at least $35 million a year if the Hughes hotels and casinos were managed by my group. You'd make a great deal more money, and still have enough left over to pay me a nice management fee. In fact, I'll manage it all for the first year for free, and take a cut the second year."

It sounded like a reasonable offer.

"Tell Howard I love him and tell him I'm glad we're back together again," Del said as I left Pat Hyland's home.

"I will," I replied, although I never gave that message to Howard.

I flew back to Miami, arriving at midnight, and called John Holmes in Freeport to ask him to let Howard know I'd be in the Bahamas the next day. He passed the message on to Howard while I was on the phone, and came back on to say that Howard wanted me to come over to the Bahamas immediately. Howard was adamant.

"Come home now," he said. "Lease an airplane if you have to, but come now."

Pilots and planes are scarce at midnight, but I managed to find someone who would agree to fly me to Freeport. However, we got lost, and ended up on Andrus Island. I did not get to the Grand Bahamas until 7:00 am, by which time I was exhausted, having been up all night. But there was Howard, waiting for me. When I told him my story of flying to the wrong island, he laughed. It seemed like the funniest thing he'd ever heard. I'd never heard him laugh so heartily, and it was all because of my misfortune.

I told Howard that I wasn't successful in getting Del to help with the Maheu problem, but I didn't tell him about Bill Gay and what the Las Vegas casino operators thought of him. When I told Howard about the $7.6 million and Del's $35 million offer, he gave me a puzzled look, and then he searched through a pile of papers next to his bed. After a few minutes, he came to a letter, which he scrutinized with the magnifying glass that he always used to read documents. He was severely far-sighted, but he refused to be fitted for reading glasses.

"What he told you is interesting," Howard told me. "While you were with Del, I received this letter from Vern Olson [his controller in Las Vegas], which says that my hotels and my casinos made $34 million last year. I'm already getting a great deal more money than Del had promised you."

"Sorry, Vern," I thought to myself, "but I believe Del Webb and the Nevada Gaming Commission on this one. Their numbers are usually rock solid. Surely you knew that."

My concerns about the way that Gay's people were managing the Hughes Nevada Operations went back to the last week of 1971. I was in Gay's outer office with Steve Savodelli, the man who supposedly ran the hotels and casinos for Gay. Savodelli said they were trying to get in the "stockholder's" report that day, and he wanted my help with the company's airline numbers. He also mentioned that the actual earnings of Hughes AirWest were $2.65 million and that Gay said he wanted them to be $4.6 million. Savodelli wanted to know how much he had to add to the $2.65 million number to make it come out to $4.6 million. I helped him with this difficult math problem.

Steve went back into Gay's office, and returned flustered. He said that Bill Gay did not want me to be involved with any financial reports, in any manner whatsoever. Because of incidents like that, I had to question Olson's $34 million income figures for 1973.

I kept my thoughts to myself, and let Howard believe what he wanted to believe. I told Del Webb that the deal was off. Not long after that, he was diagnosed with terminal cancer, and he went to St. Mary's Hospital in Rochester, New York for treatment. In late 1975, I got a message from the hospital, requesting urgently that I contact Del. When I phoned back, his nurse said that no calls were going through to him because he was "very, very low," and that he might die that day.

"Please give him my best regards," I told her.

"Who is this?" she asked.

"It's Jack Real."

"He's been waiting all day for your call. Let me put you through to him."

When Del came on the line, I asked him how he was doing.

"Jack, I think it's all over," he said. "I don't know how many days I have left—one or two or three. But I want you to tell Howard I'm thinking of him. Just tell him."

I relayed the message to Howard, but there wasn't the same warmth and concern I had felt from him when Bob Gross died. Then, Howard had gone into mourning for three days. With Del, Howard just nodded and went on with business.

Howard never realized that he lost money in Las Vegas. Ultimately all of his Nevada properties showed losses. When he died, he owned seven hotels and casinos. They had told him that he'd made almost $40 million every year, but he never made a nickel. How can you lose money with a casino? The answer is that casinos never lose money.

CHAPTER 6

A MAN ON THE RUN

OUR FRIEND, THE GENERAL

In February 1972, Howard was under extreme pressure. He had been in seclusion at the Britannia Beach Hotel on Paradise Island in the Bahamas for 17 months, and suddenly the Bahamian government had started to harass him. Lynden Pindling, the country's first black prime minister, was under pressure from the opposition Free National Movement party to kick Howard out. The Hughes aides did not have work permits, and Howard's own residency permit had long since expired. There was an election coming up and Pindling could not be seen to be catering to the Yankee billionaire. When Pindling ordered all of Howard's entourage out of the Bahamas, Howard was in trouble.

Nadine Henley, Bill Gay and Chester Davis had convened in Miami to try to figure out a solution, but Howard contacted me for help. I had to think of a place in a hurry. He couldn't come back to the United States because of his fear that the IRS would take his money, so it had to be a third country. Finally, I sent him a message saying that I had found the best place in the world: Managua, Nicaragua.

I wrote that "The president of Nicaragua owns the Intercontinental Hotel. He owns everything, and I know him."

Howard's response was simply "Let's go."

It was early in the morning, when I phoned President Anastasio Somoza and told him, "Get the people off the top floor of the Intercontinental Hotel. Howard Hughes is coming."

Anastasio Somoza Debayle had been president of Nicaragua since 1967, when he took over from his brother, who had taken over from their father, who had come to power in a coup in 1937. They had each headed the Nicaraguan National Guard before becoming president, and they ran the country like a family business. If anything needed to be done in Nicaragua, there was only one family to talk to.

I had met Somoza shortly after I went to work for the Hughes Tool Company, when I was helping Howard dispose of some of his airplanes. Howard had bought 30 Convair 880s. He gave TWA 20 and kept 10. When he bought Northeast Airlines in 1963, he gave four of those unassigned 880s to them, but when he sold Northeast Airlines to Storer Broadcasting Company in July 1965, they didn't want them, so Howard got them back.

The 880s were stored in the desert, their tires were flat and they needed a great deal of work. One of the tasks that I had taken on was to get rid of these, and other surplus airplanes that Howard had in long-term storage around the country. He had a Sikorsky flying boat, a Douglas DC-6 parked in Santa Monica, an old Douglas B-23 Dragon bomber, and a B-26. Without telling him, I disposed of all of these because I knew that he no longer had any interest in them.

I met General, the president liked to be identified by his national guard rank, Somoza through James Golden. He was a former Secret Service agent who had been hired by Bill Gay and Chester Davis to handle security matters at Hughes Nevada Operations when they took it over from Bob Maheu in 1970. Golden had been on Milton Eisenhower's staff, and he had been security chief for Richard Nixon at the 1968 Republican National Convention. Jim was a nice guy, and one of those who was eventually fired by Bill Gay.

I had spoken to Jim Golden in the course of trying to sell the 880s, because I knew that he was well connected internationally. Jim thought for a minute and then brought up Nicaragua.

"I know that one of Somoza's jets was blown up recently," he said, "and I think if you go and make the General an offer, he'll buy it."

I made the necessary arrangements and flew down to Managua, Nicaragua to see Somoza. I told him that we would sell him the 880s at a very attractive price with very low interest, spread over a long time. During the course of our discussions, the General proposed to take the 880s in a partial trade that would give the Hughes Tool Company a 38 percent interest in his airline, Lanica, the national flag carrier of Nicaragua.

As we were negotiating the deal, he said, jokingly, "I'd do this if I ever thought I could get Howard Hughes to come and live in Nicaragua. I'll give him an island if you can get him to move here."

I said, "You never can tell."

Now, in February 1972, I found myself in Miami with Chester Davis, trying to find a friendly country to take Howard.

Back at the time that I was negotiating to sell the Convair 880s, Chester and I had gotten together for dinner one night at the Brussels Restaurant in New York City. I knew that Chester had a fondness for young women, so I happened to mention one of the nightclubs that Somoza's aide had taken me to when I was in Managua.

"The General's man took me to a nice club down there," I told Chester. "It's called The Cave, and there was a girl there that had a 44-inch bust."

"Hey, everybody, there's a girl down in Managua, Nicaragua that's got a 44-size chest!" Chester shouted, attracting the attention of the other diners in the posh eatery.

Now, Davis remembered what I had told him six weeks before in New York. "Where's the gal that's got the 44-inch bust?" He asked.

"Managua, Nicaragua."

"Send a message to Howard," Chester demanded. "Tell him why you think we should go to Managua, Nicaragua."

After the move, Somoza thought that I got Howard to leave the Bahamas and come to Nicaragua as part of the deal to sell him the 880s. It was much later that he learned the true story of why Howard Hughes came to move to Managua.

To get Howard out of the Britannia Beach Hotel in the Bahamas, we had to bring him down the back fire escape stairway on a stretcher. He was very frail and he didn't like to wear clothes, so it would have been awkward for him to go out the main entrance. His dread of media attention was also a factor, and he didn't want to have Lynden Pindling know that he was going until he was gone.

The plan was to take Howard by boat to Florida, where I had arranged to lease an Eastern Air Lines JetStar to stand by at Opalocka Airport near Miami to fly us all on to Managua. Jim Golden, our security chief, took care of the boat, hiring the *Cygnus*, an 83-foot luxury yacht owned, I was told, by an advertising man from Baltimore. With his Secret Service connections, Jim was also able to arrange for Howard and the entourage to slip through United States customs and immigration with just a nod and a wink.

Conveniently, there was a boat landing at the foot of the Britannia's fire escape, so it was possible to load Howard directly on the *Cygnus* and get under way immediately. The crossing to Biscayne Bay took 22 hours, most of which Howard spent below deck, but he did go topside at one point to thank the captain. This was one of the very few times during the last decade of his life that Howard spoke to, or was seen by, anyone other than his tiny inner circle.

After less than four hours on American soil, the aircraft was on its way to Nicaragua, where General Somoza and United States Ambassador Turner B. Shelton had done their best to make the necessary arrangements for a smooth arrival.

On February 15, 1972, Howard slipped into Nicaragua quickly and quietly, even though he didn't have a valid United States passport. We took over the eighth floor of the pyramid-shaped Intercontinental Hotel, and the windows of Howard's room were quickly covered with dark curtains to keep him secure from the prying eyes of the outside world. The General was, of course, able to arrange for the strictest security. Even Somoza himself would not see Howard for two months.

One complication was that Howard told us that he wanted to keep the airplane, which was owned by Eastern Air Lines. "I'm never going to let that airplane go back," he told his aides. "I enjoyed it too much."

Eastern was very upset with me when I told them, because they had the airplane scheduled every week. That night, without telling Howard or any of the aides, I moved very fast, bought another JetStar and had it flown down to Managua within nine hours to replace the Eastern one. This one would be kept in Managua for his next flight, which would occur sooner than anyone expected.

As soon as he was settled, Howard started to read the local papers in Managua. He had some knowledge of Spanish, and he became interested in local news, especially when it started to include him. Pedro Chamorro's opposition newspaper, *La Prensa*, which was continuously critical of General Somoza, had started to discuss Howard in a series of anti-Somoza stories. *La Prensa* said the General had gotten Howard to glorify some of his exploits by coming to Nicaragua, and that he was now going to take advantage of Howard. This made Howard extremely uncomfortable. He felt that he would be an embarrassment to the people of Nicaragua, so he called me and asked me to get him out of Nicaragua. This time, the decision was made to fly him to Canada, specifically to Vancouver, where arrangements were quickly made for him to take over a floor at the Bayshore Inn.

I'd had to take back the JetStar that I had pre-positioned in Managua, so I brought a Grumman Gulfstream down from Los Angeles. After everything was in place for Howard's departure, I went ahead to Vancouver.

On March 13, 1972, after less than a month in Nicaragua, Howard was on the move again. Before he left the country, though, he decided that he should meet General Somoza at least once. His aides trimmed his long, unkempt beard and cut his shoulder-length hair, and Ambassador Shelton arranged for the General to meet him at Managua's Las Mercedes airport.

General Somoza and Ambassador Shelton both came out at 2:00 in the morning to see him at the airplane, and they spent

about 90 minutes together before Howard took off. The General
and the billionaire had a delightful time. They kidded one another
about who was the richest and who was the best pilot.

"You know, I'll never be as rich as you, General." Howard
laughed, although they both knew that Howard's net worth was
much greater than the net worth of Nicaragua's ruling family, "but
I do think I'm a better pilot."

"No," Somoza laughed in his American-educated accent, "I'm
a better pilot than you are."

When asked later about their meeting with the enigmatic
Howard Hughes, Somoza and Shelton could not get over what a
fine, articulate man Howard was. He was indeed a charming man.
He could charm anybody.

Howard had also developed a fondness for the General. He
had formed much of his opinion of Somoza and Nicaragua from
reading *La Prensa*, which vilified him. In person, however, he found
the General to be very charming. Howard enjoyed the meeting
with Somoza immensely, and his whole impression of the General
was changed. I remember that almost as soon as we reached
Vancouver, he said to me, "Let's go back to Nicaragua and see the
General again."

While Howard was in Vancouver, I found myself back in a
familiar role, as his airplane broker. John Holmes called me to say
that Howard wanted to buy a Grumman Goose flying boat that
he had seen when the air conditioning failed and he opened the
window at the Bayshore Inn. I went to Vancouver, met with the
owner of the Goose, and got his price. I submitted the offer to
Howard, but he never got it. One of the bad aides reported the
incident to Gay, and Gay told Holmes that, one more misdeed,
and he would be fired. Holmes reported to Howard that they
could not locate me, and that perhaps I was still in Europe.

Meanwhile, another situation had come up. While I was
negotiating with an attorney up there to get a hangar, he happened
to mention that under Canadian law, Howard could remain in the
country for only 180 days without being subject to Canadian
income tax, which is even greater than that which Howard was

trying to avoid in the United States. At the time I discovered this, Howard had been in Vancouver for 150 days.

We had not been able to make the kinds of accommodations with the Canadian government that had been possible with the Nicaraguan government, and we had to move quickly. I phoned Chester Davis. I couldn't help rubbing the situation in his face after the way he had been so arrogant to me during the Texas International Airlines negotiations.

"You know," I told him, knowing that he was a lawyer, "there's a Canadian law that says that once a person like Howard lives in this country over six months, all the income from their property is taxed in Canada. Chester, you haven't read the law very well. We've got to get out of here, because Howard is going to be taxed again."

Howard did not seem to mind leaving Vancouver. He was nostalgic for Nicaragua, and for his friend, the General, so on August 29, 1972, Howard returned to the Hotel Intercontinental in Managua. Once he was back in the Nicaraguan capital, Howard let it be known he wanted to find a house that he could live in. In the meantime, it was my understanding that Turner Shelton had been looking all over Managua for a house for him. The ambassador was very accommodating. He told me that we could use the top floor of his residence at the embassy. He said he would move himself down to the bottom floor, and live there until Howard could get another home. We thanked him, and remained at the Intercontinental.

Howard and his friend Somoza never would again meet face to face, but they were involved in several business deals in which I served as an intermediary. A great deal has been said about Howard and shipping magnate Daniel K. Ludwig competing to purchase Marina Mercante Nicaraguense, SA (the Mamenic Line) from the Somoza family. The fact is that Howard was never really interested in the Mamenic shipping line. He may have *considered* sending the General an offer, but I knew about all the serious offers, and there was never an offer.

Actually, Howard was most interested in putting a resort up on Corn Island, which is located in the Caribbean Sea, 52 miles from the Nicaraguan port city of Bluefields. It had an area of approximately four square miles, and Little Corn Island, about nine miles to the northeast, is a little over one square mile. For centuries, the Corn Islands were under British domination and served as a refuge for British, Dutch and French pirates escaping the Spanish fleet. They each have white sand beaches and are ideal for swimming, snorkeling, and other water sports. Today, there are some primitive hotels there, but Howard talked about a sort of casino resort, rather like Las Vegas or the Bahamas' Paradise Island. I conducted the Corn Island negotiations with Somoza for Howard, but we never closed the deal.

As soon as Howard was settled in back at the Intercontinental, I returned to Encino, but I got a call the next day saying that Somoza was disappointed that I did not stay. The General wanted me to fly back down to Managua to discuss his airline.

Bill Gay intervened, sending me a verbal message telling me that he did not want me to return. With this, I went to his office, where I told him that I had an impossible situation with him which continued to get worse. He said he didn't have time to speak with me. It was after 5:00 and he had to get home to a formal dinner party that evening. He told me that his daughter had her fiancé and his entire family as guests. We stayed, however, screaming at each other until after 10:00 pm. The meeting was regularly interrupted by calls from his wife regarding his dinner commitment.

"I've known all about you for years," I told him. "I'm prepared for the worst. I'm prepared to eat a yard of your crap, but you are pushing down 37 inches and there are only 36 inches in a yard."

At one point, he pretended to pull the drapes off the wall.

The upshot of the shouting match was that a meeting was arranged in Managua that included General Somoza, Jim Golden, Bill Gay and myself. Chester Davis and two ladies also joined us. We all had a good time except Bill Gay. He looked strained during the whole affair, and had no understanding as to what we were doing with Lanica Airlines. He also had a deep jealousy of the excellent and cordial relationship that the General had with Jim and me. To indicate his displeasure, Gay told Golden that he was thinking of transferring him to Jack Real's staff—the kiss of death. It was obvious that Gay and Somoza did not get along.

LOSING HIS BIRTHRIGHT

Howard may have made half a billion dollars selling his 78 percent interest in TWA in May 1966, but in April 1970, a federal court had ordered him to forfeit $145.5 million in damages in the TWA antitrust suit. The judgement was for triple damages, because Howard refused to make an appearance in the courtroom. His fear of being seen in public was costing him dearly. Howard had appealed this judgement and had fought TWA for more than two years. By the autumn of 1972, there seemed to be no end in sight, and no chance to escape except to just pay them off. However, Howard didn't have the money.

Most people believed that Howard was a billionaire, but, contrary to popular belief, he could no longer produce hundreds of millions of dollars on short notice. Although he had hundreds of millions of dollars in assets, most of it was tied up in his businesses, such as the Hughes Tool Company—in vast parcels of undeveloped property in Nevada and California, and in his extensive Las Vegas hotel holdings. The mismanagement of the Las Vegas properties had greatly depleted Howard's cash reserves. Records from that period show that these holdings lost $131 million from late 1970 through his death in April 1976. In all that time, his casinos never turned a profit, even though all the other hotels in Las Vegas were showing consistent profits.

Howard had half the cash that he would need to cover the penalties per the court-approved TWA judgement, but in order to raise the full amount, he had to sell something. He couldn't sell the Las Vegas properties because, with no profits, they had minimal value. He couldn't sell the Hughes Aircraft Company because it was owned by the Howard Hughes Medical Institute. This left the Hughes Tool Company, his birthright, the company that his father had created in 1909.

The Hughes Tool Company sale was consummated in late 1972, and as Merrill Lynch was pushing through the sale, I sent a message to George Francom asking him to tell Howard that I thought the sale was immoral. First, I did not want to see Howard having to sell his birthright, a company which Howard had, since 1925, publicly insisted that he would preserve and nurture. Second, I thought that the $28 per share price that Merrill Lynch came up with was too low. They had used Hughes Tool Company's 1971 earnings rather than a pro forma on the Hughes Tool Company earnings for 1972. This share price would yield $140 million, which was far less than the company was worth with the oil industry going into an upswing.

I suggested an alternate plan. I recommended that Howard counter by offering to sell Hughes Tool Company in two parts. He needed to sell assets worth $75 million to cover the shortfall in the payout, so he should take that much out of the sale immediately, but I recommended that the remaining $50 million commitment should be put in trust for one year and sold at the market value of the publicly offered stock for Hughes Tool Company as reported that day by the New York Stock Exchange. He would have to agree to sell the second block of stock in one year at the then-going price—up or down. I was certain the $50 million would bring a substantially higher profit.

I was right on all counts. By November 1972, the quarterly earnings in the first 10 months were significantly higher than the 1971 earnings, and Howard had lost millions in potential stock growth. When Merrill Lynch offered the stock for public sale on the New York Stock Exchange on December 7, 1972, it quickly went up to $30, so Howard netted $150 million, but that was still less than it was worth.

As of December 7, the oil tool-making component of the Hughes Tool Company became Hughes Tool Company, Inc., but Howard retained ownership of the other components, such as the Hughes Tool Company Aircraft Division and the Las Vegas properties. These were organized under a new holding company that Bill Gay named "Summa Corporation," after the Latin word that implies "the greatest."

Howard hated the name "Summa," and even complained that he didn't even know how to pronounce it. But, by the end of 1972, Gay's power had become, in a word, "summa."

The Aircraft Division of Hughes Tool Company, which ultimately was known as "Hughes Helicopters" until it was sold to McDonnell Douglas in 1984, was not included in the sale. The helicopter company officially became Hughes Helicopters, a division of the Summa Corporation in 1972.

The stock price, however, would nag Howard more than Bill Gay's word games. In mid-1973, while we were living in London, Howard asked me to check the current price of Hughes Tool Company stock.

"If I tell you, you'll just get mad," I replied, trying to avoid answering his question. But Howard was persistent, and I ultimately gave in.

"It's selling for around $90 a share," I told him.

His face turned red as he screamed out, "No. No! No!"

"I told you that you'd get mad," I reminded him. "I warned you."

Howard grinned as he calmed down. He then recounted that George Francom had reported my opposition to the Merrill Lynch offer, but by the time he got the message, it was too late. Since I didn't have direct access to Howard at that time, it was clear that the Encino team had stuck my message on the back of a snail and let time do the rest. Actually, I was just a little amazed that Howard even got the message.

A year after Howard died, Charles Tillinghast, the TWA president at the time of the trial and judgement, told me privately that TWA would have been willing to wait at least a year for the payment. If he had asked for such a delay, Howard would have won.

The final, hellishly bitter irony in Howard's sale of the Hughes Tool Company was that *just 27 days* after the stock went on sale, the United States Supreme Court found in Howard's favor, and threw out the TWA judgement. After fighting TWA for 12 years, if Howard would have held out for just 27 more days, he never would have lost his birthright.

THE EARTHQUAKE

Throughout the latter half of 1972, I spent most of my time in Nicaragua working on the Lanica deal. I even took my daughter Patty down with me.

In late December, I flew back to Encino for a board meeting and to pick up a Gulfstream I that was in Van Nuys, and which I'd bought from United States Steel for $600,000. I was anxious to get back to Nicaragua, because Howard had finally made the decision to start flying again. During the first week of December, with General Somoza's help, I had leased an airplane, and gotten a hangar ready. We were scheduled to start flying between Christmas and New Year's. Howard was looking forward with great anticipation to resuming his flying, because he was going to show Somoza who was the best pilot. Unfortunately, other factors would intervene.

It was at the December board meeting that two of Howard's inner circle, Levar Myler and John Holmes, asked Chester Davis to put me on the Hughes AirWest board. By now, it was common knowledge that Howard thought I *ran* the airline and that he assumed I was on the board. For their protection, it would have seemed wise for them to actually have me on the board. Chester agreed, and he came to my office to tell me that I had been appointed.

When Bill Gay heard this, he literally screamed. Then he told me that if I ever opened my mouth at a board meeting, he would see that I was kicked off. I said nothing. After Gay left, Chester paused for a moment and thanked me for keeping my cool.

It was as though Gay had been hit by an earthquake, but two days later, a real earthquake would strike at the heart of the Hughes empire.

Just after midnight on December 23, 1972, a magnitude 5.6 temblor struck Nicaragua, its epicenter in Managua itself. The damage and destruction was staggering. Entire sections of the city simply disappeared into fields of rubble. The scene was chaotic. Members of the national guard were involved in the looting, and they did some things they shouldn't have. The death toll, which was in excess of 10,000, made it one of the two deadliest earthquakes to strike the Western Hemisphere in nearly a century. The Intercontinental Hotel was a newer building and did not collapse, but it suffered severe damage, and it was affected by a power outage that would keep most of the city dark for days.

Howard was sitting in his lounge chair in his room when it occurred and he remained calm, as furniture toppled around him, until it was over. His aides feared that the hotel was coming down. They were running around screaming that they had to get outside. When it was over, he simply told the aides to get the room cleaned up. His four decades in California had given him a respect for earthquakes, but he was not afraid. He just said, "We're over the worst part. I don't have time to run outside."

I had gone home four days before the earthquake, but I had left my daughter in Nicaragua. Patty was there, and she put on a pair of fatigues and became a nurse. She was giving blood transfusions for eight or nine days.

When the earthquake occurred, my foremost concern was for Howard's security. I couldn't telephone him because the phone lines were down, but I realized that I would have to get him out of Nicaragua right away. However, just as there were no telephone communications, there were no flights going into Managua's Las Mercedes Airport. The runways were cracked and the lights were out. It was December and the daylight hours were short. I called several people before I found someone who would agree to fly down and get Howard out. Finally, Bob Graf, a fixed-base operator with a charter service out of Fort Lauderdale, said that he would fly down immediately.

Meanwhile, I had gotten word that the United States Treasury Department wanted to query Howard in the matter of the TWA case, so I was afraid to bring him back into the United States.

When Bob Graf's LearJet whisked Howard out of Managua, I had the pilot file a flight plan for New Orleans, and then divert to Fort Lauderdale. The Treasury Department probably figured we would do this, and they had people at all the spots. When the jet landed at Fort Lauderdale, the Treasury Department agents were there. The aides kept Howard in the airplane and out of sight for four hours while they argued with the agents. It was Christmas Eve, and Howard's 67th birthday. He hadn't slept for days. He was almost devastated by exhaustion.

Finally, the Treasury Department relented and said that they would let him alone and query him "in a couple of days." We drove Howard to a company-owned house on Sunset Island, where he rested, while I spent Christmas Day negotiating with Dan Haughton to use a Lockheed-owned JetStar to fly in from California to pick Howard up. Howard owned more than 30 aircraft, including a dozen JetStars, but, as a course of habit, he seldom used his own airplanes.

A great deal has been written about how Howard Hughes went through the earthquake and then simply ran away without offering to use his resources to help his fellow victims. Even his friend, General Somoza, criticized him for that. Somoza said at the time that he was disappointed that nobody from the Hughes organization had called offering sympathy or condolences or putting forth any tangible offer to help. In fact, Howard wanted to help and even tried to help. When he reached Florida, he left instructions for what he wanted done.

"Because of the devastation of the earthquake," he said, "I want a water distillation plant funded immediately, so Somoza can have fresh water for all those people. I want it on an expedited basis. I want a plant built that could get distilled water for everybody that was devastated by the earthquake."

Those instructions were never carried out. They were passed along to Bill Gay, and it would have been in his interest to carry them out, but nothing happened. Nobody was ever told that Howard had really intended to be part of the relief effort.

The Lockheed JetStar arrived on Christmas night, and on the morning of December 26, they filed a flight plan for London. I hadn't made any arrangements in London prior to Howard's going there, but somebody within the Hughes organization had. They were also looking at least one move ahead at places where he could go. I didn't go on the flight to London, but Lockheed had a London office, and I worked through them. I had to alert those people and arrange for special handling for Howard. They did a good job of getting him through customs and immigration, and they greased the whole thing. This was especially sensitive, because Howard didn't have a passport.

Howard had been happy in Nicaragua and he had a good relationship with Somoza. However, in the wake of the earthquake, we knew that communications would be out for days, if not weeks, and Howard couldn't function under those conditions. It was simply time to leave, and he could not stay in the United States, because he had so many lawsuits there, and he had federal agents wanting to question him.

I didn't think he would ever come back to the United States. Indeed, when he boarded the JetStar that morning in Florida, it was the last time that Howard Hughes would set foot on American soil.

The author, Jack Real, in 1987 when he was president of McDonnell Douglas Helicopters.

Jack Real along with Senators Barry Goldwater
and John McCain at the opening of the
Hughes Helicopter facility in Arizona.

Jack Real accepting the Hughes Award from William Lummis,
Los Angeles, California, January 1984.

Painting by Cynthia Blythe Schemmer, based on Jack Real's
description of Howard Hughes in 1968.

THE AVIATION HALL OF FAME
AWARD

HOWARD ROBARD HUGHES
1905-

DEVELOPING AN INTENSE INTEREST IN AVIATION, HUGHES TOOK FLYING LESSONS WHILE IN HIS TEENS. IN 1925 HE BEGAN A CAREER AS A MOVIE PRODUCER AND IN 1930 PREMIERED HIS MOVIE "HELL'S ANGELS," WHICH GENERATED A WORLDWIDE INTEREST IN AVIATION.

SETTING A STRAIGHTAWAY SPEED RECORD OF 212 M.P.H. IN 1933, HUGHES LATER WON THE SPORTSMAN PILOT EVENT OF THE ALL-AMERICAN AIR MEET. IN 1934 HE BUILT HIS H-1 RACER THAT GAVE BIRTH TO THE HUGHES AIRCRAFT COMPANY AND IN WHICH HE SET A WORLD'S SPEED RECORD OF 352 M.P.H. IN 1935. HE SET A TRANSCONTINENTAL RECORD OF 9 HOURS 27 MINUTES IN HIS NORTHROP "GAMMA," FOR WHICH HE RECEIVED THE HARMON TROPHY. IN 1937 HE SET A NEW TRANSCONTINENTAL RECORD OF 7 HOURS 28 MINUTES IN HIS MODIFIED H-1, AND HE ACQUIRED CONTROL OF TRANS-CONTINENTAL AND WESTERN AIRLINES (TWA). IN 1938 HE AND A CREW OF FOUR COMPLETED A FLIGHT AROUND THE WORLD IN 3 DAYS 19 HOURS, FOR WHICH HE RECEIVED THE HARMON AND COLLIER TROPHIES AND THE CONGRESSIONAL MEDAL. HE BEGAN THE DEVELOPMENT OF THE XF-11 WAR-PLANE IN 1938. HE INITIATED THE DESIGN OF THE LOCKHEED "CONSTELLA-TION," AND DURING WORLD WAR II FLEW THE FIRST MODEL FROM COAST TO COAST IN 7 HOURS. DURING THE WAR HE BUILT THE "HERCULES," A HUGE FLYING BOAT THAT HE SUCCESSFULLY FLEW IN 1947. AFTER THE WAR, HE WAS SERIOUSLY INJURED IN A CRASH OF THE XF-11. AFTER RECOVERING, HE CONVERTED HUGHES AIRCRAFT COMPANY INTO A SUCCESSFUL ELEC-TRONICS FIRM. HE CONTINUED TO EXPAND TWA, CONVERTING IT TO JET-LINERS IN THE 1960'S AND DEVELOPING IT INTO ONE OF THE WORLD'S LEADING INTERNATIONAL AIRLINES. LATER HE FORMED THE HUGHES AIR-WEST AIRLINE.

TO HOWARD ROBARD HUGHES, FOR OUTSTANDING CONTRIBUTIONS TO AVIATION BY HIS DEVELOPMENT OF ADVANCED DESIGN AIRCRAFT, BY SET-TING AERIAL RECORDS THAT DEMONSTRATED THE CAPABILITIES OF AIR-CRAFT, AND BY DEVELOPMENT OF DOMESTIC AND INTERNATIONAL COM-MERCIAL AVIATION, THIS AWARD IS MOST SOLEMNLY AND RESPECTFULLY DEDICATED.

AWARDED DECEMBER 14, 1975 AT DAYTON, OHIO

The Aviation Hall of Fame Award
Presented to Howard Hughes Dec. 14, 1973.

Hughes Flying Boat. Generally known as the "Spruce Goose" (although there was almost no spruce used in its construction) it is now housed inside the Evergreen Aviation Museum McMinnville, Oregon.

The Howard Hughes flying boat ("the Spruce Goose") is now housed here at the Evergreen Aviation Museum and the Captain Michael King Smith Educational Institute, McMinnville, Oregon

The 1938 Collier Trophy being presented to Howard Hughes
for his record setting around the world flight
by President Roosevelt.

CHAPTER 7

BACK IN THE AIR

REACHING LONDON

Howard arrived in London on the day after Christmas 1972, and took up residence in Suite 901 at the Inn on the Park, overlooking Hyde Park, with Buckingham Palace in the distance. In January 1973, shortly after the entourage arrived in the British capital, I received a phone call from Howard Eckersley in London, saying that Howard desperately wanted me in London. We had made plans to start flying again in Nicaragua, and the hangar and aircraft had all been arranged by General Somoza. The earthquake had spoiled that idea, but Howard's enthusiasm for getting back into the air had not diminished in the slightest.

He hadn't actually taken the controls of an airplane since our Electra flights back in 1960, and he was very eager to get going again. He wanted to fly and he wanted me with him in London to make all the necessary arrangements. For the next six months, that would be my sole occupation. I would be very much involved in making the necessary arrangements for his going flying.

I joined Howard at the Inn on the Park in the early part of February 1973. It was the first time that I had seen him in many years. All that while, I had repeatedly tried and failed to get together with Howard, but now the opportunity had arisen and I took it. I would remain with him until he died, more than three years later. I checked in to a room at the Inn, and I dedicated myself to the man, and to the idea that he was going to fly again.

Life now became beautiful. I was with Howard again, but,

from the greeting I got from the aides, I knew that I was not the most welcome addition to Howard's inner sanctum. Even though I had known Howard well for more than a decade and was closer to him than virtually any other Hughes Tool Company executive, I was treated by the aides as a distrusted outsider. They had become the architects and builders of the bubble of isolation that surrounded Howard, and they feared that I was the bridge to the outside world that would disrupt their inside world.

Before I arrived in London, Howard had been a virtual shut-in for several years, programmed to stay bedridden while he passed the time watching mindless movies over and over again or poring over occasional reports from Chester Davis. By orders from Howard's staff in Encino, he was not permitted to view television or read magazines or newspapers. During his stay in London, I don't believe he had more than two or three phone conversations with anyone other than his aides or the Encino communications center headed by Bill Gay.

LOOSE ENDS

Before we were able to focus our attention on getting him flying again, Howard had to turn his attention back to his longstanding problems with his Nevada operations. Since November 1970, when he had pulled the rug out from under Bob Maheu, Hughes Nevada Operations had been under the control of the triumvirate of Raymond Holliday, Chester Davis and Bill Gay, but they had run things for over two years without the official approval of the Nevada Gaming Commission. During the 1960s, Nevada officials seemed to have been more cooperative with the Howard Hughes interests, but the incoming governor, Mike O'Callaghan, was under a great deal of pressure from people who were suspicious of a reclusive billionaire who was perceived to have fled the United States. Because of the Clifford Irving affair, there were also concerns about whether Howard was really in control, or whether he was being manipulated by others who were using his name and forging his signature.

At the beginning of 1973, the conflict with the state government of Nevada reached a climax. Governor O'Callaghan and Nevada Gaming Control Board chairman Philip Hannifin demanded a face-to-face meeting because of "recent events focusing on the authenticity of Hughes' handwriting [the Clifford Irving book]."

Chester Davis told me that if Howard refused such a meeting, "He had better be prepared to liquidate everything in Nevada."

Finally, Howard relented, and the meeting was arranged for St. Patrick's Day. Howard spent most of the day watching movies, and just before midnight, Mell Stewart, the barber who was on retainer for Howard's extremely rare haircuts, was brought in to trim his shoulder-length locks and shape his rather scraggly beard.

In the meantime, Bill Gay and Chester Davis had arrived for the meeting. Chester had never met Howard face-to-face, and Bill Gay had not laid eyes on our boss since 1958.

At 1:00 am on the morning of March 18—after the men from Nevada had waited outside Howard's suite for 12 hours—the aides told O'Callaghan and Hannifin that Mr. Hughes would see them now, and they were brought into Howard's darkened inner sanctum in Suite 901. In the widely reported version of the meeting, Davis and Gay participated in the meeting, but that is not true. I was in the suite at the time, and, although I did not participate in the meeting, I saw enough to see that Davis and Gay didn't either. They sat in an adjoining room with the lights off and said nothing. Howard didn't know they were there, but they would later tell everyone about the meeting they had with him. They could see Howard, but Howard couldn't see them.

During the meeting, which lasted more than an hour, O'Callaghan and Hannifin found Howard to be very lucid. They would report that he was very much in command of the situation and knowledgeable about his interests in Nevada. They even reported that Howard said he was looking forward to returning to Las Vegas.

At the end of the meeting, Hannifin and O'Callaghan agreed to sign the clearance to have the Las Vegas casinos under the

management of whomever Howard designated. As had happened
a year earlier on the tarmac in Managua with Somoza and Shelton,
the Nevada men could not get over what a fine, articulate man
Howard was. As I had seen many times through the years, Howard
was a charming man could, when he wanted to, win almost anyone
as a friend.

GETTING A PLANE

While Howard was still embroiled in his Las Vegas affairs, I
had been spending nearly every day looking for an airport within a
30-mile radius of central London where he could resume his flying
operations. Having ruled out the two big airports, Heathrow and
Gatwick, because they were in constant use by the scheduled
airlines, I drove out and toured Luton, Hatfield, Stansted,
Southend, and even the old Battle of Britain-era fighter field at
Biggin Hill.

On March 21, I had a meeting with Howard, at which I
reviewed the various airfields near London that I had visited. We
reviewed the various aircraft to start his flying program. Howard
told me to bring one of his Convair Model 240 aircraft over from
the United States so he could use it to start his flying. I explained
that the Convair 240 had never been certified in the British
Commonwealth, and to bring it to Britain would be an irritant to
the British civil aviation authorities.

"Instead," I said, "Let's get a British-made turboprop, base it
at a nearby airport and hire a good pilot to get you up to speed."

He listened carefully, and then said, "Go ahead."

I jumped at the opportunity. I recommended the Hawker
Siddeley Aviation HS-748, which I felt was the ideal airplane for
Howard. It was similar to the Fokker F-27 that was then in use by
Hughes AirWest. Both accommodated 40 passengers, and both
had the same Rolls Royce Dart turboprop engine. The HS-748
was never certified in the United States by the Federal Aviation
Administration, but it was sold worldwide outside of the United
States under a British airworthiness certificate.

Meanwhile, of the airports that I considered, my first choice was the one at Hatfield, in Hertfordshire, just north of London. Coincidentally, one of the three main facilities of Hawker Siddeley Aviation was located at Hatfield. The other two were farther north in Britain, one at Woodford, near Manchester, and the other at Chester, near Liverpool. We could use either of these in an emergency, and I felt that this was an important consideration. I knew the weather could be a problem and I wanted alternate runways in case Howard needed them in an emergency. Hatfield was the ideal choice for our base, though, because it was a short drive from central London, where we were living, and because its runway was in the midst of a large farm owned by Hawker Siddeley, and this made it very secluded.

I made contact with Jim Thorne, the Hawker Siddeley manager at Hatfield, and when I told him that Howard Hughes wanted to lease one of his airplanes, he almost fell over. The myth of Howard Hughes was so unbelievable. In those days, just the mention of his name evoked awe. When he got over the shock, and ascertained that Jack Real was for real, he promised that he would do everything he could.

Less than a week later, on March 27, Howard came up with the idea to replace the Fokker F-27 short range turboprops that were being used by Hughes AirWest with the HS-748. He told me to go to Manchester and review the HS-748, and to lease a demonstrator. The purpose of the demonstrator would be to evaluate it for use by AirWest, but Howard could have it to fly in the meanwhile.

The following day, I flew up to Manchester to discuss this idea with the general manager of Hawker Siddeley Aviation, Humphrey Wood. He agreed to the proposal, and said that Howard could use Hawker Siddeley's own demonstrator for a nominal fee with an option to buy. Wood wanted to know whether this was agreeable so that we could ink an agreement right away, so I phoned Howard at the Inn on the Park, and he gave me a one word answer: "Go!"

I said that I would send the HS-748 performance data to

Hughes AirWest, and asked that the airline's London attorney, Jim Leaver, come up to Manchester the next day to help me work up the lease agreement. Leaver flew up, and we spent the entire next day writing up a lease for the Hawker Siddeley HS-748, with the civil registration G-AYYG.

On March 29, I was back in London at the Inn on the Park, and I met with Howard in Suite 901. He asked me about my visit to Manchester, and I handed him all of the operation manuals on the Hawker Siddeley HS-748 so he could study them. He also asked for additional books from Rolls-Royce regarding the engines, and I requested these to be sent over. The next morning, I received a message to "go slow" on the HS-748 lease, as he would prefer a "straight buy" on a new aircraft, or to go straight to pure jet aircraft. He specifically expressed interest in the HS-146, a medium-range, four-engine jetliner that the company had under development, and for which it was soliciting support from the British government. On April 10, however, after reading through the contract, he decided to go ahead with the HS-748 lease, providing that I checked the contract with his tax attorneys.

Three days later, I visited the Hawker Siddeley facility at Hatfield, near London, and met with Jim Thorne. On this visit, the talk turned from the HS-748 lease to other ideas, such as their new Hawker Siddeley HS-146 jet. They hadn't even begun building the prototype yet, but they were projecting a first flight in 1975, and a serious interest from Hughes AirWest would give them a strong bargaining chip in their negotiations with the government over financial support for the project.

I told Thorne that we were "interested" in looking at the HS-146. I never said we were going to buy it. I merely intimated that Howard, because he owned Hughes AirWest, always had an interest in new types of airplanes. I said that I knew Howard would like to be involved in its development.

I discussed the HS-146 with Howard that evening, who told me that he was definitely interested, but that he wanted to wait awhile before involving anybody else at AirWest in the discussions. Ultimately, both Hawker Siddeley and Hughes AirWest would cease to exist before the 146 made its first flight. Five months later, in August 1973, the British government would announce its support for the project, but the following year, Hawker Siddeley would put a hold on the 146, and it would not make its first flight until 1981, four years after Hawker Siddeley was taken over by the government-owned British Aerospace, and five years after Howard was gone.

A follow-up meeting in London, at the St. James Street office of the Hawker Siddeley organization, was arranged by Thorne. I told the Hawker Siddeley people that I had surveyed the local operations in Britain and had come to the conclusion that the Hawker Siddeley aerodrome at Hatfield would be the ideal location for Howard to start his flying. I explained what I wanted and how Howard demanded secrecy of the highest level. I gave the group the background about Howard's XF-11 accident, the success of the Hughes Flying Boat and his long-time involvement with TWA. I told them that I felt that the HS-748 would be the best aircraft for Hughes to use to start.

I proposed that we enter into a lease-purchase agreement for one of their demonstrators, so Howard could start to fly with a Hawker Siddeley pilot. There was some reluctance to do this, because the company feared some adverse publicity because of the attention from the media. I assured them that we'd apply all the security safeguards we'd always used, which should satisfy their requirements. Once we had decided that they would provide the airplane, we discussed how long Howard could use the Hatfield airport without being seen and without the press leaking the news. Tony Banham from the Hatfield facility, then jumped in to explain what back roads to take to avoid arousing suspicion.

Our next task was to identify a pilot. Ward and others at Hawker Siddeley recommended Tony Blackman, the company's chief of engineering flight test, who was based at Manchester. I immediately took to Tony Blackman. My background as the chief of flight test for Lockheed had helped train me to spot people who were ideal for a particular job, and I knew Tony was perfect for Howard. He was well educated, and, after graduation from Cambridge, he became a college professor. Later, he took up flying and eventually went to work for Hawker Siddeley.

We got the aircraft lease-purchase agreement signed very quickly, but I had to break the news to the people at Hawker Siddeley that Howard had that one idiosyncrasy that prevented him from flying an aircraft he owned or was leasing. I explained that it was like a man who would not wear his new suit since it would no longer be his *new* suit if it was worn. What had seemed to be a simple lease-purchase agreement now had become a fairly complicated arrangement because I wanted them to provide us with *another* HS-748 demonstrator for Howard to fly.

Like a stage actor being called back for another curtain call, the HS-748 aircraft that Hawker Siddeley identified was in high demand. It was even scheduled for performances at the Paris Air Show. We were persistent in our demands, and it was agreed that the aircraft would be available after the show.

After the details of the contract seemed to be ironed out, the issue of Howard's pilot's license was raised. We would have a problem licensing Howard in Great Britain, particularly if Howard was to use his license legally. He'd need check-flights with the United States FAA-approved examiners, and he would need to be photographed for the license. We considered getting Howard a British license, but that required a photo as well, and we knew that Howard would never pose for a picture. This was something he hadn't done in three decades.

Tony Blackman, meanwhile, noted that the HS-748 flight manual required two pilots to fly the aircraft. However, it did not require that the pilots be licensed. There was no doubt that Howard was a pilot of great reputation, so the issue, per Tony's interpretation, was resolved. Hawker Siddeley concluded they were not breaking the air and navigation rules. As for the insurance issues, Howard and Hawker Siddeley would have entered into a contract, so there was no way that Howard and/or any members of his staff could take legal action against the Hawker Siddeley Company should there be an accident.

With our strange lease agreement finally in place, I told Jim

Thorne that Howard had expressed an interest in coming up to Hatfield to tour the Hawker Siddeley factory. He promised that he would do anything to accommodate the great Howard Hughes. I told him that Howard would come at a moment's notice, and that the plant should be open and ready to be toured whenever Howard wanted to make his visit. This meant that if Howard came on Saturday or Sunday, the plant should be open and ready for his visit. In England, in those days, they didn't believe in working on weekends. Jim Thorne balked, but I painted a picture of what he would do if this big Daimler car rolled up to the gate and it was locked.

The plant was open that weekend, and the next. For six weeks, they had kept it open seven days a week, and they were getting pressure from the factory floor to go back to the old schedule. I took this concern back to Howard, telling him: "Howard, they're not going to keep the place open on Saturday and Sunday for you anymore. They've opened it for the last six weeks, and you never came."

He said, "You haven't tried hard enough."

"I've tried hard," I told him. "I've gone up there. I've done everything. I can't do it. I admit the failure."

He said, "What's going to happen?"

"Well, we have to do the one thing that I know you don't like to do, but the only way you can get it open on Saturday and Sunday is, you've got to call Jim Thorne, the general manager, and you've got to give him a little charm. You've got to tell him what aviation does for the world, and you'll get it open on Saturday and Sunday."

Howard agreed, and I prepared Thorne for the call that he was going to receive from Howard Hughes. First, Howard was going to make the call on Tuesday, and then, on Thursday. I had to get Thorne ready to receive the call. I had to tell him "It's going to · come today—no, it's going to be tomorrow—then it's going to be tomorrow."

Finally it came. I was in the Hawker Siddeley offices with the door ajar, and I knew what was going on.

When Thorne hung up, I went in and asked: "How was the call?"

"Oooh, brilliant!" He said. "I've just established a relationship with Howard Hughes. I'm moving the phone up here, and it's going to be painted green or red. That's his phone, and when that phone rings, I'll be on it."

Of course, I knew that he would never get another call from Howard the rest of his life, but he got a red phone installed in his office. And of course, the plant was open on Saturday and Sunday after that. Howard Hughes was the most charming guy in the whole world. He could charm anybody.

Shortly after he established his "relationship" with Howard Hughes, Jim Thorne invited me to be his guest at the 1973 Paris Air Show. He clearly saw this as an opportunity to spirit me away from Howard for a couple of days and to make a sale. Thorne was still optimistic that he could seek my help in having Howard launch the HS-146.

"It's going to be quite a show this year," Thorne said. "We're taking the HS-748 to Paris. And we've reserved plenty of rooms. We can accommodate you easily."

"Forget it," I told Thorne. "Howard will never let me out of his sight. But it's a tempting offer.

"Wait a minute," I said as my creative juices started flowing. "Why don't you invite both Howard and I. He obviously won't be able to come, but he'll say, 'Jack, why don't you be my surrogate?'"

Thorne followed through with the plan and, sure enough, on May 25, Howard received an invitation. Howard called me to his bedroom. He was holding the invitation.

"Thorne from Hatfield has invited us to join him at the Paris Air Show. But you can't go. I need you here. You know why, don't you?" He continued. "That's the week you and I are going to be closeted doing advance planning for all of our companies."

I frowned just a bit and clenched my fist behind my back. I did a poor job of hiding the fact that I was upset. Howard could see that I looked dejected.

"Well, maybe we could get the Paris Air Show postponed for a week," Howard said in a deadly serious tone—one that almost made me believe he could pull it off.

I never did get to the Paris Air Show that year. And, true to form, we didn't do any advance planning that week either.

This was the year that the Tupolev Tu-144, the prototype Soviet supersonic transport, crashed at the Paris Air Show, so the show was closed a day before it was supposed to have. When I got a message on June 3 that the Hawker Siddeley people that I wanted to see were coming home a day early. I decided to go up to Manchester to see them a day earlier than I had previously planned. Howard was asleep, but I told George Francom to tell him where I had gone, and why I went early. George gave Howard the message when he woke up, and he asked George what a Tu-144 was. He had never heard of the aircraft.

The fact that Howard, who was extremely interested in aviation, had never heard about one of the most talked about aircraft of the year came as a shock to me. It demonstrated graphically how strictly his aides controlled his access to information. When George brought him a copy of *The Daily Express* newspaper that told about the crash, he was like Rip van Winkle. When he finally got to read the newspaper, he learned about many things of which he had no knowledge. How terribly long he had been completely out of touch was demonstrated when he looked up from a page that he was studying with his magnifying glass and asked innocently, "What's Watergate?"

The Watergate scandal that ultimately brought down the presidency of Richard Nixon—to whose 1968 campaign Howard had donated $50,000—had been on the front page of nearly every American newspaper, and most European dailies, for a year or more. Howard had never heard of it. Much was written during the 1970s about a secret role that Howard himself might have played in the cabal behind the Watergate scandal, but in fact, it was two years after the Watergate break-in and months short of the scandal's dramatic climax before Howard read his first mention of it in a London newspaper!

When the other aides found out that George had shown Howard a newspaper, any newspaper, they were livid. He had violated the wall of security that they had constructed around Howard. The original intent had been to keep the news media from reaching into Howard's own privacy, but it had been twisted so as to cut off Howard's access to all forms of news media. They had deliberately stopped bringing him newspapers and magazines, and they had removed the television set from his room before he had arrived. He was totally isolated.

Soon, however, I would break that wall of isolation that had been constructed around Howard, and get him back to a world he loved. I went up to Hatfield to make the final arrangements with Jim Thorne to keep G-AYYG in the Hatfield flight shed, so that it would be more convenient for Howard's flight program. The stage was now set. The only hurdle remaining would be actually getting Howard out of Suite 901, out of the Inn on the Park, and out of the clutches of the bad guys.

With all the arrangements having been made at Hatfield, I had to prepare Howard for his first prolonged appearance in public in 15 years. This would include buying him a suit of clothes. For all of those years, he had spent all of his time in his bedroom, and he didn't like to wear clothes, so he had no clothes. Like many people, he'd sleep without clothes, and since he stayed in bed most of the time, he never wore them. He was just more comfortable this way. Many of those who have written on Howard's life have regarded this as abnormal, but I don't. He was in bed, and alone in his room, so it didn't bother him.

He would have the top of his pajamas wrapped around his shoulders to keep the draft off, and occasionally he wore a robe. When he had moved to and from Managua and Vancouver, he just wore pajamas or a robe and sandals, because he spent most of the trip sitting in a car, a boat or an airplane. These were all the clothes that he needed, and all that he had owned for many years. For the flying, though, he would need a conventional suit of clothes. Gordon Margulis, one of Howard's bodyguards, and I took it upon ourselves to go to Simpson's in Piccadilly in London where we outfitted him. Gordon and I had a great time. He pretended he was gay and wanted me to have everything he could get for me. Instead of buying one shirt, he bought me five, and he bought Howard a leather flight jacket and a pair of Bally shoes that fit me. I figured they would fit him if they fit me. He never wore them. Instead, he wore his sandals. Because he liked to keep his toenails fairly long, shoes were hard for him to wear.

We also went to Dunn's, another store in Piccadilly Street where they sold hats and I bought him a black fedora. Later that day, we bought him a lightweight seersucker suit with a very comfortable coat.

A PERFECT DAY

The next day, Sunday, June 10, blossomed into a beautiful summer day. That afternoon, Howard abruptly decided that we were going to go flying, now. It was amazing to see a man who had been practically bedridden for a decade suddenly decide to go flying.

Levar Myler had taken his wife and daughter out to Windsor Castle, so the Daimler car that we had hired for the use of the Hughes entourage in London was gone. I called a rental agency and reserved a Rolls Royce, expecting it to be a good one. I was wrong, it was built before 1950.

We called Tony Blackman, who had been taking advantage of the sunny day to do some work on the hedges at his home. I told him today was the day, and he got into his little de Havilland Dove aircraft, which he kept near his place—and flew down to Hatfield. Luckily, he got there about 20 minutes before we did.

When the Rolls Royce arrived at the Inn on the Park, I had it moved to the basement and asked that the garage doors be shut. With George Francom's help, I got Howard out of bed and dressed. Because he hadn't done any serious walking in years, I was afraid he'd fall over then and there, but he stood, unsteadily, on his feet. He was unused to walking farther than from his bed to the bathroom, so he was very shaky on his feet at first. We put chairs at eight or nine foot intervals ahead of Howard so he could sit down frequently. Using this method, we slowly moved down the ninth floor of the hotel and finally got him to the elevator.

Leaning against him whenever I could to prop him up, we finally got into the antiquated Rolls Royce. Just as we were moving out, Levar Myler pulled up with our driver, Alan Trelogan. Howard was already in the Rolls, so we decided to stay with it and our contract driver. Levar Myler climbed into the back seat, and I joined the driver in front to guide him to Hatfield.

Just as we were leaving, Howard said angrily, "Is that sonofabitch Bill Gay in the front seat?"

"Jack," Levar interjected, "please turn around and show him that it's you and not Bill Gay."

I turned around. Howard recognized me and became totally relaxed. We then headed toward Hatfield, where we entered by the back way, through an old, decaying farm, onto the Hatfield aerodrome perimeter track and onto the airfield. Tony was at the hangar door, and as the Rolls drove in, he shut the hangar door.

There was complete silence. The Hawker Siddeley engineers stood as far back as they could, keeping out of the way. After a few minutes, I got out of the front of the car and confirmed that everything was in order. Levar Myler was the next man to get out. I had a feeling he didn't relish this event at all. He was a white-knuckle flyer.

At last, Howard got out of the car. He was wearing an open-necked shirt, blue trousers and his fairly flimsy sandals. When I introduced him to Tony, Howard spoke slowly but firmly. I warned Tony that he was deaf, but that day it wasn't obvious. He walked unsteadily to the steps at the bottom of the front entrance of the aircraft, where he waited for Tony and me to join him.

He had walked around the front end of the airplane and discussed the need for flush rivets on such an aircraft. Tony pointed out that it was British design philosophy on a slow aircraft like the HS-748 to use flush rivets only where they were needed, or where the flush rivets would help the aerodynamics of the design and reduce drag. Consequently, on the HS-748, flush rivets were used just on the top surface of the wings.

Howard reluctantly agreed to the logic of the design and then slowly climbed the steps. He briefly inspected the flight deck and then proceeded to make himself comfortable. His unfamiliarity with walking caused him to bump his head on a temporary antenna. I held my breath, but he acted as if nothing had happened.

Then he moved to the cockpit. Howard was about to begin his journey back from beyond the fringes of reality.

The story has circulated that Howard got undressed before we went flying, but this is untrue. He opened his shirt, and he would unbuckle his belt and unbutton his fly, but he never took his pants off. He felt more comfortable with nothing around his waist, because he hadn't worn pants for years, but he never exposed himself or anything like that. It was just a little freedom from being tied up with a seat belt on.

Much of the myth of Howard Hughes that existed in the 1970s was constructed out of innuendo by people who had never met him. Another aspect of this myth was his fear of germs or contagion. Having grown up on the Gulf Coast before the development of antibiotics, he had a healthy concern about contagious disease. He may have been a bit obsessive, but he was nowhere nearly as pathological as many people have reported. When we went flying, there was none of that. There was never any issue about germs or wrapping his hands in Kleenex. Tony Blackman just couldn't get over what an average guy he was.

It also has been reported that Howard was deaf. He may have seemed to be hard of hearing in his later years, but curiously, Howard could hear fairly well when we were talking about aviation aboard the aircraft. It seemed that he could hear fine when the discussion involved subjects that he liked to talk about—and he liked to talk about aviation, particularly when aboard an aircraft.

Howard got into the left seat and Tony started the engines. I looked at my watch. It was 4:10 pm. It had taken just two hours from when we left the Inn on the Park to get Howard settled in and ready to fly. In the right seat, Tony had completed the preflight checks and he opened the throttles. The Rolls Royce Dart RDa-7 turboprop engines made their characteristic whistling whine.

From my vantage point in the jumpseat between, and slightly behind, the two pilots, I glanced at Howard. He had his hand on the nose wheel steering tiller trying to steer the aircraft on the taxiway. Unfortunately, the HS-748 provides nose wheel steering by the pilot in the left hand seat only, so even if Tony wanted to help with the steering, he couldn't reach the tiller. He was obviously frustrated, but couldn't do anything while seated in the right seat. It reminded me of the infamous passenger-side emergency brake that people often use to help control a car when not in the driver's seat. Tony couldn't help himself. He was reacting to a reflex that we all share.

The control tower gave Howard and Tony permission to enter the runway, and Howard lined the aircraft up for takeoff using the inadequate nose-wheel steering device. Tony opened the throttle and the aircraft accelerated down the runway, weaving from side to side.

Tony called "rotate" and Howard slowly pulled the wheel back. The aircraft left the ground. Thirteen years after Howard's last flight as a pilot, he was airborne and in control again.

Howard wasn't familiar with British instruments, but he quickly got a feel for the layout of the cockpit. He clearly was absorbing even the slightest movement by the plane, breathing in the cabin air like it was an intoxicating perfume.

The plan called for a 15 minute flight to Hawker Siddeley's Bitteswell airfield, about 40 miles north of Hatfield, where the aircraft would be in controlled air space. Here, we intended to "shoot" a series of "touch-and-goes," where we would touch down, take off and come around to do it again. Initially, Tony would help Howard to land the aircraft because he hadn't had the experience in such a long time.

As we approached Bitteswell, Tony took the controls and

demonstrated his idea of a typical landing and takeoff. Howard then took over without difficulty, but made a very slow turn downwind on his landing approach. They were much farther away than Tony wanted when Howard proceeded to do a big circuit. We were a long way out when Howard reached a final straight-in approach. I sat there as Howard prepared to land. I was confident that he could do it, especially with Tony there to assist, but the thought crossed my mind that I could end up as a statistic on Howard's lengthy resume.

Tony realized he was acting as Howard's automatic throttle. That wasn't such a bad thing, Tony thought, since the HS-748 was very speed stable.

Howard started his descent to the runway, but he got too low, and Tony had to keep pulling the stick back to prevent him from landing short of the runway. As we were running out of runway, Howard finally touched down. Tony politely, but firmly, told Howard that the correct way to land was on the first part of the runway.

They made several more circuits, landing each time and taxiing around for the next takeoff. Tony adopted the strategy of taking over control of the aircraft at the bottom of the downwind leg, and putting the aircraft in a position where Howard couldn't get to his favorite undershooting position before touchdown. Howard gradually began to accept the fact that if he wanted to land the aircraft without Tony interfering, he would have to touch down farther up the runway.

Bitteswell was not equipped for night flying, so as it began to get late, Tony got permission to go to nearby East Midlands Airport so that Howard could continue trying to master the HS-748. After several touch-and-goes with the benefit of runway lights, darkness had fallen, and Howard agreed that he had done enough. Howard had rationalized that he should not be flying on instruments without practice, especially in the dark. They decided to make one more takeoff and head back to Hatfield.

Meanwhile, another aircraft was coming in to land, so they waited for takeoff. Tony had left the landing lights on, shining a bright, distracting light toward the inbound plane. Howard suggested we should turn them off to avoid confusing the pilot. Tony and I now realized that Howard was beginning to think like a pilot again.

As we started back to Hatfield, Howard told us how much he enjoyed flying again. It was wonderful to hear his voice beam with excitement. It was like old times. Howard made a fairly reasonable landing. Not bad for a man who hadn't flown in 13 years and had only now piloted an unfamiliar aircraft for three hours and 10 minutes. I could see that Howard and Tony were both delighted as they began taxiing. Tony breathed a sigh of relief, and Howard seemed justifiably pleased with his effort.

After we had completed the flight, Tony said Howard's flying had been "sloppy," but that he was improving. Tony pointed out that correct air speed was just as important as landing in the right part of the runway. He didn't think Howard was convinced.

Levar Myler, who had ridden as a passenger in the cabin, left the aircraft visibly shaken. He had much less confidence in his boss than either Tony or I.

I helped Howard get back in the Rolls Royce, and we started back to London. I have never told Tony, but on the way back to the hotel in the Rolls, Howard told me that he was embarrassed by the way Tony had treated him.

"I don't like having anyone teach me how to fly," Howard said. "I have my own way of landing and taking off. I've always liked to hit the numbers right on the edge. Tony wants me to fly like a student pilot. I think you're going to have to look for a new copilot for me."

Fortunately, this feeling went away as the two of them developed a rapport with one another. Howard would develop great respect for Tony, both as a man and as a pilot.

At the time, Tony was busily involved in other projects and didn't have time to waste, but he didn't want to give up the job as Howard's pilot to anyone else. He knew that Hawker Siddeley was about to launch the HS-146, to which he had been assigned as the test pilot, and Hawker Siddeley would love to have Howard as the launch customer.

RENEWING HIS VISA

It's not easy to renew a visa for a man who travels with no passport, but for me and for Howard, it was a job that had to be done. In June 1973, Kay Glenn, Bill Gay's assistant from the office in Encino, called Tony Blackman and told him that Gay wanted Howard taken out of Britain, so that they could extend Howard's stay in the country. At that time, an American citizen could stay in Britain without a visa for six months, but a longer stay required more paperwork and the kind of intrusion into his privacy that Howard abhorred. If Howard wanted to stay, the immigration laws dictated that he apply for a renewable six-month visa that required a photograph, and Howard adamantly refused to be photographed.

However, if Howard left Britain, even for a few hours, and reentered the country, he could theoretically stay for another six months without having to go through those complications.

Tony asked where they wanted him to take Howard, but Glenn didn't know. The Encino team simply felt that Howard had to get out of Britain so that he could stay in Britain. Of course, Howard had no passport, so he had to be taken somewhere within the European Community of nations, where he would not need one.

Glenn further told Tony that he and Bill Gay did not want me to be involved. When Tony asked why, Glenn told him that I was "seriously ill." As Tony knew, because he and I saw one another on a regular basis, this was untrue.

They just didn't trust me. The Encino people wanted to circumvent my access to, and influence over, Howard, so, to guarantee success, Gay sent Kay Glenn to London from California to run this specific operation of taking Howard in and out of the country. When Tony met Glenn and told him that he didn't know the front from the back of an airplane, Glenn reluctantly told Tony they needed me. They waited for me to "recover."

Tony never trusted Kay Glenn and the Encino people after that episode, so he and I worked together to plan the flight. We decided that we would fly from Hatfield to the airport at Ostend, across the English Channel in Belgium. We would land and return immediately to Hatfield. The round trip would take approximately four hours. Hawker Siddeley's Tony Banham would, meanwhile, make certain that the immigration and customs officials would be present at Hatfield to witness our departure and return, thus avoiding the need to leave from an international airport where it would be necessary to obtain customs clearances.

Meanwhile, Howard's plane sat ready for flight at Woodford, near Manchester. I had Howard's California-based flight mechanic, George Larsen, and his family come to England to make sure the aircraft was always in flight-ready condition, even though it was never to be used. As usual, Howard would charter an airplane rather that fly one that he owned.

Hawker Siddeley looked everywhere for an HS-748 they could charter for the trip and finally found one in France that was operated by a small French airline known as Rousseau Aviation. Once we located the aircraft, things began to deteriorate. First, Howard's staff at the Inn on the Park could never decide what day we were going to take off. When I was assigned the task, I picked June 27, and planned for "wheels up" at 10:00 am. Hawker Siddeley made all the arrangements using Bob Stubbs, one of Tony's pilots, as their operations manager. His assignment was to fly the French airliner into England at Hatfield before 9:00 am.

Tony Blackman left his home in Woodford at 4:30 am, and arrived at Hatfield four hours later, only to discover that the French HS-748 was delayed, and we'd had to put a 12-hour hold on the flight. Unfortunately, those were the days before cellular phones and pagers, and he didn't get the word that the flight had been delayed until he arrived at 8:30.

Meanwhile, Tony Banham was told by British customs authorities that they wanted the aircraft to land at Stansted en route to Ostend, and then check back at Stansted after our landing and take-off at Ostend. At 7:00 pm Tony Banham and I had signed the contract papers for a lease of the French HS-748 aircraft. I called Tony Blackman and said the program was a "go" for that night at approximately 11:00 pm.

I arrived at the Inn on the Park at 10:00 pm and made the arrangements to move Howard to Hatfield. Before leaving the hotel, I checked in with Tony Blackman, who told me that he would not make the night flight unless he could have Bob Stubbs along as a back-up pilot. Howard didn't want this, but after I explained that Tony really needed an experienced man with us for a flight across the English Channel, he agreed, but he insisted that the additional pilot not be allowed to see him. We did not leave the hotel until 11:00 pm. We were now behind schedule, but the French HS-748 was also late, and it had not arrived until five minutes before we reached Hatfield.

When we arrived, Tony Blackman had bad news. The weather at Hatfield was zero-zero. You couldn't see 50 feet in front of yourself. Tony recommended that we should not go until the weather improved, or reschedule the flight for another day. I had to argue with Tony not to cancel, as we had worked too long to arrange this flight.

He reluctantly agreed, and we climbed aboard. We seated Howard's aides in the aircraft. They all looked scared when they saw Howard seated in the pilot's seat. I was never told why Gay had ordered three aides to go on the flight, but I surmised that Gay thought I was going to kidnap Howard to a foreign country. After what happened over the next three years, I think that would have been a very good idea.

I handed Howard his headset, which he had used before, and which we now kept at the hotel. The weather still looked impossible, and Tony again suggested delaying the flight until another day. Howard would not hear of it, so Tony started the engines and Howard taxied the aircraft to the runway. When the aircraft was lined up for take-off Tony made one last appeal to postpone the flight. Howard just shook his head.

The aircraft slowly gained speed. The runway lights appeared and disappeared in the fog. As Howard left the ground, Tony took over the controls and headed for Stansted. The weather had not changed. Tony received permission to make an approach and put the aircraft on the ILS (Instrument Landing System) localizer, using the autopilot coupled to the glide slope. Howard sat there in amazement.

Fortunately, Tony had been flying simulated minimum approaches on the company simulator. He had determined that an approach speed of about 150 mph and visibility of about 200 feet was necessary to get sufficient guidance from the runway lights to be able to touchdown and to keep the aircraft straight after landing. This was providing that the aircraft was lined up on the ILS system when the lights came into view.

Tony had also determined from the simulator test that with a good glide slope, the aircraft would not become unstable. Instead, it would remain on the glide slope until about 50 feet above the ground. Tony realized that under these conditions, the aircraft should be operated by two crewmen. Howard's unfamiliarity with the aircraft meant he could not help, so Tony would have to do it alone. As Tony reached the glide slope, he turned to watch the altimeter and look out at the same time. When he reached 200 feet above the ground, a light appeared briefly through the murk below. He disengaged the autopilot and reduced the rate of descent. To his surprise, he was lined up properly and we were on the ground.

He stopped in the middle of the runway. There were no other alternatives. He could see nothing but the runway lights 50 feet ahead. The tower sent out a "follow me" van and Howard taxied slowly to the ramp.

The aides exited the aircraft as soon as it came to a stop. Bob Stubbs took the ship's papers to the customs and immigration office, which was just a few yards away, but which we could barely see in the fog.

The weather could not have been worse. A warm sector was lying across southern England, with very low clouds, rain and very poor visibility. Howard was still sitting in the pilot's seat and showed no intention of leaving it. I went outside and had a "What now?" session with Tony.

"Enough is enough," he said. "I won't continue the flight unless I sit in the left seat and Bob Stubbs sits in the right seat. Mr. Hughes will have to fly as a passenger."

I carried the ultimatum back to Howard, who was still seated on the flight deck. He refused, but suggested that Bob Stubbs could sit in the jumpseat as an observer.

"I'm learning a lot watching Tony," Howard said proudly. "And I don't want to sit back in the cabin. It's too cold back there. The only warm place is the cockpit."

For the next hour, I became the arbiter of the ensuing argument, going back and forth to the cockpit with offers and counter offers. All the while, the customs and immigration people were wondering what the delay was about.

At one point during the discussion, Howard smiled at me and said: "I consider you one of aviation's finest salesmen. You hate to admit defeat. Use this same charm and talent to convince Tony to allow me to sit in the left seat."

I hated to admit defeat, and so did Howard, but after almost an hour, he climbed back into the cabin and sat down. I eventually turned two of the cabin seats around and made a bed for him, and he slept through most of the flight.

We took off with Tony in the left seat, and were swallowed up by the clouds as soon as we rotated. Tony set a course for Belgium.

After a long, bumpy flight, we suddenly found ourselves in the clear, with the lights of Belgium in the distance. Tony decided to make a touch-and-go landing. After touching down, he opened the throttles and lifted off again. He declared a hydraulic emergency and asked for a clearance to Stansted. With approval granted, he headed back for another approach into Stansted. For the record, this declared emergency proved that the airplane carrying Howard Hughes had landed and taken off from a foreign country.

As we approached Stansted, the weather had cleared, and dawn was starting to break on the eastern horizon. The autopilot made a perfect approach down the glide scope. We dropped below 200 feet, but this time Tony was better prepared and had just enough visual clues to close the throttle and pull the stick back.

After a perfect touchdown at Stansted, we bundled all of the passengers out of the aircraft. As we disembarked, Tony asked me, "Do you think he will ever forgive me?"

"Not tonight, he won't," I said.

I had previously arranged for the two cars that took us up to Hatfield to be repositioned at Stansted so we could go back to the Inn on the Park from there.

One of cars was a Rolls Royce limousine that Kay Glenn had gotten from a London rental firm through the efforts of Grant Mannheim at the Rothschild Bank. It was a real attention-getter because all the windows were covered with newspaper sheets from the current *Times of London*.

As we drove away, Howard fell asleep with his head on my shoulder.

LET'S FLY FOREVER!

Howard loved flying again. He loved it like a baby. He came alive when he was flying. I never knew a man on whom flying had such an effect as it had on him. His life had become livable again.

Two days after the June 27 Ostend flight, as we reminisced about the flight, Howard said it was the worst weather in which he had ever flown. He described every minute of the flight from Hatfield to Stansted, in which he'd occupied the left seat, but there was no mention of the Stansted to Ostend leg of the flight. He was complimentary in his remarks about Tony's airmanship and candor. He told me to tell Tony he would like to fly the Hawker Siddeley HS-125 business jet as soon as possible, with Tony as the co-pilot. All was forgiven.

I was instructed to buy a low-time, used HS-125, which was to be delivered to the Hawker Siddeley plant at Hatfield. As was the case with the HS-748, the aircraft was to be kept ready for flight, but not to be flown.

In anticipation of flying the HS-125, Tony contacted the former de Havilland facility in Chester, where the HS-125 was assembled, and asked the chief pilot, John Cunningham, to have one of his pilots check Tony out in preparation for flying Howard in the HS-125.

The HS-125 is a small, nine-passenger, twin engine executive jet. Originally launched by de Havilland in 1960 as the "Jet Dragon," it was the first aircraft designed specifically as a business jet. The prototype de Havilland DH-125 made its maiden flight in 1962, with the first customer delivery in September 1964. Shortly after introduction of the DH-125, the de Havilland Aircraft Company became part of Hawker Siddeley Aviation, which led to the aircraft becoming the HS-125. Eventually, 358 aircraft were made with the Rolls Royce Viper turbojet engine, before 1976, when it was reequipped with turbofan engines and redesignated as the Hawker 700.

We kept putting Tony off on the date, and he was losing credibility with his management, who wanted to know when—if ever—the mysterious Howard Hughes was going to fly their HS-125. Finally Tony gave me a "now or never" ultimatum, which I passed along to Howard, who agreed to go the following day, July, 17, 1973.

Since it was in the middle of a working week, there were a great many prying eyes who might see Howard, so we positioned the company HS-125-400 (tail number G-AYOJ) on the far side of the Hatfield airfield near the back entrance.

Howard really enjoyed flying the HS-125, and he seemed more active and more responsive than he had been when we started the flying program. The flying was obviously doing his physical condition a great deal of good, especially since he was up and around more than he had been in years. He talked to Tony and me much more freely, and it was possible to have an open and warm conversation with him. I enjoyed that brief period, especially since Howard seemed to be smiling a great deal more, and his conversations, which were filled with life, reminded me of the first night we met in 1957.

July 17 was a great flight. We took off at 6:28 pm and went back over to Stansted. Howard still tried to land on the numbers, but after a discussion, his touch-and-go flying improved. He loved the flying qualities of the HS-125 jet compared to the HS-748 turboprop, which exhibited much heavier control forces. I suspected that I was right when I suggested to Tony that Howard should start with the HS-748 because it was slow. But the problem with the HS-748 was that the control forces were high and had excessive speed stability on the approach pattern.

During his flight that day, Howard pressed for touch-and-goes rather than what Tony wanted, which was to get Howard to land, stop and then take off again. Howard knew that he could get more landing in if we immediately took off again after touching down. Consequently, most of the flying was touch-and-go. Each time we touched down, Tony raised the flaps and retrimmed the elevator and then opened up the throttle so we did not come to a stop after we touched down. From Howard's facial expressions, you could see he was enjoying himself.

After seven landings and takeoffs at Stansted, we made the 20-minute flight back to Hatfield and touched down at 8:47 in the evening. As we taxied in, Howard seemed very pleased. We then went back in the cabin and had a 15-minute talk all about flying, with Howard telling us how much he enjoyed flying.

Tony took the opportunity to pitch the turbine-powered HS-748 and talk about the soon-to-be-launched HS-146. Tony played salesman, pointing out repeatedly what an ideal aircraft it would be for Hughes AirWest. Howard listened with an open mind and a closed pocketbook. Tony mentioned that Hawker Siddeley had constructed a mock-up of the aircraft there at Hatfield, and that Howard was invited to visit it the next time we flew.

The flying bug had really struck home with Howard. It brought him alive. He was truly taken by the program that Tony and I had working, but we both realized the long trip to Hatfield was a deterrent to his flying. I knew that Hawker Siddeley owned on-site residences at both Hatfield and Woodford airports, and I told Tony that it would be great if he could get the management to host Howard for three or four weeks at one or the other of these. I had visited the Woodford "Clubhouse," and felt it would be ideal. The home had been built in the sixteenth century as the home of the Duke of Wakefield, but it had been totally modernized with five bedrooms. It was under the care of a couple who could provide meals and services.

With some trepidation, Tony approached Humphrey Wood, the Manchester general manager, suggesting the possibility of turning over the Woodford Clubhouse to Howard for three or four weeks. Humphrey was not too happy, but he finally agreed that Howard could have the Clubhouse for a limited time. Humphrey believed Hatfield would be the big winner if Hughes went ahead with the HS-146, so he had urged the Hatfield team to turn over its similar facility, an Elizabethan manor called Nast-Hyde, to Howard.

In turn, Tony had approached Jim Thorne. Although he was impressed that Howard was interested in coming to visit the mock-up on his next visit, he said that it would have to be left to Woodford to host Howard.

Howard, meanwhile, was quite taken by the idea of getting out of the hotel and living in a private location next to his aircraft. He was absolutely delighted with the proposed move to Woodford.

"Let's go today!" he demanded when I told him of the arrangements.

I was afraid to tell him that it would not be ready for a week to 10 days, so, instead, I reported that the manager and his wife were on a short vacation.

"Nobody knows exactly where they went," I lied. "All we know is that they were headed for Scotland in a trailer caravan."

"What a break," he said. "Now we can hire a helicopter and search for them in Scotland. We'll land the helicopter when we see a parade of housetrailers. You'll jump out, find the manager and his wife, get the key to the clubhouse, and we'll return home victorious!"

Foiled again, as my mother would say. You always will get caught in a lie. I escaped admitting my falsehood by telling Howard that we located another key from Humphrey Wood, the Woodford general manager. Tony had another key, so that day I called him while he was on vacation at Dartmouth in Devon. I told Tony that Howard wanted to visit the clubhouse at Woodford the next day, and also would like to visit the mockup of the HS-146 at Hatfield.

We arranged to meet Tony at Hatfield at 4:30 pm on July 27. We arrived right on time, almost like a scheduled airline flight, and were airborne an hour later. We flew straight to Woodford in the company's HS-125-400 demonstrator, arriving at 6:10 pm. We taxied right to the walkway leading to the Clubhouse, about 30 yards from the front door. Howard was truly taken with the facility when he viewed it for the first time from the flight deck windows. He was in a quirky mood, though, and decided not to get out of the aircraft.

After being on the ground for just 10 minutes, we took off and flew to Stansted, where we did seven touch-and-goes. Howard continued to argue with Tony over whose landing technique was better, but he was beginning to concede that Tony wasn't so sloppy after all. We returned to Hatfield in a rain shower just as it was getting dark, where we landed at 8:20 pm.

We then drove over to view the HS-146 mockup. By the time we got to the hangar where it was kept, the weather had changed and it was getting cold. Tony loaned Howard his jacket, since, as usual, Howard was wearing only an open-necked shirt.

Howard, Tony and I crawled all over the mock-up. Howard's chief worry with the HS-146 design was that the landing gear geometry with the high wing configuration meant strengthening the fuselage at the wing/fuselage intersection. With my experience in the Lockheed C-130 program, I could not see the problem. Howard conceded that the Hawker Siddeley design kept the bulges on the fuselage to a minimum, but Howard still pondered over the overall weight problem.

The summer of 1973 was turning out to be the best that Howard had experienced in years. He was relaxed, and he just told me that he was going to start living again, and I could really see it. Six weeks earlier, he could barely walk down the hotel hallway. This night, he climbed up old wooden stairs to look at the mock-up. The elevator had jammed, and he had to walk up three flights, with me trying to stay up with him. He had come back to living and I was delighted.

We stayed up until midnight talking. He had devoured the wooden mock-up of the HS-146. He made some suggestions for the landing gear, and Hawker Siddeley made some changes as a result of his observations. They created new blueprints and sent them to me for his approval.

Howard waved goodbye that night still wearing Tony's jacket. I retrieved it after Howard got to Suite 901 at the Inn on the Park, and returned it to Tony.

The day after our flight up to Woodford, I chastised Howard for not going inside the Clubhouse.

"I'm in love with it," he said. "I love everything, including the flowers along the walk. I wanted to move in on the spot, but I knew if I went inside, there might be something I don't like."

He did not want to be disillusioned. It was perfect, and he didn't want to spoil the vision.

"I want you to get ready for us to move in immediately," he told me decisively, "but don't limit us to three or four weeks. We may want it forever!"

Howard Eckersley and George Francom were the only aides that respected Howard's decision to move. All of the others objected violently. Of course, I'm sure the Encino folks had a great deal to do with the decision not to move.

Tony resumed his vacation, but felt that it would be interrupted in a few days because of Howard's excitement about flying, and his desire to move into the Woodford clubhouse as soon as possible. Two weeks later, I had to tell Tony that Howard had broken his hip. His flying days were over.

Tony Blackman never saw Howard again, but in his farewell to Howard, Tony wrote: "During that summer, as we flew together, Howard gained mental strength and alertness and seemed an entirely normal, if slightly elderly, gentleman. He seemed a lonely man, quiet and courteous, and I felt very sorry for him. There is a picture of him in his famous Flying Boat, all alone on the flight deck. To me, this picture epitomizes a famous aviator who broke many records. It was the man as I knew him, alone on the bridge. I shall always remember him with pleasure and feel pleased to have had the chance to have met him and to have given him a few hours of enjoyment."

After Howard died in 1976, I needed to sell three aircraft we had purchased in England. Howard never flew any of them. They simply joined the fleet of aircraft that I had to sell for the estate. He bought one HS-748 and two HS-125s while we were in England. I asked Tony to help me sell these aircraft. The HS-748 was sold to Mount Cook Airlines in New Zealand, and one of the 125s was sold to Short Brothers in Belfast. I sent the other HS-125 to the Hughes Tool Company in Houston. I asked Tony to fly this HS-125 to Las Vegas and paid him a commission for his help. It was just a small effort on my part to say thanks for all the wonderful things that Tony did for us while we were in London.

Getting Howard Hughes airborne and flying again in June and July 1973 was among the most satisfying experiences I have ever had. There was virtually no way to express the elation and sense of victory I felt when I saw the life and sparkle flow back into Howard's eyes when he lifted off for the first time. His lust for flying remained strong and could not be extinguished.

During those weeks, we talked for hours about aviation. We would get down to the nitty gritty of every little detail. That was his thing. Having spent my life in aviation, I never knew a person who was so consumed with aviation as Howard Hughes. We mainly discussed turbine engines, certain things he would like to see improved in airplanes, particularly turbofan engines, and how the rules were, how three-spool engines work.

He had plans to see improvements in the airplanes that he was fond of, and I knew he'd end up buying the airplanes that he flew. This was fine when he was buying Lockheed JetStars, but one day he asked me, "Who builds the Concorde?"

I said, "British Aerospace."

"Do you have any contacts there?" He asked.

At that point, I steered him away from wanting to arrange a flight on the Concorde, because I could just see us buying a Concorde. I hoped he was joking when he asked whether I knew anybody at British Aerospace.

Howard loved anything to do with flying. It had been his one true passion. He demonstrated his boundless love for flying in the late 1950s when we flew Electras and JetStars out of Burbank. By 1963, he had logged 10,000 hours as a pilot, but had not flown one hour from the cockpit in the next 13 years.

He was reborn in England in 1973. He was like a child, living out a fantasy that he carried with him throughout his remarkable life. Had he not broken his hip after only four times, there's no question that the remainder of his life would have been dramatically different. He was becoming a new man, gaining strength and confidence every time he walked to the aircraft and climbed into the cockpit. He had flown four times for a total of 10 hours in the pilot's seat and treasured those moments over the British Isles for the rest of his life.

I cherish the memories of his rebirth as a pilot and thank the Lord I was able to fulfill my friend's desire to soar with eagles once again. He had been a total recluse before his flights over England, but everything changed once he had stepped into the cockpit. His strength returned. He was vibrant and alert. He was Howard Hughes again, and he wanted to fly forever!

HOWARD'S ADDICTION

In April 1973, after I had made the initial arrangements with Hawker Siddeley for Howard to go flying again, I had made it clear to Tony Blackman that, as Howard's pilot, he would have to make himself available almost full-time to meet Howard's needs. However, as the weeks passed, Howard had frequently postponed our going to Hatfield to make our first flight in the HS-748. For two months, we had delayed every flight after setting it up with Tony and the Hawker Siddeley ground crew at Hatfield. I'd had to stretch the truth and make excuses. I was profoundly embarrassed that we could not deliver Howard when promised, and could not tell them why. I was frustrated because I could not be honest. I couldn't tell them that Howard was a drug addict.

It wasn't until I got to London in February 1973, and started living with Howard full time, that I began to learn the full story of Howard's addiction to narcotics. After the XF-11 crash in July

1946, they had given him morphine to ease the pain and to prevent him from dying of shock, but the doctors never weaned him off the morphine like they were supposed to. Instead, as he had demanded more and increased morphine dosages because he could not stand the pain, they gave it to him. Gradually, however, they were able to substitute codeine, a milder narcotic, for the morphine.

Howard was never able to kick the codeine, though. It was a monkey that remained on his back for the rest of his life. He never really recovered from the 1946 crash. It's that simple.

He had functioned fairly normally until around 1960, when the side effects started to take their toll. Mixed with the valium that he was taking to relax, the codeine made him confused. Prolonged use of codeine also causes constipation, which led to all sorts of internal problems. He was taking Empirin, an analgesic containing phenacetin as well as codeine, and this led to kidney problems also. Of course, any kind of narcotic use leads to depression, which leads to the urge to increase the dosage. Of course, Howard was also cursed with the means to get anything that he wanted, and aides who would not argue with his wishes or demands.

By the early 1960s, Howard's dependence on drugs had increased dramatically. This was the time when he cut himself off from the outside world and retired into the tiny world of his darkened bedroom. This was also when his marriage to Jean Peters began to fail. After they moved back to Bel Air from Rancho Santa Fe, Howard deliberately cut himself off from Jean, and forced her to make appointments through the Romaine Street switchboard just to telephone him. When he had moved to Las Vegas, she refused to go. They never saw one another again. It is hard to know whether the increased drug addiction led to the reclusivity and the failed marriage or vice versa, but certainly one thing fed the other all around.

When I had first started to spend time with him in 1957, he was still very alert. By the time I caught up with him in London in 1973, his health had become totally shattered. I had found him sick and addicted, but nobody would take him to a hospital.

I wanted to get him to stop taking the drugs, but I couldn't. He was totally addicted, and I could tell that the addiction was increasing.

I heard some of the aides would joke with him. Once I heard Howard being told that the usual supply had been cut off and the only place that they could get the drugs would be in Tanzania.

Howard just responded feebly, "Let's go to Tanzania."

I imagine that you can do wonders with drugs when you want to get control of someone. I belive that he would have gone to Tanzania to chase the dope. He would have gone anywhere.

Throughout the time that I lived with him on a daily basis, from 1973, through his death in 1976, I never personally observed Howard taking codeine phosphate, which he reportedly diluted in water and self-administered by injection. I never saw him taking Empirin tablets, which contain one gram of codeine, but I did watch him taking valium tablets, which the aides referred to as "blue bombers," because of their color and their large size.

I would always leave his room when he was injecting himself. The sight of it made me sick. I didn't want to witness it or be any part of it, and made it a point to disassociate myself from that part of Howard's life.

When I heard the aides talking about it, I'd walk away. I would hear them saying, "What is he doing? Does he have his playthings?" This meant his needle and the codeine pills that he dissolved in fluid so that he could shoot himself up.

I'd just walk away. Perhaps it was a form of denial, but I felt better pretending that I could isolate myself from this horrible reality if I never actually saw it happen.

I think that Howard didn't want me to know how bad it had become, because it was a part of his life that he knew disappointed me. John Holmes once told me that Howard had asked if I knew he was on drugs. John told him emphatically, "No!" and Howard smiled. The subject never came up again.

I didn't want Howard to know that I knew, and I wish to this day that the world would have never found out about it. Every man has his thing, but I never wanted *this* thing to be known about Howard Hughes.

As I could sense by his behavior, Howard was in and out of drugs. He could have days to "med out," and then have days of alert activity. Howard was handcuffed to the drugs every Thursday, Friday, and Saturday. He was just gone. Then he'd have the rest of the week to work. Even after 1973, though, he would still have these windows of alertness in his week.

If we were going to do any flying, it always had to be during these windows of alertness, and, if I had my wish, he would discover that the joy that he derived from being aloft would totally transcend the numbness of the drugs.

THE TURNING POINT

Just as aviation had brought Howard back to life, the project of keeping Howard flying became *my* life. As July turned to August in 1973, I was consumed with negotiations with Hawker Siddeley aimed at leasing an HS-125 (tail number G-AZAF), and purchasing an HS-748 (tail number G-AYYG). Howard and I talked for hours about the HS-146 jetliner and about the changes to the landing gear that he had suggested, and which they would implement.

In the meantime, I was also trying to figure out a way for us to get in even more flying. We still expected to move to Woodford, but even living at the edge of the Hawker Siddeley runway, we'd be restricted in our flight activities, because the weather in the English Midlands is not the best flying weather. Howard knew where the best flying weather was. He suggested: "Why don't you call Chester Davis, and find out when I can go back to Nevada and start flying every day. The weather is nearly always perfect there. We won't have all these problems."

I had followed through on this. I did phone Chester, but his reply simply underscored Howard's deep isolation and the bridges that had been burned behind him.

"Tell Howard that when he left, he had 20 lawsuits against

him in the United States," Chester Davis reminded me. "Now he has 40 lawsuits. I don't know if he will ever be able to come back."

I never conveyed this to Howard, because I knew it would disappoint and depress him. I just kept things rolling as they had been in London. Little did I know that the hourglass was rapidly running out for Howard's flying. Indeed, by August, his flying days had already ended.

On August 6, two Hughes AirWest executives flew in from California to study the HS-146. I took them up to Hatfield to meet Jim Thorne and to examine the wooden mock-up. Howard did not join us for this visit to Hatfield, but he took a great interest in all of the technical details.

Two days later, on August 8, the Hughes AirWest men flew back to Los Angeles, and I briefed Howard in detail about our progress. He and I discussed the leasing of G-AZAF, and the following morning, I sent them his latest counteroffer. I also sent a down payment of £532,000 to Hawker Siddeley in Manchester for the purchase of G-AYYG, the HS-748.

Then, our whole world turned upside down.

It was just before 10:00 am on August 9. I had just sent the down payment package off to Manchester, when suddenly, Levar Myler burst into the outer room of Howard's suite at the Inn on the Park.

"Find a doctor, quick!" He said, obviously in a panic. "Mr. Hughes has fallen and he can't move!"

My first thought was that we were surrounded by doctors. By this time, Howard typically had at least one doctor travelling and living with him as part of his entourage, and on this particular day, there were two present. Dr. Wilbur Thain was the "on call" physician at the time, having just taken over from Dr. Norman Crane, who had returned to the United States at the end of his two-week "shift" in London. At the same time, Dr. Homer Clark had just joined us for a few days. He had been an occasional member of Howard's entourage since 1971, but on this day, he just happened to be stopping over in London on his way home from a vacation in Yugoslavia.

Dr. Thain was in the hotel dining room at the time, but Dr. Clark was in the immediate hallway when I rushed out with Myler, so I asked him to come with us to Suite 901.

We found Howard lying on his bedroom floor near the door to the bathroom. His eyes were open and he was staring at the ceiling as though dazed. I noticed that his left leg and foot were twisted to the side at an odd angle.

The room was swarming with aides describing the fall in nervous, contradictory half sentences. He had tripped on a rug. No, he had slipped on the bathroom floor. He hit his hip on a side table as he fell. There were conflicting versions, but I soon ascertained that nobody had actually witnessed the fall. Howard had apparently fallen sometime early in the morning, and had lain on the floor with nothing covering him until Levar Myler discovered him just before 10:00.

"Howard has sprained his ankle," I heard Dr. Clark announce, quickly diagnosing the problem. "It's a good thing that *I* was here. Some other doctor might have diagnosed it as a broken hip. It was through the grace of God that I was available!"

Dr. Clark then helped us lift Howard back into his bed. He left later that day for his home in Utah. A pathologist by training, Dr. Clark had come to us through the recommendation of his brother, Rand Clark, who had been on the Hughes Tool Company staff at Romaine Street in Los Angeles since 1958, and who was now one of Bill Gay's principal aides.

Meanwhile, it had been Dr. Thain who was technically "on duty" when Howard suffered his fall. Bill Gay's brother-in-law, Dr. Thain was in general practice—with a secondary specialty in anesthesiology—in Logan, Utah when Bill Gay and Kay Glenn had invited him to join Howard's medical "staff" in 1972. However, he had never actually met Howard until the day of the fall. He claimed that he had met Howard in the 1950s, but Howard told me that he had no memory of that. As I understand it, the Hughes Tool Company had paid his tuition at the University of Southern California Medical School.

The doctors in Howard's entourage—usually Dr. Clark, Dr.

Crane and Dr. Thain—were rotated about every two weeks. The "doctor in attendance" would be on for two weeks, and then home for four weeks before his next "shift" began. As I observed, these doctors were not present to monitor his condition and to keep him healthy, but rather, like the other aides, to cater to his whims. That Dr. Thain had not seen Howard was not atypical. It was my observation that many months would go by without the doctor "on duty" being called in.

Early in the afternoon of August 9, after Dr. Clark had departed and was unable to come "now," Howard's pain began to increase. We summoned Dr. Thain to what I believe was his first examination of a man who had been his "patient" for nearly a year. Unsure of what to do, but suspecting a broken hip or ankle, Dr. Thain contacted a London practicing specialist who acted as a sort of medical broker. He, in turn, contacted Dr. William Young, who was a radiologist. Dr. Young moved a mobile x-ray unit up to Howard's suite. I think he was probably the first doctor outside the "medical staff" component of the entourage to have seen him since Las Vegas.

The X-rays confirmed that there was a clean break in Howard's left hip. Surgery to insert a metal pin to repair the hip was required, and Dr. Walter Robinson, a noted orthopedic surgeon, was contacted to perform this operation. At first the aides demanded that the surgery be performed in Suite 901, but Dr. Robinson insisted that it be done in a hospital, and they finally relented.

However, it was not until August 12 that Howard was moved— under the tightest security—to the London Medical Clinic. Dr. Robinson inserted the pin in the hip socket, and from all appearances, the operation was a success.

In the course of moving Howard in and out of the hotel and the hospital, Gordon Margulis was the man of the hour. Gordon was a husky man who had been a prizefighter when he was growing up on the bad side of London, but he had a warm heart and a ready smile. In contrast to Howard's aides, he was a breath of fresh air. Howard had always admired Gordon's strength, and Gordon would assist in Howard's lifting operations "in and out" of a hospital chair and from the chair to the bed. For the rest of Howard's life, through the various location moves, Gordon would be the man who literally moved Howard. As was the case with me as well, the aides were jealous of Howard's personal fondness for Gordon, and would severely limit his access to Howard unless he was absolutely necessary. Like me, he spent three years within 20 feet of Howard, but at least I got to actually see Howard regularly. George Francom, the good, nonconformist among the aides, would occasionally violate the rules, and I am sure he welcomed Gordon's help.

As soon as Howard knew that his hip was broken, he had asked me to bring Dr. Lawrence Chaffin to London immediately. I relayed the message to Encino, and Nadine Henley and Bill Gay went to Dr. Chaffin's house asking him to go. For some reason, Dr. Chaffin was not immediately sent to the Inn on the Park, but, instead, he was told to register at the Dorchester Hotel under an assumed name, Hugh Winston.

Larry Chaffin had attended Howard as far back as 1932. He had been one of the doctors who had patched him up after the 1946 crash, but he would not see Howard again until February 1971, when he was in the Bahamas.

I had heard of Dr. Chaffin but had never met him before London, and I would get to know him very well during the next three years. He had a brilliant mind. When he died in 1997 at the age of 103, I gave the eulogy at the church. Like me, he would be at Howard's side all the remaining time that he was in London, and for most of the rest of his life. However, until the very last days, Howard would refuse to see him, even though he was on the payroll and standing just a few feet away for much of the time.

He later told me he came to London immediately in 1973, because he hoped that Howard would still be in the hospital, and he could use this as an opportunity to break him of the drug addiction. But it was too late. Howard was back in the hotel.

Dr. Chaffin also told me how poor Dr. Clark's diagnosis had been. He said: "Physiology 101 in medical school states that if an individual is lying on his back with one foot pointing upward and the other foot turned 90 percent—such as Howard's was when Homer examined him—then the patient has a broken hip."

Dr. Homer Clark may have not been a great doctor, but he was a fine watercolorist. That morning, it was too bad that Howard needed medical attention and not a watercolor painting.

CHAPTER 8

THE LOCKHEED DEAL

HOWARD'S MONEY

When I got to talking with Howard in the days when he was thinking of flying—the days before he broke his hip—I could sense the same spirit of creative enthusiasm that he had exhibited back in the years before the 1960s, before the drugs had started to cloud his mind. We always had two or three conversations simultaneously. He always had a great deal going on in his mind, and we covered a lot.

One of the themes that we kept coming back to was his dream of owning Lockheed. He still took pride in having been the "inventor" of the Constellation, Lockheed's greatest commercial aircraft, and he considered that he had a most special relationship with the company. As we were sitting there in Suite 901 at the Inn on the Park one day during early June 1973, he told me wistfully, "Jack, I'm still disappointed in you. After all these years, you never got Lockheed and the Hughes Aircraft Company together."

Coincidently, I had just had a meeting with my former boss, Lockheed chairman Dan Haughton, on a related subject that I thought would play neatly into Howard's plan. He was in London, and had invited me for lunch at the Hilton Hotel. Of course, there is no such thing as a free lunch. I listened carefully. Dan had a problem.

In the late 1960s, Boeing had announced the development of its 747 "jumbo jet," the largest production jetliner ever conceived. It was capable of carrying up to 500 passengers, more than double the capacity of the Boeing 707 or Douglas DC-8. When the 747 was announced, both McDonnell Douglas and Lockheed looked at the market and each decided to build a somewhat smaller jumbo jet of their own, with a passenger capacity between that of the Boeing behemoth and the existing jetliners. Announced in the spring of 1968, both of these aircraft had a passenger capacity between 250 and 300 (depending on configuration), so they were competing for exactly the same customers. The McDonnell Douglas DC-10 first flew in August 1970 and started carrying passengers (for American Airlines) in August 1971. The Lockheed L-1011 first flew in November 1970 and started carrying passengers (for Eastern Air Lines) in April 1972, eight months after the DC-10 began service.

Now, a year later, Dan's woes were compounded. They had sold only 190 of the 300 L-1011s that they had forecast. Sales were down, he said, because Lockheed did not have a long-range version that could compete with the long-range version of the DC-10.

He told me that 80 percent of the DC-10 sales had been for long-range versions, while only 20 percent were for the original DC-10, which had approximately the same range as the L-1011 aircraft. Dan said that Lockheed was planning its own long-range version, to be designated as the L-1011-2.

Finally, he got to the point. "Jack," he said sheepishly, "I need $100 million to produce a long-range version."

He wanted Howard's money. He wanted me to tie the bell on the cat.

"It will take more than $100 million to produce such an aircraft," I argued.

I'm sure that's all the money I'll need. The Lockheed board said they'll allow me to go ahead with it if I have an order for 25 of these new aircraft. I've just logged a letter of intent for 20 from BOAC [British Overseas Airways Corporation] and 10 from Air Canada, so I'm ready to go—if I can get the money."

I told him that I would discuss it with Howard and get back to him the following day. In the meantime, I looked up the current stock prices. Lockheed shares were selling for $5.00 each. For an investment of half what Dan Haughton was asking, Howard could own the company.

I was convinced we had a winner, and that night, I told Howard of the fabulous opportunity he had. I reminded him of our recent conversation, and about his being disappointed that I had never gotten Lockheed and Hughes Aircraft Company together.

"You don't have to combine them. I think you can buy Lockheed for nothing today," I said, almost casually. "For not too much money, you could literally own Lockheed, the company that you've courted for 40 years. You can merge it, sell it or do what you like. It's yours to control. You've dreamt of this for years. This relationship with Lockheed, they're closer to you than to anybody."

Together, we strolled down memory lane. We discussed his successes with the Lockheed Model 14 during his around-the-world trip in 1938, and his "invention" of the Constellation series. I touched on his heady involvement with the Electra, and reminded him that he had launched the L-1011 with his order for 100 back in 1968, and the sale of 12 JetStars. I played on his great personal relations with his friend Bob Gross and his rivalry with Kelly Johnson.

"This is your dream of dreams." I told him. "You can buy half the company for $50 million and also give Lockheed a $50 million loan. But we would get the debentures. We'd buy the convertible debentures in two years, when the debentures would mature. It'd be a dollar above the price that we paid. The conversion price would be $6 instead of $5. The $50 million loan—we'd make it a street loan. After they use the first $50 million, they'd have to come to you for all the additional money."

Howard smiled broadly and seemed lost momentarily as he fantasized about attaining a lifelong dream. I could see his mind racing, devouring the possibilities like a good meal, that he hadn't eaten in years.

On June 25, after I spoke to Haughton, I met with Howard and told him that he'd soon have an offer from Lockheed regarding his participation. He brought in George Francom and pledged him to secrecy on the offer. He coined the word "West" for the transaction in order to maintain better security.

Howard knew that most of his aides were loyal to Bill Gay, who would try to kill the program. Although Howard had lost touch with the outside world to a great extent, he hadn't lost his faculties. He knew that if Bill Gay and his troops at Summa headquarters in Encino got wind of the deal they could—and would—kill it. Gay monitored and managed everything that came in and out of the head office. I believe that not being in control would have driven him to the brink, but with Howard's funds tied up, Gay would not have been able to fulfill his plans for Las Vegas.

At that time, neither Howard nor I knew how bad the financial affairs were regarding his Las Vegas operations. His financial records later showed that he would have been able to cover the Lockheed loan, but beyond that, financing anything else would have been difficult, if not impossible.

If he wasn't fully cognizant of the situation in Las Vegas, Howard certainly expressed the concern that having Encino in the know regarding "West" was an invitation to disaster, because the faction there had the wherewithal to outmaneuver him on the Lockheed loan matter. I feel that it is a pity that his dependency on drugs prevented him from fully comprehending how little control of his empire he still had, and how the Lockheed deal might have helped him get into a situation where he might regain that control.

I was instructed by Howard to involve Chester Davis in the "West" negotiations, and to conduct them through his office in New York, rather than London or Burbank, as Lockheed had proposed. He would be a key player and I would be the conduit between Howard and Chester. I pledged Chester Davis to secrecy. I conveyed to him Howard's insistence that, under no conditions, could Nadine Henley or Bill Gay, who, along with Chester, were on the executive board, know about the Lockheed deal.

Chester argued with me. "I'm in trouble," he said. "I'm on the board of a company. I've got the two other executive members and I'm not telling them a thing."

"Don't worry about it," I replied. "It's not a public board, and the only stockholder does *not* want you to talk to them."

I told Howard that we had to pledge each of the aides to honor the security requirement surrounding "West," and I told them that Howard and I had made them "insiders" involving a major company listed on the New York Stock Exchange and they could all end up in a court proceeding if they talked to anybody about the deal.

Howard was excited. He almost giggled when he said, "I'm making you insiders. Now, you're going to live with a prison record if you talk about it. If you talk in your sleep, don't let your wife hear you. Have her sleep in another bed, because this is heavy stuff."

I met with Haughton the next day, and I told him that the program was a "go." Dan wanted the negotiations to take place in London with both of us working out of the Lockheed office there. I told him that was impossible. The negotiations, per Howard's wishes, would be in Chester Davis' office in New York City. I also told Dan that I did not want any conversation between us until the deal was canceled or consummated. Dan agreed.

Lockheed's negotiation team included Vince Marifino, who would become the vice chairman of the merged Lockheed-Martin Company a quarter century later, and Bill Rieke, an executive vice president of Lockheed Corporation. They would spend most of the next two months in New York City at Chester's office.

On August 1, I talked with Howard about a special Lockheed board meeting that would take place the following day in New York City, to consider his offer. He then asked me to phone Chester with some last-minute changes. He didn't want his $50 million loan subordinated to bank loans, so to get around this, he wanted the option to apply this debt against L-1011 aircraft purchases. Chester told me to tell Howard that he thought he could do this.

Late the next day, Howard started to get cold feet.

"Call Chester," he told me. "Call Chester and tell him to tell Lockheed that I need more time. I've still got some worries. Tell Chester and Lockheed that I'm still interested, but I want more time."

Unfortunately, by the time that I got this message to Chester, the Lockheed board meeting had already broken up. Equally unfortunate was that this would be the last meeting that Howard and I would have on the subject of "West" before he broke his hip on August 9.

In the weeks before the fall, Howard had been lucid most of the time, but in the weeks following, the situation turned around completely. His world would once again become a medicated haze, that was now and again punctuated by pain that demanded more medication. Before the accident, he was self-medicated out of habit, but now, like in 1946, when it all had started, he seemed to be using drugs to fight the pain. Before we started flying again, he had been sedentary out of choice. After the fall, he had no choice. He was now truly bedridden.

The next meeting that I would have with Howard regarding "West" would be on August 20, when he asked me to start studying plans to merge Hughes Aircraft Company into Lockheed after we had closed the deal. Two days later, we discovered by way of a memo from Chester in New York City that Dan Haughton was pushing Rieke to take a hard line on the involvement of the Hughes Helicopter Company in the deal. As part of the deal, Howard wanted to sell his helicopter company, then a part of the Summa Corporation, to Lockheed for $10 million, with the payments spread over four years. Dan Haughton was emphatically against including the helicopter company in the deal. I apparently had soured Dan on helicopters while I was at Lockheed. Haughton had told Rieke to tell Chester "No," and Chester's recommendation to us also came down to one word: "Disengage."

This upset Howard. He did not want the deal to slip away as it had before. He insisted that I make it clear to Chester that "Disengage" was not in our vocabulary. However, when Howard and I met on August 26, he said that he was thinking about agreeing to pull the Hughes Helicopter Company out of "West" if he could think of something to ask in return to make up for pulling out the helicopter company.

In the meantime, Dan Haughton had yielded to save the deal,

but suddenly Howard agreed to drop the helicopter aspect of the deal. I recall thinking at the time that he was just testing Lockheed, but I was never sure. He was asleep most of the time and groggy much of the remaining time.

Howard's next window of alertness and lucidity came on August 29, when I had three sessions with him regarding "West."

"This ought to get Lockheed to sweeten the package," he said. "Call Chester and tell him to ask them to go for $50 million in debentures and only $25 million of debt—and maybe another $25 million later."

"The Lockheed board won't approve the deal for the go ahead of the 1011-2," I said, shaking my head, "Unless there's a commitment for $100 million."

During the first week of September, we were back and forth with Chester practically every day, polishing and modifying the deal to a place where we felt Lockheed would accept it. At the same time, Howard insisted that I stay with him to discuss, not only "West," but a wide variety of related topics. On September 4, I had three long sessions with him, talking about such things as the range capability of the L-1011-2 and the status of the Rolls Royce RB211 turbofan engines that we were recommending. He also brought up his fear that I would go back to Lockheed if the deal was made. To this, I assured him that I would not leave his side.

We were up all night in Suite 901, as Howard carried on endlessly, obviously keyed up as the ramifications and nuances of "West" spun through his mind. With the blackout curtains sealing the windows completely, one never knew whether it was night or day. This was how he liked it. Howard was not a slave to the clock. He worked when he felt he needed to, and I worked with him. I hadn't slept in 24 hours and it was my turn to feel a bit groggy as Howard leapt from one idea to the next. At one point he even decided to insist that the Hughes Helicopter Company be put back into "West," but he added, "Don't tell Chester—yet." I didn't.

Eventually, Howard drifted off and I was able to get some rest. I awoke on September 6 to a message from British Prime

Minister Edward Heath. He wanted to express his personal pleasure that Howard had chosen to specify the British-made Rolls Royce RB211 engines for the 1011-2. To match Howard's bold step, Heath said he had approved funds that week to develop a new and more powerful Rolls Royce engine, the RB211-524, which would greatly enhance the L-1011-2's performance. He concluded his note by inviting Howard to have lunch with him at 10 Downing Street.

When I showed the letter to Howard later, I didn't mention that I had engineered this communication with the help of Chuck de Bedts, who headed up Lockheed's London office. This little pat on the back of British industry was a feather in Howard's cap that might pay off later. The letter also stiffened Howard's resolve to proceed.

On September 7, the "West" final offer was ready. The plan was pretty simple: Howard would buy $50 million in debentures. When converted at $6.00 a share in two years, the debentures would give him 50 percent of the company. He'd also make a straight $50 million loan that included an option for this money to be applied as a down payment against future long-range L-1011-2s at a "favored" price. The second $50 million would be on call and would be available only as Lockheed needed it, but it would never exceed $50 million. Howard's agreement required that none of the second $50 million could be drawn upon until the first $50 million had been spent.

The next day, Howard called me into Suite 901.

"Jack, let me ask you personally," he began. "Do you think I should go ahead on 'West?'"

"There are probably 10 or 12 places where you could put your money and do better," I told him frankly, "but you've chased this thing for 30 years, and you'll never get it cheaper. You'll have a legal battle on your hands to keep in commercial transport aviation because of the Justice Department's interpretation of conflict of interest. You may lose AirWest, but you'll own Lockheed."

"Promise me one thing, Jack?" He asked.

"What's that, Howard?"

"Promise me you'll stay with me. Promise me you won't let Haughton get you to go back with Lockheed. I need you here."

"Don't worry, Howard, I'll stay."

THE LONGEST DAY

Of all our long days and long night sessions discussing "West," nothing would compare to the marathon climax of the affair that began on the morning of September 13, when I received a call from Chester Davis, saying that they had just finished the negotiations with Lockheed, and that he was sending by facsimile, a text of the essential items of the proposed Memorandum of Understanding.

The Lockheed board was supposed to be meeting in Burbank at 2:00 pm London time, and we needed Howard's approval before the board met. He was asleep, so I sent the memorandum to Howard's suite, along with a message telling him that we had to have an answer regarding his approval.

At 11:00 am, George Francom woke Howard long enough to have him read the memorandum. Howard pencilled in four changes:

1. Remove the serial number "later than 5" from the option to buy 1011s.
2. Remove any reference to quantity to buy. Use the "whatever number."
3. Howard must have the right to re-sell his L-1011s on the open market if he so chooses.
4. The money for the debentures would be spoon-fed along with the money for the straight debt obligations of $50 million.

During the final days of negotiations, Howard had also let us know that he wanted a "kicker" in the contract. In exchange for having monopolized all of my time and his for the past two months, Howard wanted some safeguards to ensure that Lockheed would proceed with the long-range L-1011. He proposed to give Lockheed six months to launch the program. If they did not, he wanted to be able to buy 10 percent of the company for $5 million. Chester told us the kicker would be hard to get, but if Howard wanted it, he would try.

Howard then told George we could sign the deal without waking him any more—*if* we could get the four items approved, plus the "kicker." He then rolled over in his bed and went back to sleep. It was now 2:00 pm London time.

We promptly sent Howard's comments to Chester in New York City for him to review, and two hours later, at 4:00 sharp, we received a message on the facsimile from Chester. He was negative on most points that Howard had asked for, and he backed up his response with a legal opinion. It was Chester disagreeing on these issues, not Lockheed, and he apparently had good legal reasons.

We attempted to wake Howard immediately, but didn't get his attention until 4:30. After reading Chester's message, he looked at George and said: "Retire from the field with honor. We'll form a committee to work out the deal, and make a new proposal at the next board meeting."

George and I then decided to get Chester on the phone and tried to work out the differences. Between us, we pumped handwritten messages between Room 902 and Howard's Suite 901 discussing all of these points. George was the most effective negotiator that afternoon.

Finally, we came up with a "new" proposed solution to all the problems—except the spoon feeding of the first $50 million—that was acceptable to Howard.

He then went back to sleep. A half hour later, at 6:30, we tried to wake him up again, but he was virtually comatose. I shook Howard's bed nonstop for almost 10 minutes. At times I lay on the floor forcibly rattling the bed from below in a frantic attempt to wake him.

Howard finally awoke and said, "We'll do it tomorrow."

"NO! NO!" I yelled out. "We've got to act immediately or lose the deal."

Howard pulled himself together.

"Did you get the 'kicker?'" He asked sleepily. "The deal still hinges on the 'kicker.'"

"I talked to Chester in New York City while you were asleep. He assured me that Lockheed has agreed to the 'kicker'."

Then I got him to agree to go along with the Lockheed proposal, if we could delay the closing until about half of the $50 million was gone, and if monthly payments to cover actual costs were made, and there was an indication each month that the program was "tracking per schedule."

If we could get something as good or better than this, he would "go."

In the meantime, I had advised Howard that Nadine Henley and Bill Gay would not support the Lockheed program.

"Maybe we should hear what they have to say before you commit yourself," I told him.

"No," he said. "I've made up my mind. We *will* go forward with this."

I had George Francom witness Howard's verbal commitment and quickly notified Chester. It was to be a done deal, thanks in large measure to George Francom.

Unknown to any of us in London, certainly unknown to me, Bill Gay and Nadine Henley already knew about the deal//////. A few days earlier, Chester had told me that he felt that he was betraying Gay and Henley—the other two members of the Summa Corporation Executive Committee, by not letting them know that he had participated in such a bold step. I later reminded him that I had strict orders of secrecy from Howard and that he would be in violation of the orders that I had received from Howard and passed on to him. I also reminded him of his obligation to maintain client-attorney privilege.

The day before the Lockheed board meeting, Chester got the vote of John Holmes and Levar Myler, giving Howard, along with Chester's vote, three of the five Summa Corporation votes needed to secure the program. Chester told me that he had told Bill Gay and Nadine Henley about the plan on the night before the Lockheed board meeting. Chester said that Gay had gone ballistic, and had ordered one of Howard's JetStars fly him to London immediately so that he could personally intervene to stop the deal.

Just before 7:00, with Bill Gay winging his way toward London to surprise us, we finally got a reply to the wire that we had sent to Chester 20 minutes earlier. By this time, Howard was fast asleep again. Chester assured us that Lockheed would allow him to buy the $50 million debentures, $5 million at a time, and monitor the program as it went along.

"I've got 'West' on the other line." Chester told us impatiently. "And they're saying that the board meeting is going to break up in five minutes."

George and I looked at each other.

"Okay," I told Chester. "Under the authority Howard gave me 25 minutes ago, sign it."

George and Levar Myler, who had just arrived in the room, both agreed and we told Chester to sign. I wrote Howard a message telling him that Chester had signed, and left this memo in the outer room of his suite.

In the midst of this three-hour drama, a call came in from Kay Glenn in Encino. George told the switchboard that we were busy, and Howard was asleep—and to take a message. This was fortunate. When the dust settled, we found that the message was one that was marked "forward with great speed" to Howard—and the subject was "West."

It appeared to me to be Glenn's attempt to stall the negotiations until Gay arrived in London.

The following morning, Bill Gay did arrive, but it was too late. "West" had been signed, and Howard was fast asleep. Gay climbed back in the JetStar and filed a flight plan for California.

In New York City, Chester would spend most of that day, September 13, incorporating all the changes into a Memorandum of Understanding. Basically he was adding the "kicker" option allowing Howard to get 10 percent of Lockheed if they did not make the decision to go ahead on development of the 1011-2 within six months. Meanwhile, Lockheed had to poll its board on this item after the board meeting was adjourned, and as some of the board members were on their way to the Los Angeles airport.

The Memorandum of Understanding was finally signed at 3:00 pm Pacific Time on September 15, but the press dispatch went out at 2:30. The Lockheed stock would open and close at $6.00. I had lunch with Dan Haughton the next day in his suite at the Hilton Hotel in London after the market had closed in New York. He offered me a spot on the Lockheed board, which I declined. He made the same offer to Howard, asking him to allow me to join the Lockheed board of directors.

Typical of any Howard Hughes decision, finalizing "West" had not been an easy task. Howard looked at every possibility and pitfall and would often study his options for days before making a move.

I met with Howard when I returned from the Hilton. The man's spirits were in great shape because of "West." I told him about Haughton's invitation to me to join the Lockheed board and my refusal. Howard thanked me and said that, since I now worked for him, I was to represent him personally on both the Hughes Aircraft Company and the Howard Hughes Medical Institute boards.

"When?" I asked.

"Not now," Howard said. "We're too busy. If you went to board meetings, you'd be away from me for a whole week at a time."

Howard paused a moment, and then added, "but someday. I promise!"

Of course, that never happened. However, it was satisfying to know that it was a possibility, especially since to be on the Howard Hughes Medical Institute board was a uniquely prestigious job. It was also one where I could have assured that Gay would never gain control of Howard's medical research programs.

EXERCISING THE KICKER

After "West" was signed, Howard was in the catbird's seat. He could envision himself at the helm of Lockheed and changing the course of aviation. In the meantime, we discussed his continuing to fly, and on September 27, I showed Howard drawings of a special seat to accommodate his injured hip, which I had designed for his HS-125 (G-BAZB) that would allow quick exit and egress. He was delighted. Two days later, at his instruction, I signed an agreement with Hawker Siddeley to rework the cockpit of G-BAZA per my drawing.

Time was running out though. Howard's position of power changed quickly. The world was about to be turned upside down by the biggest blow to the world economy since World War II, the "Energy Crisis" of 1973-1974.

On October 6, 1973, less than 30 days after the agreement with Lockheed was made, Egypt and Syria, backed by the Soviet Union, invaded Israel. It was the Jewish holy day of Yom Kippur, and the Israelis were caught off guard. Having suffered severe initial losses, the very survival of the Jewish state was threatened. The United States undertook a marathon series of resupply flights, and gradually Israel was able to stabilize the situation and push back the Arab armies.

Even before the fighting ceased on October 24, the Arab oil producing countries, to show solidarity with the defeated Egypt and Syria, retaliated against the United States and its Western European allies by cutting off oil supplies. The immediate result of the Arab oil embargo was rationing, skyrocketing prices and a severe jolt to the world economy. Even after shipments were resumed in March 1974, the price of oil would increase from $2.50 to $10 per barrel. This action helped bring on the recession of 1974.

There were serious side effects throughout the aviation industry. The high oil prices and uncertain financial future would cause Lockheed's only two customers for the long-range L-1011-2, BOAC and Air Canada, to cancel their orders. The long-range Lockheed jetliner was dead. As a result, Lockheed would not consummate any of the $100 million in support from Howard Hughes. He had, in effect, lost his last chance to control Lockheed.

Fortunately, his foresight left him in a position to exercise the "kicker," and buy 10 percent of Lockheed for $5 million, before it expired on March 13, 1974. All he had to do was act on the provision that he himself had demanded be included in the loan deal.

In March 1974, I received a phone call from Dan Haughton asking what we were going to do about our option, since the company had announced it was not going to proceed with the L-1011-2. He was very guarded in his inquiry.

Meanwhile, Chester called me twice a day for four days pleading with me to have Howard agree to exercise his 10 percent Lockheed option. I told Chester to send Howard daily messages, and I put messages in to Howard's suite twice a day myself.

"Jack, get your message in," Chester insisted desperately. "We've got to get that kicker before the date lapses."

By now, Howard was asleep most of the time, and the only way to communicate with him was by written messages that he could read when he woke up. The aides were in control of delivering the messages, and they decided when he received the memos.

Unfortunately, George Francom was not on duty, because he was the only one among the corps of aides with whom I could work. I felt that he was one who kept Howard's interests above those of Bill Gay. Instead, it was Jim Rickard who was on duty as time was running out on the "kicker." It seemed to me that he was perhaps the most loyal to Gay of all the aides, and I was certain that he was under orders to keep any messages from Chester or me away from Howard. I would go into the suite, and plead with him to act, because it was such a good financial opportunity for Howard. Rickard just positioned himself between me and the closed door to Howard's bedroom, and smiled, "Jack, he's not reading any of your messages."

"Isn't he reading any of Chester's notes?"

"No, he's not going to read any of Chester's either."

In the end, it was the will of Gay that prevailed. His commands were transmitted to Howard's aides through Kay Glenn. Gay purposely would not give instructions to the aides. Instructions were always given by way of Kay Glenn, and in all my years with

Howard I never saw anything that was actually written by Bill Gay.

The irony of the situation was that, while Gay wielded great power within the Hughes companies, he was strongly disliked by Howard, who had fired him in 1962, only to keep him on the payroll so that he wouldn't talk publicly about Howard's personal affairs. More than once, when Gay's name came up, Howard had screamed at me "Haven't you fired that sonofabitch yet? Why are you keeping him on the payroll? Get rid of him!"

The day after the option expired, Rickard gave me back the messages that Chester and I had written. As I had suspected, they had never been given to Howard.

"You might as well just take these back," he laughed. "It's only going to embarrass him to see that you didn't try to get these to him in time."

If George Francom had been working that week, there is no doubt in my mind that Howard would have received our notes and been aware of the opportunity to exercise his option to purchase 10 percent of Lockheed for $5 million.

In retrospect, and as a stockholder of Lockheed Martin Corporation, I am glad that the option was never exercised, but what about the heirs of the Howard Hughes estate? Interestingly, at the time the terms of the option were being reached, there were 10 million Lockheed shares. As a result of two stock splits, there were 78 million Lockheed shares on the eve of the corporation's merger with the Martin Marietta Corporation in 1993. The date that the option *would have* been exercised, the stock was selling at $3.50 share; thus the 5 million dollars to acquire 10 percent of the company would have grown from $5 million to $635 million. That is more than the $565 million Howard received when he sold his 78.28 percent interest in TWA on May 13, 1966.

Frank Carlin, who was a Summa employee and later served as my chief of staff at Hughes Helicopters, provided some valuable insight into the matter. He reported second-hand to me that there had been a meeting in Gay's office in Encino where the question was raised as to whether the messages from Chester and I would be given to Howard.

It was reported that some smart lad jokingly said, "If it goes through, you know who someday would be the new CEO at Lockheed."

He was, of course, referring to me. That glib remark was all that it took to light Gay's fuse.

About a year after Howard died, I visited Haughton in his Lockheed office in Burbank. He was moving out of the company. He was no longer the chairman because of the scandal surrounding the Japanese deal on the L-1011.

"Dan, you talked to me with forked tongue regarding our exercising Howard Hughes' option," I said. "You should have asked whether we were going to buy it or not."

He answered that Textron, who owns Bell Helicopter, was considering the purchase of Lockheed at the time, and they were playing cat and mouse. Dan felt he had an ace up his sleeve if Howard made a move first, since he felt Textron would never move against Howard with his vast money source if Howard owned 10 percent of Lockheed.

"My ace in the hole," he explained, "was that they felt the same way that other people did, that they wouldn't touch anything that Howard Hughes owned even 10 percent of!"

More than a decade earlier, in 1964, when I had become Chief Research, Development and Testing Engineer for Lockheed, Kelly Johnson had told me, "If you do everything I tell you, someday, you'll be the president of the company."

I never did want to become that, and it was a good thing. After the problems with the L-1011 TriStar program in the early 1970s, Lockheed would go through seven presidents in nine years.

CHAPTER 9

THE EASTERN DIVISION

SOMEPLACE WARMER

The summer and early autumn of 1973 had been marked by a roller coaster of activities for us in London. There was the genuine thrill of getting Howard back into the air, which was cut short by the tragedy of his broken hip. The frenzy of the Lockheed deal had culminated in the crushing blow dealt us by the Arab oil embargo.

Although the operation on his hip had been successful, and Howard should have been walking again in a few weeks, he continued to lie in his bed, apparently self-medicating himself and gradually growing thinner and weaker, and more susceptible to the chills and head colds that would be virtually inevitable during the damp, cold London winter.

The nights had grown longer and colder, and the urge to leave London was in the back of everyone's mind. On October 22, 1973, Howard had talked to me about wintering in a warmer climate and returning to England in the spring. At the same time, across the globe in Encino, talk had also turned to the notion of getting Howard out of Britain. I wasn't fully aware of it at the time, but as I discovered later, the word had come in from California that Bill Gay and Nadine Henley wanted Howard out. For reasons that I never fully understood, they had decided to move him back to the Bahamas.

The aides were instructed to sell Howard on the idea, and they were handed the perfect pretense in the form of the British coal strike that occurred in the wake of the Arab oil embargo. In response to this, the British government had instituted a policy of turning off the heat in large buildings at 10:00 every night. Howard was a night person. He was awake when he wanted to be awake, and often, that was after the coal-fired furnaces were shut off for the night. When he was awake, he naturally wanted to be warm, but there was no heat. He was easily convinced of the need to go south.

While the aides were looking for an excuse to move the entourage to the sunny climes, I had been vainly trying to get Howard back into the cockpit. On November 1, I told Howard that the seat modification project in G-BAZB was finished, and he asked me to set up an inspection trip to Hatfield in two days, so that the two of us could inspect the seat and look at the landing gear changes that Hawker Siddeley had made to the HS-146 mockup.

When the day came for the Hatfield trip, however, Howard was too heavily medicated to move, and he slept the whole day. This inspection trip would never take place, but on November 16, with Howard's approval, I signed an agreement with Hawker Siddeley which said that we intended to lease G-BAZB.

By November, though, the general sense among the entourage at the Inn on the Park was that we would be going to the Bahamas, although no firm plans had been made, and we really did not know where exactly in the Bahamas we would go. As the discussions went back and forth, a set of code words developed as a sort of shorthand for locations in the Bahamas. For example, Nassau and Paradise Island were referred to as "Southern Spain," while Grand Bahama Island, and the stretch of beachfront hotel development near Freeport were "Northern Spain." During his 1970-1972 stay, Howard had lived in "Southern Spain," and that seemed to be where he expected to go. This was also the general preference among the aides. However, by the time that we got around to making our inquiries, the top floors—which was a Howard requirement, at all the hotels in Nassau and adjacent Paradise Island were fully booked for the winter season.

This left "Northern Spain." A few calls were made, but the

results were the same. The wealthy Europeans and Americans, who liked to escape the snow and sleet of the northern winters for the warmth and tranquility of the Bahamas, had already booked every penthouse in Freeport through February. I recalled my earlier conversations with the Daniel K. Ludwig people regarding the Mamenic Line deal, and I remembered that Howard's fellow billionaire recluse owned a hotel in Freeport. I knew that we could purchase the Xanadu Princess outright.

I recalled that Ludwig had been in the midst of negotiations with an organization called American Bulk Carrier, which owned the Xanadu Princess, and that he had picked it up as part of the deal. I phoned the Ludwig people and found them very open to our buying the property, as they had no use for the hotel.

I asked Chester Davis what he thought we should offer for the Xanadu Princess, and he said, "I don't care what the price is, just give me the terms."

We paid 10 percent down, with a low interest rate on the rest, and Mr. Ludwig let us pick it up for $7.5 million.

The other problem that I had to sort out in the Bahamas was the political situation. England's rule of the Bahamas was coming to an end in 1973, and the prime minister, Lynden Pindling, had not been too friendly to Howard the last time that he was in the Bahamas. In 1972 when Howard was there before, the British were making Pindling stand for election as Prime Minister, and there was a great deal of pressure from the Bahamian voters for Pindling to treat the American billionaire like anyone else when it came to permits and papers.

In 1972, for the sake of politics, Pindling had decided to force Howard out by pulling the work permits of his aides. Pindling was willing to let Howard stay, but without his aides. Without work permits, they couldn't stay in the islands. He couldn't stay without them, so we'd had to pull him out as well.

Almost as soon as he had kicked Howard out, Pindling and his cronies, who had been running the place since 1967, realized that they had made a mistake. After their Progressive Liberal Party had won the election, they figured out that Howard, and his presumed billions, wasn't such a liability after all. Now, almost two years later, Pindling was more secure in his power base, and he was very receptive to having Howard and his money back. In fact, they would be delighted to have him back.

The plans for the move quickly developed momentum, so Chester Davis flew to Nassau to meet with Pindling. The prime minister had clearly changed his tune in the 23 months since we had carried Howard's stretcher down the fire escape at the Britannia Beach Hotel. Pindling greeted Chester warmly and kept saying over and over how very, very sorry he was that his people had been so tough with Howard during his previous residence. He promised Chester that this would not happen again. In the course of their conversations, Pindling recalled that Howard Hughes had been a big land investor in Nevada, and it didn't take a world leader of his caliber to realize how this could help the Bahamian economy. The Yankee billionaire would be good for business. What was good for Hughes was good for Pindling and he made it very clear that he knew that.

Meanwhile, back in London, the shorter days and worsening weather made it clear that Howard and I would not again, at least for the next several months, fly English skies. On November 18, though, I was able to see Howard and to discuss continuing our flying in the Bahamas. So much had happened in the year since we were in Nicaragua, where he had made the decision to go flying again. Although he hadn't walked a step since he broke his hip, Howard still imagined himself flying again.

The plan was to go to Freeport on Grand Bahama Island, where there are big hotels, but where there is no hangar space. He told me that I should rent a hangar at Nassau as soon as we arrived in the Bahamas, but to immediately begin construction of a permanent hangar at Freeport. Through my contacts at Lockheed in Georgia, I was able to get a six-month lease on the large Bahamas Air hangar at Nassau, but I decided to wait until we arrived to start thinking about the hangar at Freeport.

On December 4, we discussed the impending trip, and Howard requested that I personally set up all the departure plans.

"Jack, I want you to take care of the whole bit," he said. "Getting us to the airplane, getting the vans, getting the cars, and arranging the parking for the airplane. You decide when the airplane leaves. And you're in charge of working with the immigration officials."

Through my Lockheed contacts, I arranged to lease a DC-9 belonging to Adnan Khashoggi, the Saudi billionaire trader and arms dealer who later played a role in the Iran-Contra affair. This DC-9 had been a familiar fixture at McCarran Airport in Las Vegas during the years that Howard was there, because Khashoggi was a frequent high roller at the Las Vegas casinos, especially the Sands. Parenthetically, Adnan's sister, Samira, was the mother of Dodi el Fayed, who was, two decades later, the consort of Princess Diana. As for the 24-hour lease of his aircraft, Khashoggi was absolutely delighted to be linked with the mystique of Howard Hughes.

On December 6, I told Howard of the arrangements and that I had scheduled our Bahamas flight for December 19. Three days before departure, Aileen Walker, Adnan's secretary, and I met with the British Customs and Immigration officials at London's Heathrow Airport to make sure that everything was ready for our departure. A nod from Prime Minister Heath cleared up any potential problem that Howard's lack of a passport might have caused, and, of course, Howard would be allowed to board the aircraft without having to be seen or inspected. The day before we were scheduled to leave, I met with Howard to lay out the plans for the trip, and I showed him the layout of Khashoggi's well-appointed DC-9.

Before we departed, we had one last task to complete. Everyone talks about Bob Maheu's opulent lifestyle and his grand schemes for Howard's properties in Las Vegas. However, he was every inch the realist compared to Bill Gay, who produced a grandiose scheme far more elaborate than the Desert Inn. Gay had a plan for a shopping center and covered walkways. It was a huge project that he called "Gateway." I remember that in some of the memos, it was even referred to as "*Gay*teway" to work his name into it.

Gay spent a great deal of money having architects draw up the plans, and more on a huge, very elaborate, model. The model was flown to London in four sections and set up in the outer room of

Howard's suite. It took days to assemble it, but Howard refused to look at it. He told me later that he thought it was a ridiculous idea, and a bad notion for Gay to name it after himself.

On December 19, the day that we moved Howard out of London, Gordon Margulis and I spent about two hours tearing up this model and chucking it down the garbage chutes. On the way to the airport, I told Howard that "Gayteway" had been destroyed. He laughed and made a ring with his thumb and forefinger, indicating a job well done.

We quietly slipped out of the Inn on the Park and went directly to a secure corner of the airport, from which we departed at 10:00 pm. We were the last flight to take off that night, because takeoffs from Heathrow were not permitted after that hour. We stopped en route at Labrador for fuel, and landed at Freeport, on Grand Bahama Island at 4:28 am local time on December 20.

I'll never forget when we touched down at Freeport. It was raining, but the plucky Pindling had literally rolled out a red carpet. He had sent his deputy prime minister and a group of about two dozen dignitaries—as well as a marching band—to welcome the great Howard Hughes back to the Bahamas. They were dressed in their dress uniforms, and they all stood at attention as the airplane landed.

I had to go to the bathroom, so I was the first one out of the airplane. Since I am a tall, skinny guy, they thought I was Howard, so I went through the receiving line. Pindling was extremely happy to have Howard back I could tell that from all the smiling faces of his staff. I shook hands with the deputy prime minister, the local Parliament member, Kendall Nottage, and everyone down the line. I didn't say anything, I just shook hands with them and let them think I was Howard Hughes. Because it was raining, they all got back in their cars and drove away as soon as I had worked my way through the line. I went to find a bathroom while Gordon Margulis and the aides unloaded the real Howard Hughes.

He was in his wheelchair when we got him to the Xanadu Princess, and I pushed him around the balcony. It was about 5:30 am, and the sun was beginning to come up. We spent an hour there, with him telling me what we were going to do. He had decided to put me in charge of a new entity that he called the Eastern Division that would be based in the Bahamas.

"We created a new division," he explained happily. "Jack runs the Eastern Division, and this island is Jack's."

Shortly after, Howard heard that Bill Gay and his wife had come to Freeport to spend the New Year's holiday, and he ordered them off the island. I remember his voice when he told the aides to send Bill and Mary back to the mainland. They left the same day. They loved the Bahamas, but not by the rules of Howard Hughes. Chester Davis and his wife Jean had joined the Gays for New Year's, but they were not ordered off the island, so they remained for four or five days.

Howard was truly excited by the prospects for our Eastern Division, which we discussed at great length during our first days in the Bahamas. We were going to buy an airline. We were going to travel all over the world. We were really going to make a great deal of money. He wanted me to buy more hotels and he wanted me to buy islands. He imagined that it would be just like it had been in Las Vegas, but with someone in charge whom he could trust implicitly.

Unfortunately, Bill Gay would never let go. He seems to have had a long memory for the events of the first week of 1974.

SETTLING IN

"I'm going to hold you responsible if you don't get me flying again," Howard smiled. "I've got a broken hip, but I'm going to fly again. Buy us an Aero Commander. The Aero Commander sits just 17 inches above the ground. You can lift me up and put me in the seat."

I remember when we went into his bedroom after spending that first hour on the balcony watching the sunrise. The aides were already sealing the windows with blackout curtains. He looked at me and said: "Jack, if you don't get me flying again, I'm going to hold you totally responsible."

We had taken over the whole top floor at the Xanadu. A man named Jerry Goldsmith was still living in one of the suites, and we agreed that he could stay while we helped him locate a house. All the other suites had been vacated, and Jerry was out within a month. The only thing that delayed us, and the maintenance folks took care of that within hours of our arrival, was the installation of a bidet that Howard wanted, but never used.

When we put him in his bed, both Gordon Margulis and I realized what a Herculean task it would be to get him out again. It would be almost three years before he next left this bedroom suite. He never even went back to the balcony.

Nevertheless, I would operating under the assumption that we would fly again. We had done it in Britain, and in Freeport we had better weather and we were closer to the airport. I proceeded to follow all of his instructions. I bought him an Aero Commander 690 just so he could start flying. He looked at the calculations of the pedal forces, because he knew his left leg was very weak. We discussed how, when he was doing his trimming up, he would always have to keep the right foot on the rudder, so if anything happened, if he lost an engine, for instance, all he would have to do is lift his foot off the right rudder. He had it all figured out. Then he had me lease a part of the airport from the Port Authority, and arrange to bring a house trailer out to the site. He imagined that we were going to move into a trailer so we could be close to the airplane when we started flying again.

I also leased about 40 acres from a lawyer named Edward St. George who was a key man with the Port Authority. He had been the a government official on the islands when the British ruled it, and he would become a very useful member of our team during our years in Freeport.

My new role as head of the Eastern Division was analogous to Bob Maheu's in Hughes Nevada Operations, except the latter was Bob's creation, and Howard himself had invented the Eastern Division and he had personally named me to head it. With the airport lease behind me, my role in the new division was to investigate business opportunities for us, specifically in the

Bahamas. I looked into many of them, but I think Howard was disappointed when I rejected many of them as being bad investments.

In July 1974, he had me looking at a television network throughout the Islands, and even at the possibility of a communications satellite dedicated to broadcasting exclusively in the Bahamas. I investigated this idea thoroughly throughout July and August. I had discussions with the satellite people at the Hughes Aircraft Company and at the government, as well as the owner of a cable television operation on Grand Bahama Island, and of the system in use at West End. However, by this time, Freeport was beginning to get cable from Palm Beach, Florida, so putting up his own station in the Bahamas just didn't make sense.

Howard also wanted to buy an island and he had me look over several. I found one cute little island, Great Harbour Cay, but nearly all the lots surrounding the golf course and airport were already sold, so it wasn't such a good opportunity unless he could have bought all the land contiguous to the airport. I turned that down.

When I told him that I didn't want him to waste his money buying an island, he said, "You think the money is yours."

"No," I said, "I just don't want you to put your money in things like that."

Another thing that Howard wanted the Eastern Division to do in the Bahamas was show the Bahamian people that he wanted to become a part of the community. He wanted to invest money in visible projects. It was my job to come up with the deals. One of these involved a man that had been with Coors Brewing in Colorado. He had tasted the water in the Bahamas, and he said that the water would be ideal for making beer.

He had a convincing argument. "All the beer in the Bahamas is imported," he reasoned. "And the Bahamian natives drink a lot of beer. Grand Bahama Island has plenty of water, so we could just raise hops and set up a brewery."

However, when I discussed this proposal with Howard in January 1974, Howard didn't want to do it.

"I don't want to do anything that could contribute to the worsening of the natives," Howard said. "This is a poor idea."

I decided to go back to projects in areas where Howard was more comfortable, so I started looking into airlines and hotels.

BUYING AN AIRLINE

Howard agreed that maybe he ought to be putting his money into an airline, and this soon became one of the major directions that I would take the Eastern Division while we were in the Bahamas. Howard and I had numerous meetings to discuss airline acquisitions. On July 28, 1974, Howard outlined his desire to become involved in an airline serving the Bahamas, Central America and Europe, and a week later he asked me about extending our position in Central American airlines, such as Lanica, the Nicaraguan national carrier, in which he'd had a position since we were having our dealings with Somoza in 1972. Throughout the summer and fall, we discussed taking over both Bahamas Air and Bahamas World Air Lines, as well as Lanica.

On October 5, Howard agreed to drop both efforts in the Bahamas and start "afresh," but by the first week of November, we were informed that Bahamas World Air Lines was bankrupt. Pindling's people offered to transfer the airline's rights as a carrier to Summa, but I told Howard that we should decline the offer because of the many legal problems involved, and he agreed.

Meanwhile, the Bahamas Air people had gotten wind of Howard's interest. On November 28, the vice chairman of Bahamas Air, Sherlock Hackley, came to me with an offer to sell his shares in Bahamas Air. Hackley had a 12 percent interest, which he told me was the largest slice of the pie that was not owned by the Bahamian government. When I passed this offer along to Howard, we agreed that the shares were not worth making an offer, but a week later, Pindling phoned me to say that he really wanted the Eastern Division to take another look at the Bahamas Air operation. I promised the prime minister that I would, but after I met with the top management of the airline, I hadn't changed my mind, and I still recommended to Howard that we not get involved in ownership.

Howard was still anxious to get back into the airline business, and on November 15, he called me in to discuss an idea that he had come up with. He wanted the Eastern Division to buy Shawnee Airlines and Mackey Airlines, both of which operated between Florida and Freeport. On November 25, I met with the new owner of Shawnee, but we didn't discuss numbers. That evening, when I told Howard about this meeting, he said: "They probably know how excited I am about having an airline. They'll surely want too much money, so we'll just wait six months and make them hungry."

We didn't discuss Shawnee again in six months, or ever, but Howard kept pressing me to look into Mackey. It was not until March 3, 1975 that I finally met with Colonel Joe Mackey. He flew over to Freeport and we met in my room at the Xanadu. He had been putting me off by saying that the airline was not for sale, but during our meeting, it became obvious that he wasn't even the real owner, because Fred Ayers, the New York City financier, held the paper on all of Mackey's old aircraft.

However, in the course of my chat with the colonel, he mentioned that the airline owned some property in Bimini that he might want to unload. I was pretty cool on both Bimini and the airline, and when I met with Howard the following day, I told him so. He agreed with me about the Bimini property, but he was still interested in the airline and he urged me to pursue it. Rather than argue the point about this small, shaky airline, I let the whole Mackey affair slide, and eventually Howard forgot about it.

Meanwhile, Pindling was continuing to hound me periodically about getting Howard involved with Bahamas Air. On March 8, at the request of the prime minister I met again with the airline people again. The sale of shares, however, was just a smoke screen for what they really had in mind. As I soon discovered, the true purpose of the meeting was for them to ask me for Howard's money.

As with many people—from Dan Haughton to General Somoza—they were intoxicated by the aroma of Howard Hughes' billions. They wanted to re-equip the airline so that they could apply for routes into the United States. In exchange, they said that they would give the Eastern Division up to 49 percent of Bahamas Air.

"This is a bad idea," I told Howard when I reported on the meeting. "Bahamas Air is losing a bundle of money every day. The general manager is a former cab driver from New York. This is absolutely a bad thing for the Eastern Division to get involved with financially."

Howard nodded in agreement, but he told me to let the prime minister know that we would be glad to help him technically to improve the airline's operation.

Pindling was not happy when I relayed this to him, but he held his temper because he was anxious not to upset Howard at a time when the Eastern Division was starting to pour money into our Bahamas real estate ventures.

Another airline with whom we were negotiating during this period was International Air Bahamas, which was a part of Icelandic Airlines. They had flown in on April 14 to meet with me at the Xanadu, and to lay out their proposal. They were looking to sell us their permit to fly between Luxembourg and Nassau, but in the course of our discussions, they offered to sell us the airline for $2.5 million, plus the equity they had in the DC-8-63 jetliner that they were using on the route. Their license was about to expire, but they assured me that the Bahamian government would renew it. They wanted to sell us the airline, but they had a "kicker." They wanted us to hire them back to operate the airline after the sale.

This was actually the first airline deal that I had seen since we came to the Bahamas that made sense to me. International Air Bahamas had made money for five years in a row with a load factor of 82 percent, and this looked very good for the Eastern Division.

I liked the deal and I told Howard that we ought to go for it. This was assuming, of course, that our friends in the Bahamian government would renew the license for us for another five years. I also wanted to see some of the flights coming into Freeport, and I suggested that we alternate the flights, with four flights a week going into Nassau, and three a week into Freeport. I would, of course, have to convince Edward St. George and his people at the Port Authority to make a commitment to extending the Freeport runway from 8,000 to 10,000 feet to accommodate the DC-8-63.

Howard agreed with me that this was the only air transport system that made sense here on the islands, and he told me to pursue it. For the next three months, this was to be the major focus of my activities.

By July, we had the deal ready to go when International Air Bahamas abruptly withdrew its offer. Lynden Pindling had agreed to give them another five-year lease. What had happened was that they were expecting the prime minister to deny their lease extension, and they had been hoping to unload it to us before that happened, and to let us take our chances with Lynden. They would have won either way. If Pindling had approved the extension after we had bought it, they'd have had a management deal with us, but if he had denied it, they would be gone, with us holding the bag.

GETTING HELP

Even though I didn't see Howard every day, he always insisted that I stay close by. Even when I flew over to Miami for a meeting, he always wanted me back in Freeport in the evening. At the same time, the Eastern Division was becoming more deeply involved in numerous and varied projects in the Bahamas. I told Howard that I was going to need help if I was going to run all of his affairs—and he would not allow me to leave him. He suggested that I hire Dan Haughton, the chairman of the board of Lockheed, or Carl Kotchian, the corporate president, as an assistant.

This was not very realistic, of course, but I did hire Tom Morrow, a former Lockheed Corporation executive vice president with a background in finance. His name was familiar to Howard from the work that he had done with Chester Davis and Raymond Holliday on the proposed merger of Lockheed and Hughes Aircraft Company in 1971, so, with Howard's approval, I hired Tom at a ridiculous salary of $30,000 a year. He insisted on low pay for the first three months, but expected a raise after he proved himself. He had an office in Miami in our Lanica/Hughes building, which made sense, since Howard still had a 38 percent interest in Lanica.

I sent Tom to Las Vegas to size up the operation there, and then on to Encino. He submitted a good report to me. It had 32 action items. The first one was the shortest: "Fire Bill Gay."

I couldn't tell him why that was impossible.

The remaining 31 items detailed the problems with Howard's Las Vegas operations. As I recall, Tom's memo also included problems with the bookkeeping at the Desert Inn, and a few personnel and staffing problems.

After working for less than six weeks in early 1975, Tom visited me in the Bahamas and asked for a leave of absence. He had severely constricted arteries, and his family had long been urging him to have a heart bypass operation. He told me that he had finally agreed.

I put him on an Eastern Airlines flight home after our visit, but somewhere on the 20-minute flight between Freeport and Miami, he died.

I was deeply saddened by Tom's death and mourned his sudden passing. Tom had been my friend and associate for many years at Lockheed, but beyond that, he was a wonderful man who could have done Howard, and me, a world of good.

Howard was depressed with the news of Tom's death and sent me to California for the funeral, and to make sure that Tom's widow was adequately provided for. When I was convinced she would be okay, I headed back to the Bahamas. Howard was aware of Tom's activities in Las Vegas, and while I was at the funeral, Howard asked the aides whether Morrow had submitted his findings. When I returned, I sealed a copy of the report in an envelope and asked the aides to pass it along to Howard's room.

When I asked him the next day whether he had read the report, he pointed to his ears and said, "Write it down." I had my usual yellow pad with me and wrote him a note. He looked at it and said we'd discuss the Morrow report after I helped him gather information about a Westinghouse surveillance system that he wanted installed on a hot air balloon that would be kept on the east end of the island. Like many of Howard's later plans, the surveillance system was never installed, and a balloon was never purchased. But it gave Howard pleasure to pursue those types of fantasies, and everyone just played along.

Howard's attention drifted from Morrow's report and we never discussed it again. I kept looking for someone to fill Tom's slot, but I never hired another assistant. Nobody of Tom's caliber materialized as a viable, and available, candidate during the last year of Howard's life.

After Howard died, I was talking to Dan Haughton and jokingly told him about the job that Morrow took. Dan said he was disappointed that I hadn't made him an offer, because by that time, Dan had resigned his post as Lockheed chairman after being tainted by a scandal involving the sale of L-1011 aircraft to Japan.

"I'd have taken it," Dan confided.

I didn't believe him for a second.

SABOTAGE

Throughout the whole time that we were in the Bahamas, I was constantly being sabotaged by Howard's aides. With the exception of George Francom and John Holmes, the aides were constantly undercutting my authority and my ability to do my job. It was my understanding that this was partially on orders from Bill Gay in Encino, and partially through the general jealousy and distrust that they had felt toward me since I had entered the inner sanctum in London. Neither they, nor Bill Gay, seemed happy with the access that I had to Howard.

Ironically, while Howard asked for me nearly every day, he told me that he had specifically ordered that neither Bill Gay nor Nadine Henley should even set foot in the Bahamas while he was there. Bill Gay would frequently fly 3,000 miles to spend time in nearby Miami, but he would never travel the last 100 miles to Freeport. Of course, he didn't really need to. He had his surrogates in place.

One day, during the middle of 1974, when George Francom was on duty, Howard called me in to read me a memo. In fact, he called me in three times that day to read me that same memo. Each time he read it, he laughed with greater gusto.

Written by his newest aide, Jim Rickard, this document suggested to Howard that he send me back to California. It was a personal attack on me, saying that if Howard sent me home, all of his personal problems would be corrected. His general health would improve, but most important, his relationship with Bill Gay—which was, for many years, an adversarial one—would be allowed to blossom again. For this relationship to flourish, Rickard wrote, "we must send Jack Real home."

Each time he read it, Howard concluded by saying Rickard was to be fired.

A few days later, Howard told me that he had reconsidered firing Rickard. The other aides had begged him to forgive Rickard, and he said that he rationalized his forgiveness when he realized the source.

"The message had to have come from Gay himself," Howard whispered. "Rickard just rewrote it to make it look like it was his own idea."

Howard's dislike for Gay grew a little more intense as a result of the message. He asked me again why I did not fire Gay, but he knew the reason. He still believed that Gay knew too much about his business interests ever to be fired.

A few days later, I awoke at 7:00 am to find Jim Rickard in my bedroom. When he realized that I was awake, and that I had seen him, he got down on his knees. He said that he wanted to pray for God's forgiveness for what he had done to me. He didn't mention Gay's name but it was implied.

I told Rickard that I would forgive him, even if God didn't, if he would just stand up and leave my room.

Two weeks later, Gordon Margulis advised me that Kay Glenn had just sent the aides a dossier on me that covered my entire life, including grade school, high school, college, and my career at Lockheed. It exaggerated every negative thing about me. Glenn had ordered the aides to read it, and suggested that, in the future, there might be an opportunity to mention these negative items to Howard.

Howard then turned to George, and said, "I want Jack Real to have a desk right out here so I can look at him out of the corner of my eye. I want Jack to approve all of the business deals—any part of my business. I want Jack to approve them or make a recommendation or turn them down."

A desk for me was never placed in Howard's suite, but the fact that he said it in front of George indicates the extent to which he trusted me and distrusted the aides.

REAL ESTATE

The airline side of the Eastern Division was mostly a window shopping exercise compared to what we would eventually be doing with real estate holdings. Howard had expressed interest in acquiring lots adjacent to the hotel, but we had been in the islands for nearly a year before Howard started to take an active interest in the hotel scene.

This changed on November 5, 1974, when we had a serious meeting in which Howard instructed me to work with Chester Davis to determine if Summa could purchase the two other Ludwig Hotels in Freeport, the Kings Inn and the adjoining Bahamas Tower, and get them at a very favorable price.

As with the hotels in Las Vegas, the hotels in the Bahamas offered guests more than just accommodations, they also offered gaming. This made the hotels, and the surrounding property, especially attractive. In this case, the two hotels were served by a common casino.

One hurdle that would have to be crossed before the Eastern Division could move into the gaming business was the state of Nevada's ban on ownership of Las Vegas casinos by anyone who had interests in gaming properties outside Nevada. Against this backdrop, we realized that any negotiations that we undertook involving gaming properties would have to be very discreet.

On January 2, 1975, after some preliminary discussions, Edward St. George of the Port Authority said that he could offer a package deal for a series of adjoining properties if Howard would agree to build a beach club on one of them. I passed this along to Howard, but he ignored it at the time.

In the meantime, though, an interesting opportunity came along, and one that would consume most of my time for the next year. I got word that the Montreal Trust Company of Canada, Ltd. wanted to dispose of some property in Freeport, specifically the once-magnificent Lucayan Beach Hotel, with its wonderful casino, its yacht harbor, and the Lucayan Harbor Inn. On March 6, I met with the representatives of the Montreal Trust, and listened to their offer. They wanted to sell the three properties, although they had lost their gaming license. The asking price was $15 million, but they were quick to add that they would take "something lower."

I was very interested in this deal. Assuming that we could get a gaming license—which was possible through the connections that we had cultivated within the Bahamian government—this property could serve as the anchor for a hotel and gaming operation that would rival that which Howard owned in Las Vegas. I deliberately showed no interest, but I said that we might be in touch with them soon.

On March 23, I wrote Howard a message regarding Lucayan Beach, and told him the story, adding that we could probably get it "dirt cheap," although it was essentially a worthless investment without a casino. To my surprise, Howard replied right away, instructing me to bring Chester up to date, and contact the Port Authority regarding the land on the beach to the west.

By this time, Edward St. George had gotten wind of our conversations with Montreal Trust regarding the Lucayan Beach Hotel. He asked me to meet him, which I did on April 5. It soon became obvious that he wanted to feel me out regarding our interest in the adjacent properties. I was as evasive and non-committal as I could be.

When I reported this meeting to Howard by memo, he replied

that he wanted to see me face to face, but that he would rather talk to me by telephone because he didn't want to use his hearing aid.

"I want to buy the Lucayan Beach complex, and all the land," he told me. "I'm going to buy it and restore it to its old glory. We'll have the gaming if we can get the approval. For the time being, I want you to work with Chester but keep this all very hush-hush."

Three days later, I flew up to New York City to discuss the Lucayan Beach Hotel deal with Chester. He agreed with my assessment of the property as being worthless without a gaming license, and told me to set up a meeting with our friends in the Bahamas government. He said that he would fly down to join us.

On April 13, Chester came down for the Saturday meeting I set up in Nassau with Kendall Nottage. The following evening, we all visited the prime minister at his home. We obliquely brought up the Lucayan Beach complex, particularly the gaming license. Pindling seemed to be favorably disposed to the idea. Chester and I decided that we had better get some real numbers so that we could make an intelligent offer to the Montreal Trust.

On Monday morning, with Howard's approval, we started bringing in architects to look over the property. I hired Hal Uttke's architectural firm to start "surveying" the Lucayan Beach Hotel in order to give us some idea of the cost to refurbish it and bring it up to the standard of an international destination resort casino. On Wednesday, I also asked Chas Giller, of Giller & Associates, an architectural firm in Miami, to come over and look into designing a new 12-story hotel tower for the property. I decided to involve more than one firm because Howard did not want to select a final architect until he saw some of their proposals. Giller was the original architect of the Xanadu Princess, which was known simply as the Xanadu Hotel after we had acquired it.

Chas Giller submitted his renderings of the Lucayan Beach Tower on May 13, and I shared these with Howard in his suite at the Xanadu. Ten days later, I met with Edward St. George again to discuss our purchase of their seven acres of land west of the Lucayan Beach property. He generously offered the land for one dollar—if we could complete our proposed tower in 30 months. When I passed this on to Chester, he said that it smelled like a trap, and he insisted that we should pay a fair market price.

June 4 was to be the big day. Chester and I, with Kendall Nottage in tow, flew down to Nassau to pay a visit to the prime minister. We gave him our complete plans, our analysis of the property and its potential, our drawings of the new tower and the schedule for re-activating the Lucayan Beach Hotel. We explained, as Pindling obviously knew, that our go-ahead would be based on obtaining a gaming license. He was delighted with the presentation and asked for eight copies plus a letter from Chester setting forth our request for a gaming license.

I flew back up to New York City on June 10 for a big meeting with Chester, Edward St. George and the Montreal Trust people to firm up the memorandum of understanding on the Lucayan Beach complex. They proposed $4 million with terms, or $3.5 million if we paid cash. Edward told us to name our price for their seven acres of beach frontage, and Chester proposed $500,000 on terms or $250,000 cash. We put this in a message to Howard, and he replied that he wanted to pay $3.5 million on terms or $3 million cash. The meeting broke up with Montreal Trust telling us they'd have to get back to us.

I reported this news to Howard when I got back to Freeport, but he laughed and said that he was sure we could get his price if we waited. On June 19, however, Montreal Trust replied that the $4 million/$3.5 million asking price was firm.

Howard's reply was simply: "Tell them that I'll give them $3 million in cash. Take it or leave it."

For the moment, they did neither, but I sensed that they would eventually come around. They really did not want to be in the hotel business in the Bahamas.

With the ball rolling on the Lucayan Beach Hotel, I could see that Howard had begun to imagine that this property would become the hub for creating in the Bahamas, the type of empire he had built for himself in Las Vegas between 1966 and 1970.

Early in September, I showed him some aerial photographs of

the Lucayan Beach Hotel complex, and as he looked at these views, he decided that we might want to buy the Oceanus Bay Hotel complex. He had flown over the area on one of his visits during the 1950s, and he raved about the excellent natural yacht harbor there.

I promised that I would look into the Oceanus property, although I was not in favor of the idea of him spreading himself too thin before the Lucayan Beach Hotel was developed. By the end of the month I had contacted the mortgage holders at Oceanus Bay and received a formal proposal from them. In spite of my efforts to keep his attention focused on the Lucayan Beach Hotel, Howard continued to press me to get the Oceanus Bay property. On November 5, I gave him a proposal to digest. I had learned that about $30 million had been spent to develop the area around the Oceanus property, including the roads, the golf course, the country club and the yacht basin. I also found out that we could buy the entire Oceanus Bay property for $2.5 million, less than a dime on the dollar. When he read about this, Howard was excited, but all consideration of this property would hinge on whether we could get the Lucayan Beach Hotel and a gaming license for it.

On July 8, we had submitted the eight copies of our report, plus Chester's letter regarding the gaming license, to Nottage to pass along to the prime minister. I heard nothing for two weeks until Nottage called to say that Pindling had an bonafide offer from Shawnee Airlines to do exactly the same thing at the Lucayan complex that we had proposed. Nottage said that Pindling had told him to ask me whether Howard was serious.

Trying not to raise my voice, I related a few cautious, but choice, words about Shawnee, and told Nottage to assure Pindling that the word from Howard Hughes was definitely "go."

I then turned back to my own efforts to get a final answer from Edward St. George on the Port Authority's seven acres of beachfront. Finally, on August 7, Edward phoned me at the Xanadu to tell me, "Yes, without any qualification."

We could have the seven acres of beach frontage at our price of $500,000 terms, or $250,000 cash.

FIGHTING FOR ACCESS

By this time, the powers within the Summa organization that wanted to block Howard's acquisition of any additional properties stepped up their efforts to limit my access to Howard. The aides were instructed by their master in Encino that I was simply not to be allowed to see Howard, and he ordered them to change the locks on the outer doors that led into Howard's suite at the Xanadu.

When I discovered that my key no longer worked, I was told that from then on, I was to have no more verbal contact with Howard. From now on, the chief of his Eastern Division—the man who, on several occasions, was put in charge of the entire Howard Hughes empire, would be required to submit all of his messages in the form of handwritten memos.

Not wanting to create a scene that would upset Howard, I acquiesced. I wrote two or three long messages a day, and I wrote large because he didn't have glasses and I didn't want him to have any trouble reading my messages. I brought them to the suite to be taken to his bedroom. They would almost never reach him the same day, if they reached him at all.

Meanwhile, nobody had told him why I had stopped coming to see him. Howard would ask for me and they'd just tell him I wasn't around.

"Where's Jack?"

"Jack's gone fishing."

"He doesn't like to go fishing."

"He does it just because he doesn't care for you, Howard."

I would be sitting 20 feet away from his door and they would tell him I'd gone fishing, when Howard and everyone else knew that I didn't like to go fishing.

When he started to see that I was submitting handwritten memos, he would say, "If Jack puts in a message, I want to be woken up immediately. I have to get all his messages right away."

They would nod and smile, but the messages would reach him late or not at all.

When George Francom came back on duty after his two weeks off, the matter came to a head. Howard asked him to get me—and he did. When Howard asked him why I hadn't been coming to see him, George told him the truth.

"Jack can't get in here," George said. "Everybody but Jack has a key."

"Get him a key," Howard demanded. "Go down to the hardware store in the morning, George, and get him a key. How can he function if he doesn't have a key?"

George went down and got the key. The next day, they flew a locksmith over from Nassau and they replaced the locks. When George gave me the key for the new lock, John Holmes whispered to me, "If you keep this up, you are going to be in trouble."

"I don't think these people in California have enough guts to do this to me," I said.

"Don't push them."

I got so mad that I just handed him my new key and walked away.

THE EMPLOYMENT CONTRACTS

It was during 1975 that the issue of employment contracts for the aides and executives finally came to a head. It had been discussed off and on for as long as I could remember, but by the summer of 1975, people were nervously jockeying for power. It was during the Lucayan Beach Hotel negotiations that I found out, purely by accident, about the existence of the lifetime employment contracts for certain key people, including myself.

In July 1975, my wife, Janeth, and Dr. Wilbur Thain's wife, paid one of their rare visits to the Bahamas. Ruthie Thain had found out from her husband that there were contracts being written, and she had been putting pressure on him to make a move for his. She happened to mention to Janeth that this was the reason that she flew down to the islands.

"Wilbur is trying to get Jack's contract firmed up along with his own and the ones for the aides," Ruthie said as they were sitting by the pool one day. "Nothing moves unless I push Wilbur. That's why I'm down here this time."

That night, Janeth asked me what contract Ruthie was talking about, and I told her I knew nothing about it. I had heard rumors about contracts, but I had assumed that they were just pipe dreams. My wife never had any interest in me getting a contract, but I think Ruthie put pressure on Dr. Thain, and Howard finally caved in. According to what George Francom told me, the doctor had gone in to see Howard and had used the old Chinese proverb, "No tickie, no laundry."

It was my understanding that Dr. Thain was, at that time, a key supplier of prescriptions for Howard's "medication." If so, the implication of the Chinese proverb would seem to be that he intended for Howard to know that without a contract, there would be no more "medication."

The next morning, George Francom handed me a message from Howard. Chester Davis was, at that moment, flying to Freeport for one of the meetings with the government people, and Howard wanted me to tell Chester to "add Wilbur's name, so the 'goodies' will flow again." At the time, I didn't know exactly what this meant, but I soon found out.

It was one of the days that Chester was flying in to pick up myself and Kendall Nottage, and we were to fly on to have dinner with the prime minister in Nassau. We had our conversation about the "goodies flowing" out on the runway, as Kendall Nottage was taking a seat inside the aircraft. I remember the scene vividly because Chester was very depressed. He had just heard the previous day that his daughter had died from a drug overdose in London. Nobody had heard from her for some time, and when the police had opened her apartment door, they found that she had been dead for over a week. Such a sad day for any parent.

Chester then explained that there had been commitments for seven contracts—the six aides plus myself. Dr. Thain made eight. When Chester told me that he had agreed to Dr. Thain's name being added, I quickly called George at the hotel before we took off for Nassau. He then informed Howard that the "goodies" would continue to flow.

Later, Chester would refuse to remember me ever mentioning "goodies" or "No tickie, no laundry." He steadfastly refused to acknowledge or allow anyone to discuss Howard's drug addiction.

I now knew that I was supposed to have a lifetime employment contract, but actually getting it was to be another matter entirely.

THE MAN IN THE RED PAJAMAS

Over the years, Howard had demonstrated an uncanny knack for knowing what was going to happen. It may have been extrasensory perception or a refined case of intuition, but on many occasions, I witnessed his ability to sense a problem and deal with it before it got out of control. In August 1975, he sensed that Bill Gay was about to have him declared mentally incompetent. He feared that Gay would set up a trusteeship or guardianship to manage his holdings, with Gay in control. I doubted Howard's concerns at the time, but later was amazed to read in the book *Empire*, by Donald L. Bartlett and James B. Steele (W.W. Norton, 1979), that Gay had proposed exactly such a plan to Bob Maheu in about 1968.

On the first day of September 1975, I was awakened at 4:00 am by a phone call from John Holmes.

"Howard wants you in his room now."

I dressed quickly and rushed to Howard's suite. When I arrived in his room, Howard was agitated and clearly upset. He moved around in his bed uncomfortably. Although his hip had long since mended from the fall, Howard still refused to walk on it and had insisted on remaining bedridden for two years. Of course, the longer he remained immobile, the more likely he was to become truly unable to walk. By this time, he had probably already reached that point.

"John refuses to type a letter for me," Howard said, holding up some sheets of paper with some scribbling on it. "Damn it. If he won't do it, then it's up to you, Jack. I hope you can type. You can type, can't you?"

Apparently Howard and John had been quarreling for an hour or more about my role in Howard's affairs, and their discussion had been compromised by Howard's refusal to use his hearing aid. He looked worried. I had never seen him look that way before. It bothered me, especially since I was apparently at the root of his discomfort.

"Yes Howard, I can type," I replied, although I was still unclear what Howard was trying to accomplish. He had never asked me to type anything before, and I couldn't recall a time when an aide had refused to type something for Howard.

"They're trying to destroy me," Howard said. "They want to put me away. They want the world to think that I'm senile," he said, his voice raised. "We'll show them who's lost his wits. Jack, I want this firmed up right now. I want Chester to be the attorney. I want the company to be yours, totally yours. I want you to change this so-called writing that puts Bill Gay in charge. I've never seen it before. I want it rewritten. I want you to put yourself as the ruler of everything that I have, and I want you to stay."

"It won't be legal," John told Howard, "unless Levar Myler witnesses the statement and watches me sign it. And you'll need to force me to sign it."

Of course, this wasn't true. Both John and I could have signed the letter as witnesses, making the letter valid. Levar Myler, who was asleep at the time, didn't need to be involved. Holmes was just stalling.

As he explained it to me, Howard wanted to neutralize Bill Gay forever. The letter would have put me in charge of everything, including, for the first time, his entire Nevada operation. I would also replace Nadine Henley, who was allied with Bill Gay, on the Summa Corporation's three-member executive committee.

During our three years together in London and Freeport, Howard repeatedly asked me to take control of his aviation interests, but he never consummated his offer. He repeatedly asked me to take charge, but Howard wasn't in command of his own companies. His addiction had turned him into an invalid.

After we argued for an hour, I went to the outer room of Howard's suite to type the letter. As I bent down and started looking for a sheet of paper, John Holmes tried to stop me. His hands were trembling as he feebly tried to keep me from opening the drawer that contained blank paper. The possibility that I would get Howard to sign the letter really frightened him. He feared the worst.

"I'll be done if I let you type that letter."

I said, "John, don't do this."

"Don't do it to *me*, Jack."

John's conscience got the better of him and he tried to bare his soul. He confessed the group's mistrust of me. He recounted the many lies he and other aides had told Howard about me since I joined the company in 1971.

They had told Howard I was not available because I had left my wife and was living abroad with another woman. They had deliberately painted a black picture of me as a father and friend. John told me that Bill Gay had punished him for bringing me to Vancouver in 1972 when Howard had asked for me.

Over the ensuing years, John had helped to get me close to Howard again, and this irked Bill Gay constantly. John had obviously given his argument a great deal of thought.

"You could go out and get another job tomorrow if *you* left Howard."

With tears pouring down his cheeks, he explained: "You could get a job. You're an engineer. But if I, if *we*, allow Howard to sign this letter, I'll never work again. I'll be finished."

I admired all that John had done for Howard, and I honestly believed that Gay would retaliate against John. Howard sensed that John would try to stop me from helping, so he insisted that John and I go "off campus," and find a telephone booth in Freeport and phone Chester Davis.

"Find out what he advises," Howard said. "Find out how you and John can stop Gay, and how I can legally turn the entire operation over to Jack Real."

Thirty minutes later, after John's shift was over and he had been relieved, we were in a phone booth in downtown Freeport explaining the problem to Chester. His loud and uncompromising answer was simple: "Fire Bill Gay. Fire them all."

"That's great," I said sarcastically. "But it will never happen that way. We've got to find a more reasonable solution."

It was like a recurring dream I had, in which I always found myself peeking through the darkness, unable to muster the strength to turn on the lights.

Deep down, I had wanted to confront Chester about the drug addiction issue. I resisted the temptation and didn't. Howard would rarely fire a member of his staff, especially ones who could expose his drug addiction. He had fired Bob Maheu, but, since Bob had never actually met Howard, he wasn't privy to Howard's darkest secret. Employees who fell out of Howard's favor were simply banished to obscure jobs, but kept their outrageous pay to secure their silence.

I reiterated the request to Chester: "We need a plan to prevent Gay from taking over. We've got to save Howard."

A few days later, I went to New York at Chester's request to discuss the matter and to learn how I could assume the role that Howard wanted for me. When I entered his office, he was on the phone talking to Nadine Henley. Chester allowed me to join him, and I overheard the conversation without Nadine knowing I was there. Chester told her about the instructions he had received from Howard through John Holmes, who had made one of his very rare calls to Chester. He told Nadine that she and everybody else were working for Jack Real. There was no doubt about it. The word was out, but could the momentum be sustained? I was cynical about anything coming of this announcement. I was right.

"I know you hate Jack's guts, but Hughes picked Real to run our organization," Chester told Nadine over the phone. "And if you and Gay won't work for him, you both have problems. I know the game that Gay will play. Nadine, it's a dangerous game. Don't play it. You know how much Hughes despises Bill Gay. If he tries to move Hughes out of the Bahamas to get to Real, it will be a disaster."

Chester looked me straight in the eye. "Nadine says that Gay will try to stop you in your tracks. And she intends to support him."

Over lunch, I asked, "Chester, when are you going to put me on the board? You're the attorney. You've got a message from your employer to put me on the executive committee board. He told me that. I know John Holmes is on the board and he witnessed Howard's wishes."

"I have to think about it."

"Well, look," I said. "He's your client, and you're his attorney. You've got instructions. Unless you believe Bill Gay, who wants to think that he's senile."

"No, I don't."

"What are you hiding?"

"I've got to think about it."

Finally, Chester came up with a simple plan to reorganize the playing field. He said that he wanted to bring everyone together for a board meeting at his compound at Milfer Farm in upstate New York. The message that Jack Real was in charge would be clearly communicated to the board and, as Chester said, "That will be that."

The date was set for September 10. It would be the first board meeting in over a year.

In the meantime, Bill Gay's aide in Encino got word to Kay Nolan, my secretary in Encino, that I was *not* to come to the board meeting. When I called Chester Davis, he was livid.

"We won't hold the meeting unless you're there," he said loudly, pounding his fist on his desk. "Howard has made it clear to me that you are in charge of his properties. There will not be a meeting without you."

His support was encouraging, so I elected to go.

At the end of August, about two weeks before the board meeting at the farm, I received a call from Vern Olson, the Summa financial man at Las Vegas.

"I heard that all of Gay's staff people are writing lifetime work contracts for themselves, and many of the executives," he said. "I want you to try to get me one."

I told him that I had nothing to do with any contracts, but that I would put his request to John Holmes. An hour later, Olson called again and asked if I could also include his boss, Bill Rankin, on the list. The next day I asked Holmes if he could handle Olson's request. He said that, because Howard was adamant about Gay not getting a contract, he had been instructed by Encino that *nobody* would be allowed to have a contract. Gay would not allow the issue to be brought up at the Milfer Farm board meeting unless *he* got a contract. Needless to say, the aides were all disappointed.

On Sunday, September 7, Levar Myler told me that Howard had approved my getting a contract.

I took a Delta Airlines flight to Newark, New Jersey, on Tuesday, September 9, where I was met by Bob Wearley, our company pilot. Levar Myler and his very pleasant, outgoing wife joined me and we flew up to Binghamton in the Summa DH-125.

We were driven the last 35 miles north to the compound near Unadilla, arriving in time for the board meeting, which was scheduled to start at 10:00 am. It would, however, be delayed for 13 hours.

In the meantime, we were served lunch and dinner. When I inquired about the delay, Holmes told me that Howard had not approved the list yet, and they were waiting for a fax from the Bahamas. After dinner, the list arrived, signed by Howard Eckersley and adding Gay, Kay Glenn, Nadine Henley, and Dr. Crane to the eight that Howard had previously approved. Much to my surprise, I was still in the elite eight. To this day, I question whether Howard ever approved Gay's name. I know that Eckersley had signed it, and he usually acted at the bidding of Bill Gay.

This meeting would be the first time that I had seen Gay since he flew to London over two years earlier to attempt to scuttle the Lockheed deal at the last minute. The lock-changing incident was a clear barometer of the contempt that Gay had for me, and how deeply he despised the influence that I had with Howard. He was intent on destroying my credibility at the meeting that night.

Gay made a grand entrance to the board meeting wearing red silk pajamas.

"How privileged we all are to have Mr. Real, the new chosen one, to lead us all," he exclaimed. "This is Jack Real, our new anointed leader."

Everyone just stared in slack-jawed disbelief as the man in the red pajamas moved around the room.

"I have so many problems with torn rugs in the hotels in Las Vegas," he whined with taunting sarcasm. "Mr. Real, should I replace them or repair them? We need you to guide us, oh great leader. Will you give me any relief at all—now that you run everything in Las Vegas, now that you run everything in the world?"

I looked down and didn't say a word. Finally, Levar Myler just said, "Bill, why don't you just knock it off?"

"Knock it off?" Gay mimicked as he walked around us. "You're being disrespectful to Mr. Real. He's our new leader."

Gay then proceeded to chastise Levar for quarreling in front of me. I just let them roll on without any response.

At one point, I brought up a request to support Howard's desire to buy two more Convair 240 aircraft. The board balked at the request, but I argued successfully that, "If the boss wants to buy two more airplanes, we have an obligation to fulfill his wishes."

The executive committee approved the request, and I later bought the two planes. The meeting then started to deteriorate. Nothing was being accomplished, even though Gay had openly acknowledged that I was in charge. It did little to build my power base, but Gay was on notice that Howard wouldn't give up easily. At the same time, I sensed that Gay would redouble his efforts to destroy me.

My recurring dream that firing Bill Gay would trigger Howard's death weighed heavily on my decision not to press the issue at the board meeting. It was my nightmare embodied: If I had fired Gay, I would have been forced to fire everyone around Gay to prevent his troops from rebelling and making my job impossible.

Any move of this nature had to be done swiftly and totally. I was in New York. Who would care for Howard until I could get back to Freeport? Who would run his casinos and his aviation enterprises?

The prospects of disaster loomed heavily on my shoulders. I simply couldn't force the issues now. I needed a plan. My position in the aerospace community afforded me the opportunity to meet and develop relationships with many talented and well-respected men and women. There would be a pool to draw from, but finding the right people wouldn't be easy.

The whole plan would take time to develop. I had started to work on the plan when I hired Tom Morrow as my assistant, but his untimely death forced me to slow my efforts to take full control. Ultimately, as if God had simply pulled the plug on me, I would lose Howard to the ages and everything I had wanted to do would become moot.

By 2:00 am, the meeting became so rancorous that I left. I wasn't an official member of the board anyway. I excused myself and left. Strangely, the efforts to have Howard declared senile quickly went away. My new position wasn't the only issue to be discussed at the board meeting.

I had the flight crew fly me to Newark on the DH-125, so that I could catch a commercial flight back to Freeport. Early in the morning the board approved the contracts, with Chester excusing himself from the voting.

Two weeks later, Nadine Henley called me and read me the contract. I did not show much interest in it, as I thought it was rather immoral.

Her last words to me were, "I'll give you your copy when we meet again."

Two years earlier, Howard had strongly suggested that neither she nor Gay should come to the Bahamas, so I would not see Nadine again until December, when I flew over to Miami to visit my wife, Janeth, who was hospitalized there. After I saw my wife, I drove up to visit Nadine at the beautiful company-owned home that she and Gay used when they were in Miami.

When she moved to hand me the contract, Gay made a big show of pulling it from her hand.

"Let his good friend Chester Davis give it to him," Gay hissed, as though I wasn't standing there. "They seem to be having a love affair, and I don't want to break up the match between the two of them."

There was no doubt a serious rift had developed between Davis and Gay since Howard had gotten word to Davis that I was now in charge of the operation in the Bahamas.

I left the house with Gay still holding the contract.

CLOSING THE DEAL

Meanwhile, on September 3, 1975, we had finally come to terms with Montreal Trust on a memorandum of understanding for the Lucayan Beach Hotel. We still hadn't resolved the Nevada issue, because Howard still hadn't gotten a waiver to operate a casino outside the state, so I spoke with our friends at the Port Authority about this, and they said that they would be glad to operate our Monte Carlo Casino at the Lucayan on our behalf until we were able to get things ironed out.

While this resolved the issue vis a vis Nevada, we still had the nagging problem of getting our casino license for the Lucayan Beach Hotel from Lynden Pindling's Bahamian government. On October 19, the prime minister invited Chester and me to fly down to his fishing lodge at Andrus to talk about it.

We found Pindling acting very confused about the deal. I couldn't fathom whether he really didn't understand what was going on or whether he was trying to play games with us. On one hand, he was very anxious to see us reopen the Lucayan Beach Hotel property, but he seemed to be very wary of issuing us a casino license until the Nevada situation was resolved. The gaming industry was a major profit center for him, and he didn't want to pick a fight with that gaming mecca across the continent. On the other hand, Pindling probably relished the control that he seemed to be exercising over the legendary Howard Hughes. He knew that the world's richest man could not open a casino in the property that he owned, until Lynden Pindling said he could open the casino.

To nudge the prime minister to take action, Chester and I told him that if he gave us a green light on a Bahamas gaming license, we would open 200 rooms at the Lucayan Beach Hotel on or before February 15, 1976. This would be regardless of the problem with Nevada. In answer to this concern, we told him that there was a clear precedent for Nevada to grant us the waiver that we were seeking. We reminded him that the Pritzker interests—who owned 40 percent of the Hyatt Hotels chain and 100 percent of the Four Queens in Las Vegas—had hotels with casinos throughout the world. I didn't mention that I had already had a conversation with Jack Pritzker about having them manage our Bahamas properties.

Pindling was running out of excuses, and we pushed him for a decision. My having given him the February 15 date had seemed to get his attention, so I finally got him to agree that if we got an approval before December 1, we would have a partial opening of the Lucayan by February 15.

I realized that if we were going to make good on our February opening, I had better get the ball rolling, so on the first of November, I sent $50,000 to Chas Giller and told him go ahead with drawing up the plans and specifications for remodeling and rehabilitating the Lucayan Beach property—including replacing all the interior furnishings. We couldn't actually start any work at the property, however, because our closing with Montreal Trust was contingent on getting the gaming license, so we would not technically own the property until that happened.

A month later, when our deadline for a decision from Pindling on the license came and went, Howard demanded a status report. On December 3, I put in a long, handwritten message explaining that since we were still being stalled by the prime minister, we hadn't started any real work on the property yet. Later the same day, Jack Pritzker flew in to discuss his running both the Lucayan Beach complex and the Xanadu property, in exchange for a management fee. He was fairly noncommittal, and it quickly became obvious to me that he was really fishing to get a management contract to run and oversee our Las Vegas hotels and casinos, and that he would take the Bahamas properties only *if* that would lead to his getting into the Nevada properties.

The weeks slipped away, and we weren't getting any closer to a decision. Finally, on February 3, 1976, Chester and I, together with Ed St. George, flew down to Nassau to talk to Pindling face to face. Once again, however, he refused to make a decision, so Ed went to see the deputy prime minister. Together, they came up with an alternate proposal that they were able to sell to Pindling.

On the evening of February 10, St. George had a long dinner with the prime minister, and just before midnight, he agreed to sign our gaming license. St. George said, "Let's call Jack and give him the good news." He then phoned the Xanadu and left word for me, saying that we should have breakfast or lunch the next day to celebrate.

I wasn't in when Ed St. George called. I was taking Howard to the Freeport airport, but it was not for our long expected return to flying.

At 2:00 am, Howard left the Bahamas for the last time, bound for Acapulco, Mexico. This would be the last stop on the ten-year odyssey that had taken him to darkened penthouses in five countries.

Howard had been very, very interested in the Bahamas. He had loved it there, and he would have moved out of Las Vegas entirely to be there, but Lynden Pindling had played too hard and he had lost Howard Hughes twice. There would be no third chance.

I didn't find out that the permit was granted until the next morning after we had arrived in Acapulco, but I never did tell Howard. The prime minister was so angry when he heard of Howard's move that he cancelled the permit. I never told Howard about that either.

CHAPTER 10

HOWARD'S LAST THREE MONTHS

A SUDDEN MOVE

"We're moving to Mexico," Howard told me. "I want you to handle the whole operation. Can you do it? Show me the flight plan."

I showed him the flight plan and the map. I hated the idea of moving him to Mexico, but I couldn't tell him that he was being duped. I don't know who actually made the decision to move from Freeport, but I do know that it was not Howard, and the only parties to benefit were those in the faction that did not want us to buy the Lucayan Beach Hotel. They won.

Even a delay of two hours would have changed everything. After more than two years in Freeport, we had finally secured the license that made the Lucayan Beach Hotel a viable property, and I missed the phone call from Edward St. George by no more than two hours.

I was never told who made the decision for the move, but Dr. Norman Crane did let me in on the secret of how Howard was convinced that the move was necessary. He had been one of Howard's "attending" physicians off and on since the early 1950s, and he would be part of the entourage in Mexico as well. Howard's doctors were almost never allowed to see him, and had little to do other than wait outside his door for days at a time. The boredom of doing this had gotten to Dr. Crane, especially during the Las Vegas years. He had taken to drinking to pass the long, empty hours, and since most of the entourage were Mormons who abstained, to drinking alone.

One night a few days before the move, I was having dinner with Dr. Crane at the Xanadu. The drinks had apparently loosened his tongue, and he confided in me that Howard had been convinced that he had to move to Mexico because the drugs on which he depended could no longer be obtained in the Bahamas.

According to what I was told by Dr. Crane that night, Dr. Wilbur Thain convinced Howard that the *only* remaining source for the codeine was in the Mexican state of Guerrera. Howard panicked, but, according to Dr. Crane, his colleague reassured Howard that, fortunately, a nice hotel had been located in Acapulco, the state capital.

At the time, the Acapulco Princess Hotel was one of the most prestigious resort hotels in the city. Howard's accommodations would be the penthouse, which was occupied at that moment by none other than Mexican President Luis Echevarria Alvarez and his family. Our departure would be timed to the president's departure, and when he decided to stay an extra week, we would have to delay our departure from Freeport for a week.

When I questioned the absurd logic of moving to Mexico so that codeine could be procured for Howard, Dr. Crane admitted that the source continued to be in the United States, as it had always been, but he added: "It doesn't matter, Jack, they're all against you."

Three days before we left, Chester Davis and I were on our way down to see the prime minister in Nassau, when I told him: "Chester, Mr. Hughes is not going to survive this move. If he goes to Mexico, I give him two or three months. I'm going to make a deal with you. When we get off the airplane, if you'll agree, I want you to call Bill Gay and tell him Jack Real is leaving today. He's going to quit the company today if you keep Howard here in the Bahamas. I want your word before we get off the airplane."

"I'm not going to wait," he said. "I'll tell you right now. I'm not going to do any such thing. I need you. I agree with you. It's a bad thing to do."

"If you ever have to testify about any of this, I want the record to show that I offered to quit and leave," I told him.

When Howard asked me to set up the trip from the Bahamas to Acapulco, I contacted Bill Miller, a friend of mine who was an aircraft salesman based in Miami. He put me in touch with Roy Carver, who owned four aircraft, including a British Aerospace BAC-111 jetliner that was for sale. Carver was a very rich individual who had made a fortune by developing a cold vulcanizing process for truck tires. At the time Carver's representative for Mexico and Latin America was Darrell Kuelpman, who, as fate would have it, I met later at Evergreen Aviation.

I flew over to Miami to meet him, and he entertained my daughter and me for dinner at his place. It was four beautiful penthouse condominiums at the Palm Beach Club, put together to form a 22,000 square foot home. It was one of the fanciest condominiums I've ever seen. His BAC-111, an aircraft that can normally carry up to 79 passengers, was equally elegant. It had been redone in an executive configuration, meaning that it was beautifully furnished with plenty of space for its 16 seats. Carver agreed to a free demo ride to Acapulco if we agreed to buy the fuel.

Carver's "Girl Friday," a wonderful woman named Marcie McKellup, brought the BAC-111 to Freeport at noon on February 8, 1976. I took her to dinner at the Xanadu that night, and she returned to Miami the next day.

I spent the rest of the day arranging the vans to transport the entourage and our luggage, and getting a key to open up the airport gates, because I knew that we would be leaving in the middle of the night.

There wasn't any conversation between Howard and I about whether he wanted to leave the Bahamas. I had just decided that I did not want to get involved in that aspect of the move. He had told me to make the necessary arrangements, and that was what I did. I was disappointed to see him leave the Bahamas, but I never told him so.

We left the Xanadu for the last time just after midnight, and probably just a few minutes before Ed St. George placed the call from Nassau to tell me that we had the Lucayan Beach Hotel gaming license. As we were leaving, I got word on the two-way radio that our inflight meals would be late in arriving at the airport, so I decided to drive the "long way" to the airport to stall for time. Howard made the comment that he didn't know that the airport was so far from the Xanadu.

Before we closed the door on the aircraft, I made a local telephone call to Eric Bundy, our office manager at the Xanadu Hotel, telling him what our ETA (estimated time of arrival) would be in Acapulco, so that he could advise our advance team, who were supposed to meet us with transportation. I still imagine that the phone that I heard ringing in the background while I was talking to Eric, was Edward St. George.

We were airborne out of Freeport at 2:08 am on February 10, 1976. Howard was strapped into a seat in the rear of the aircraft and covered with a blanket. He looked terrible and appeared to be under heavy sedation. Perhaps this was by design, because they did not want him to back out of their plans to move him. He had an overcoat on, and I don't think he had anything on underneath. I don't know. He was a tragic case. He looked like a zombie.

We landed in Acapulco within two minutes of our planned arrival time. Our reception committee, which was to have included Kay Glenn and Dr. Thain, was nowhere to be seen. They had overslept.

We bundled the world's richest man into a local taxicab for the drive to the Acapulco Princess. It may have been the most elegant hotel in the city, but our arrival was like a scene from a bad slapstick comedy.

The advance team was supposed to have secured the service elevator so that we could slip Howard into the building by the back door, shielded from prying eyes. They hadn't secured the elevator, and we soon discovered that it was not working. This meant that we had to use the regular passenger elevator to take Howard's wheelchair to the top. Fortunately, there were few people in the lobby at 7:00 in the morning, and those who were had no idea that the old man with the long, grey hair and beard was the elusive and mysterious billionaire, Howard Hughes.

Kay Glenn and Dr. Thain awoke about the time that the entourage reached the penthouse, and came in to greet Howard. According to Gordon Margulis, who was in the suite at the time, Howard looked up from his wheelchair and said to them: "Something really screwed up tonight, didn't it?"

The reply was terse: "Well, that's what happens when you let Jack Real do anything. He always screws it up."

Nobody told Howard that we hit our ETA within two minutes while the welcoming group was still asleep.

When Gordon told me that story, his comment was, "They're out to get you, Jack."

I already knew that.

LIFE IN ACAPULCO

The arrival in Acapulco had a deja vu quality to it. As with our arrival in Freeport, Howard began discussing his intentions to fly again and to start buying hotels. It was almost as though he had forgotten that the Xanadu and the Lucayan Beach Hotel projects had ever existed.

Two days after we arrived at the Acapulco Princess, Howard called me in to tell me of his plans to buy hotels, not in the Bahamas or Mexico, but in Bermuda. He asked me to begin negotiations with Walter Summer, who was the president of the Princess Hotel chain and president of American Bulk Carriers, the Daniel K. Ludwig company that oversaw the Ludwig Hotels in Grand Bahamas, Bermuda, Acapulco, and elsewhere. In fact, Howard had decided that he wanted to buy the whole Princess chain. I opposed this idea because I thought it was a bad investment, but during our talks, Walter Summer would come down to the Acapulco Princess on two occasions, and we would develop a good relationship that would become important later on.

For his planned flying activities, Howard wanted me to arrange for a hangar in Acapulco, and to bring an airplane in from the United States. The poor man so desperately wanted to get back to what he loved. The hours that we had spent in the skies over the

English Midlands three years before had been the brightest moments in his years of self-imposed exile from the world.

Even though he no longer had the strength to walk across his bedroom, he was very anxious to have that feeling back—but he had been very anxious in Freeport 26 months before and it hadn't happened. I had gotten everything ready for us to fly at a moment's notice in Freeport, and I would do it again in Acapulco.

I went to the airport in Acapulco to make the arrangements to park our Aero Commander 680 aircraft at the Mexicana Airlines hangar. I told them that we would be bringing the aircraft to Acapulco in two or three weeks, but that I would pay them in advance. They showed me the section of the hangar where the Commander could be parked, and I drew a plot plan of this arrangement for Howard's approval. He devoured this little sketch with relish. He had to make changes. He wanted to be involved. He did not want it parked as shown. He wanted it near the door instead of in the rear of the hangar. I took a revised plan back to him once I had the airline's agreement, and it met with his approval. We had two of our three almost-new Aero Commander 680s at the airport in Van Nuys, California, so I phoned Jack Bauman, the fixed-base operator at Van Nuys, to alert him that we may want to bring one of the Aero Commanders to Acapulco soon.

In my heart, I knew he would never fly again, but I could hope. I had gone through the motions.

By now, the drugs that had ruled Howard's life for so long had taken it over almost completely. In all of the years of Howard's drug addiction, the only doctor who had the nerve and guts to try to get him off the codeine was Dr. Larry Chaffin—but he was never successful. He would forever blame Dr. Verne Mason, who had started Howard on the substance after the XF-11 crash in 1946. Dr. Chaffin always told me that if he were given a chance, and Howard had the desire, it would not have been difficult to clean him up, but Howard would tell him: "It's my only vice—so leave me alone."

Dr. Chaffin was a great man and wonderful surgeon, who had been there for Howard between 1932 and 1946, and who had been with Howard after he broke his hip in August 1973. He had been with us more or less continuously from then until February 1974, but then we had not seen him for a year. He was with us in Freeport most of the time from February through July 1975, and returned two days before Christmas. He would remain with the entourage from then until Howard died. By this time, Larry was 85 years old, and he should have been taking it easy, but he remained near Howard in Acapulco, like me, hoping to have an opportunity to be of help to his old friend.

At one point during 1975, Howard asked Dr. Chaffin to remove a broken hypodermic needle from his leg. Howard's hands trembled a great deal, and sometimes he had difficulty injecting himself. In this case, the needle had broken off under his skin and was causing him discomfort. Larry told Howard that he would not do it without an X-ray, so he called Good Samaritan Hospital in Los Angeles. It was arranged that a recently retired X-ray technician would come to the Bahamas with a lightweight, mobile X-ray machine. The technician stayed around for three weeks without being allowed to see Howard, and then went home, leaving the X-ray machine. Dr. Chaffin called him back again. Again, he stayed for three weeks, and then went home for good. The needle was never removed.

Larry reasoned that Howard knew he had many broken needles in his body, but he had decided that he really did not want anyone to know how many. Howard's autopsy report noted at least six broken needles. Larry later told me that they would have found more if they had really looked.

When Dr. Chaffin returned to Freeport in December 1975, after being away from Howard for five months, he told me that he was shocked by how much Howard's health had deteriorated while he was gone. He was pale, he had lost weight, and he had stopped eating regularly. He told me that he discovered that Howard was taking 35 grams of codeine every day. One of the disadvantages of taking codeine over a long period of time is that a person becomes seriously constipated, and they lose their appetite.

While Dr. Chaffin moved with us to Mexico in Roy Carver's

jet and would stay near Howard until the end, Howard's "official" doctors during that period, as far as the aides were concerned, would be Dr. Norman Crane and Dr. Homer Clark in alternating tours. Dr. Wilbur Thain also made an occasional appearance, but his visits seemed to me to be unrelated to the deteriorating medical condition of our employer.

Bill Gay always referred to his brother-in-law, Dr. Thain, as "Mr. Hughes' lead doctor," but he had always relied on Dr. Crane and Dr. Clark for Howard's medical needs. As far as I could see, Wilbur rarely took an interest in Howard's condition, other than to be sure that his patient was getting his "goodies." On numerous occasions, I had told Howard's aides that he needed more medical attention than he was receiving, and that without being treated in a hospital, Howard would die. The aides may have agreed, but they were powerless to act, since the decision seemed to rest solely with Howard's "lead doctor."

Dr. Crane also seemed to me to be generally disinterested in Howard's medical condition, but Dr. Chaffin and I often talked about getting Howard to a hospital. Dr. Chaffin tried nearly every day to schedule an examination, but every time he set up an appointment, it was cancelled. The aides would permit him to observe Howard, but only from behind a screen—a very bizarre way to carry on a doctor-patient relationship. Then again, Dr. Chaffin was not one of Howard's "official" doctors.

On March 1, Larry and I had taken public transportation to downtown Acapulco, and while we were in the city, Howard fell out of his bed while he was asleep. As he fell, his head struck the corner of the bed, shearing off a large growth, or lesion, on the left side of his forehead. This growth had been on Howard's head since at least 1971, and he and Dr. Chaffin had occasionally discussed having it surgically removed. Now that was no longer necessary.

This being the era before cell phones and pagers, there was no way to reach Larry and I downtown, so Dr. Homer Clark attended to Howard. To stop the bleeding, Homer put a very large bandage on top of Howard's head, but it did little to stop the bleeding. He was still bleeding profusely when Larry and I got back to the hotel at 2:55 pm, less than half an hour after the accident. Where the lesion had sheared off, there is a little artery that was spurting blood. Larry injected novocaine with a hypodermic syringe, putting pressure on the small artery. He applied a small bandage in the area and the bleeding stopped.

Dr. Chaffin remained with Howard until about 7:30 that evening, when Howard fell asleep. In the meantime, they had a long discussion, mainly of old times, and their relationship, which went back to 1932. Through the years, he had patched Howard up a number of times, through two automobile accidents, two serious airplane accidents, the London fall, and now this. By early March, the warm weather had grown hot and muggy, and Howard had become concerned about the air conditioning at the Acapulco Princess. As elegant and spacious as it was, the hotel had a poorly installed physical infrastructure. The broken freight elevator that we had encountered on our arrival was just the first clue. There was always at least one elevator in the building that was not functioning, the lights dimmed and flickered constantly, and the air conditioning would cut out occasionally for brief periods. Howard really loved his air conditioning, and he wanted it to never fail, so he asked me to do something. He decided that he would like to have a 100 percent redundancy on the electrical system in the penthouse, so that if any outlet, switch or electrical appliance failed, there would be a back-up one next to it that was on a completely separate circuit.

Because I'm an engineer, he asked me to design such a system, and we completely rewired his portion of the hotel so that nothing would ever happen without a back-up system.

REMEMBERING BETTER TIMES

Shortly after we had arrived at the Acapulco Princess, Howard had received a personal message from Miguel Aleman, who had been the president of Mexico from 1946 to 1952, and who was still an important person in Acapulco. He had known Howard in the 1940s, heard that he was in town and wanted to renew the old acquaintance.

Howard asked Dr. Thain and me to go to President Aleman's office to pay Howard's respects. Aleman had left early that day for Mexico City, but his closest personal friend, Lic. Rogerio de la Selva, who had also known Howard, received us.

We spent more than an hour in Mr. Aleman's office as his friend regaled us with his memories of Howard. Mr. de la Selva told us many stories, but I especially remember the one about the time in 1948, when Howard and his friend, the actor Cary Grant, had visited Acapulco. Howard and Cary had flown down in Howard's Douglas B-23, a twin-engine aircraft that Howard used as a private plane, and which I later sold for him.

At that time, Acapulco was just a small town with about 7,000 people and had only an unlighted airport that shut down at sunset. They approached the town at dusk and began searching for the airport. Howard circled for about 20 minutes, and finally, as his fuel was running out, he put the aircraft down in what he thought was a clearing. He and Grant then walked into town and found a hotel.

When the two men returned to the B-23 in the morning, they discovered that it was parked in a field of huge boulders. Howard had landed it on the *only* compass heading that would have accepted the aircraft without it crashing into one of the enormous rocks. It took Aleman and his men seven days to have oxen move the boulders and clear a runway so that the B-23 could take off. Howard's luck prevailed again.

In later years, I mentioned this tale to Cary Grant, who recalled the incident with a grin, adding some of his own memories of landing in that darkened field.

POWER PLAY

After Gay and company had completed their coup of moving Howard from the Bahamas to Mexico, it did not take them long to show their strength. I really felt as though the end was closing in on me. Two weeks after the meeting at Aleman's, Dr. Thain flew back into Acapulco from Los Angeles. While he was in California, he'd had a long meeting in Encino with his brother-in-law, Bill Gay. He had big news for me.

"There's no more Eastern Division, Jack," he smiled smugly. "I guess you're out of a job. Bill and I have decided to split the world. He'll have Las Vegas and all the United States, and I'll have the rest of the world. I'm going to be concentrating on the Far East and Latin America. I've already started planning a big beachfront condominium development down in Salinas, on the coast of Ecuador."

I was speechless. Less than six months before, Howard had placed me in charge of his entire operation, and now I was being fired by the brother-in-law of the man who Howard wanted desperately to fire. Meanwhile, poor Wilbur didn't realize that the way the money was being siphoned off, there would soon not be much of a world for him to run.

"You need to look for a new job, Jack," Dr. Thain taunted, the sides of his vast body rippling as he laughed, "but I've got a job for you. You're the smartest man here. I respect your thinking processes. You're going to be *my* man on the scene. I'm going to make you *my* assistant—right here in Acapulco."

How could I respond to his amazing offer? I just shook my head and walked away.

On March 4, a couple of days after Dr. Thain's amazing "job offer," I received a message from General Somoza down in Nicaragua. He told me that he had read in the newspaper that Howard had moved to Acapulco. He was seriously disappointed that Howard did not choose to move back to Managua. He reminded me that I had told him previously how much Howard loved Nicaragua, and that, if Howard ever moved out of the Bahamas, he would go back to Managua.

I discussed the matter with Howard, and he thought it was important for me to reply promptly to our old friend and host. However, through the haze of drugs, Howard anguished and procrastinated for more than a week composing an answer to Somoza's letter.

Finally, he turned the matter back to me. "I want you to write the letter and I'll sign it," he told me. "Then go see General Somoza and deliver it personally. Make it a fast trip. I don't want you gone more than a day, but I want you to patch things up with him."

I wrote a letter. It was a difficult letter to write. I tried four times, and the fourth time, I got what he wanted to say, which was really what I should have written in the first place. It was a "thanks, but no thanks" letter, one that made it appear as though we were seriously considering a move to Nicaragua, even though we had no intention of going back. I showed it to Howard, but he was too drowsy from his "medication" to concentrate on it. In fact, the poor man was so groggy that he referred to me in the third person, even though I was standing about four feet away.

"Tell Jack that I'm going to sleep now," he stammered. "My hands are too shaky right now, but I'll be up in nine hours, and I'll sign this thing then."

I waited 13 hours and he didn't wake up, so I left for Nicaragua on March 15, with the letter unsigned. Howard would be very disappointed that I went without him signing the letter, but I had set an appointment with the General, and I felt obligated to be there on time, especially since I had been told to "patch things up."

In the meantime, Dr. Thain had found out that I was going to Managua to see General Somoza, and he insisted on accompanying me. Nicaragua was now part of his "new world" that his brother-in-law had given him. Fortunately for him, he didn't say anything during our meeting with the General. I'm sure that if he had told Somoza that he was Bill Gay's brother-in-law, the General would probably have put him in jail. When I reported to Howard about the visit, he was angry that I took Thain with me. I did not tell him that I now "worked" for Dr. Thain.

When we returned to Acapulco from Managua on March 16, I was still haunted by the news that Gay had abolished the Eastern Division and had assumed total control. He was now in the catbird's seat. I had to make a move. My wife, Janeth, was home from the hospital, and I needed to get her some help because of her poor health. Now was the time to exit. I wasn't going to work for Wilbur Thain.

I decided to discuss the situation with Howard Eckersley, who was the aide on duty that week, and to vent my rage at Dr. Thain to him.

"I'm getting out," I told Eckersley. "I've been with Howard nearly every day for three years now—almost three and a half. My wife is in tough shape. I should spend some time with her. She's diabetic, and she's lost all her blood vessels. While I've been with Howard, she's been in a hospital. Now I've had my son take her home to Los Angeles, and I'm going home too.

"I must join Janeth. I've deprived myself of her love for too long. I should have returned to her when we left the Bahamas. I regret what I've done to our marriage for the last 31 years. I love this woman and I want her to feel that love, to make up for the time we missed while I attended Howard. Now it's Janeth's turn. I miss her and I need to be with her. I'm going!

"I don't want to work for Wilbur Thain. He's not going to run the world. Bill Gay can fool him that they're going to split up the world, but everyone else knows better. I'm going home to be with Janeth."

"How are you going the break this news to Mr. Hughes?" Eckersley asked coldly.

"I'm not going to. I don't want to. I want you to tell Howard. I want you to tell Howard for me that I love him, and that I wish him all the luck in the world, but I have to go home. Tell him that I have family problems. Don't tell him about Wilbur."

Eckersley did as I had asked, and at about 4:00 am the following morning, he phoned me back.

"I know you told me not to tell him about Wilbur, but I did," Eckersley began. "I told him Wilbur was your new boss. He just got violent. He said, 'I'll take care of that fat slob when I see him, but please don't let Jack leave me. I need him. I want him. Anything he wants, he can have.'"

I said, "Why didn't you call me up to come up to Howard's room, and let me hear that from him?"

"I didn't want him having a heart attack when you told him that you were leaving," Eckersley then told me. "I'm flying out today on my two-week leave. Promise me that you won't do anything until I get back."

Eckersley was usually decent and fair with me, and would support Howard when he could, so I agreed.

"Go back and tell him that I'll stay for three weeks," I said. "Let's see if we can't resolve the subject."

I realized then that I could never leave Howard. With a deep sadness, I now knew that returning to Los Angeles would have to wait.

Later that same day, Chester Davis phoned me to say that Bill Gay and Nadine Henley had just left his New York City office.

"Bill said that he had a nice telephone conversation with Howard saying that after all the years that they did not talk, he was asking Gay for his forgiveness for neglecting him," Chester explained. "Bill said that Howard had put him in charge again. There's no more Eastern Division, and Jack Real is finished."

I asked Chester what he thought of this.

"It's unadulterated bullshit," Chester said. "He is, and always has been, a damned liar. When I last saw you on that airplane flight to Nassau, I told you that this is what Gay would try to do to you. I checked with the aides individually to see if Howard had used the phone. Of course, I knew that he hadn't, and this fact was verified. Howard made only one phone call in the past two years, and that one was to me—and you were there when the call was made."

For the rest of my life, I will be haunted by something that Eckersley told me. He said that from the day that I told Howard that I was leaving, until the day he died, he ate no solid food and had very little fluids. I hope that I was not the cause of this, and that I did not hasten his death. Dr. Chaffin assured me that his health was in a fast decline by then anyway, but I will never know.

THE BEGINNING OF THE END

Bill Gay's blatant play for control of the Hughes empire would not have been possible if Howard had not been so heavily medicated most of the time. Even after he had broken his hip in London, he was still lucid for two or three days a week, but by the time we had reached Acapulco, his moments of clear thought were few and far between. He slept for days and was disoriented much of the time that he was awake. I believe that Gay would never have been able to make a play for control of Howard's holdings if Howard had not been in such pitiful shape.

He was a virtual prisoner of those whom he had trusted to protect him. Through the drug addiction that he himself had helped to initiate, the bad guys around him appeared to be mastering their own master.

His health was deteriorating. It was going downhill fast. He had stopped eating. He was just wasting away. I don't know whether he was suicidal, but he was very morose and deeply depressed during the brief periods that he was awake.

On March 15, as we were leaving for Managua, I told Dr. Thain that I had been with Howard that morning, and that he looked terrible.

"Wilbur, have you looked at your patient today?" I asked. "Doesn't he look desperate? Why don't you do something for him? Why don't you cut him off the drugs, give him some placebos? That will fool him. He doesn't need the drugs you give him."

"I can't do that," Dr. Thain told me pointedly. "It's against the law in a foreign country to give a man placebos without telling him."

"You mean to say you can't give a man placebos instead of the drugs?"

"That's right," he said. "It's an international law."

CHAPTER 11

HOWARD'S LAST 72 HOURS

TIME TO MOVE

By the end of March, Howard was in a state of rapid decline. I would look at him every day, and I could literally see him deteriorating before my eyes. He hadn't eaten for days, and he looked dreadful. His skin had lost its color, and his six-foot frame weighed less than 90 pounds.

Finally, on Friday, April 2, after discussing the situation with Dr. Larry Chaffin, I decided to act. I said to John Holmes, who was the aide on duty that morning, "You know, I think we'd better start planning to get him out of here to a good hospital."

I didn't ask him, I told him.

"Where would we take him?" Holmes asked.

I said, "Well, we can't really take him back to the United States, so what about Bermuda?"

"Oh, go ahead," he shrugged. "Do what you want to do."

I phoned Walter Summer of American Bulk Carriers, who was based in Bermuda.

"This is very, very hush-hush," I cautioned him, assuming that he could probably guess that I wasn't just making idle conversation when I asked: "What is the situation of the hospitals in Bermuda?"

"They're the finest in any of the British Colonies," he said. "My wife is on the board at the main one, and they had a $5 million capital budget last year. They have a good cardiac arrest department, a good kidney machine, and good X-ray equipment. It's as good as any you will find in the world."

"Now," I said, taking a deep breath. "Tell me whether you can get Howard a private room on the top floor."

He said that he would call me back, and I added, "While you're there, see if you can't put the crew, myself, and others in the Princess Hamilton."

He said he would call me in 30 minutes to confirm the hospital availability and the hotel as well. In less than half an hour, he called me back to say: "You're all set. I won't leave home Saturday and Sunday. I'll stand by and wait for your call."

I then called Marcie McKellup, who controlled Roy Carver's BAC-111 jet, the same aircraft that we had used to transport our group to Acapulco six weeks before. She said that she would make it available, but asked for six hours' notice so she could get a crew, fuel the aircraft, and provide food for the flight.

I told her to stand by, and I asked whether the BAC-111 had the "legs" (range) to make the trip to Bermuda without our having to stop off for fuel in Florida or the Bahamas. An hour later she called and assured me that there was no problem. This could be done even with very heavy head winds, and there were no head winds predicted. I told her that I would give her plenty of notice.

With everything ready, I explained the situation to John Holmes, and told him that we were taking Howard to a good hospital in Bermuda. He clearly had not expected me to have proceeded so swiftly with the plans to move Howard, and it disturbed him greatly that I had done things so quickly that he hadn't had a chance to alert Encino.

"Not so fast," he said. "We have to get Bill Gay's permission before we do *anything*, and I doubt whether Kay Glenn can locate him on a Friday afternoon. And even if Kay does find him, I doubt that he'd approve moving Mr. Hughes."

He proceeded to demand that I cancel the flight, or at least postpone it until Kay could find Gay.

"In the past three years," I told him, "you've heard Howard say repeatedly that I'm supposed to be the number one man in charge. This is a life or death situation, and I'm saying that we have to get Howard to a good hospital immediately."

"You may be the 'number one man,'" he said, crossing his arms across his chest proudly. "But it's Bill Gay who signs my paycheck. It's him who signs all the paychecks. That's all that counts."

I knew that without the staff's support, I could never get Howard out of the hotel, so on Saturday morning, I reluctantly phoned Walter Summer to cancel the Bermuda hospital and Marcie McKellup to turn down Roy Carver's generous offer to let us use his BAC-111.

John Holmes was in the room when I got Walter on the phone and told him that Howard had taken a turn for the better, and that we were not going to need the hospital in Bermuda after all. I then looked at Holmes and said: "Okay John, now it's on you."

"I think if he'll start eating today," he said nervously, "this whole thing will go away."

"I don't think so, John. I think we should still keep the Bermuda option open."

He just shook his head.

In retrospect, I don't know whether Howard would have lived if I had gotten him out of Mexico bound for Bermuda on Saturday morning, but I still believe that it would have been worth the try.

By Saturday morning, Howard looked considerably worse, so Dr. Larry Chaffin phoned his secretary in Los Angeles to ask her to send some intravenous fluid to Acapulco as quickly as she could arrange for a Summa employee to fly down with it. This was done and Larry was able to attach the intravenous feeding tubes by Saturday evening. In the meantime, we also had Howard on oxygen, using a tank that we had carried with us.

The only support that I had in my efforts to save Howard came from Dr. Chaffin. He would not leave Howard's side again until his death. Dr. Norman Crane was also present during these final days, but he was of little help. Even the aides ignored poor Dr. Crane.

On Sunday morning, Holmes told me that he had finally located Kay Glenn, who was going to try to find Bill Gay. Later in the day, the two spoke again. Gay had still not been found, but this time it was Kay Glenn's turn to bring up the subject of hospitalization. He brushed off the Bermuda scenario, and insisted that the only two choices were Salt Lake City and Houston—both in the United States.

Glenn was also adamant that Howard should not be told that he was going to go to a hospital. He added that hospitalization was the last resort, and to be considered only if Howard "turned for the worse." Dr. Chaffin and I thought that he had already "turned," but we were outvoted by Holmes and Glenn.

I realized that Salt Lake City was mentioned because it was Dr. Wilbur Thain's home turf, but I didn't understand why Houston was suggested. I knew that Howard did not like the city, and I was never aware that he had ever given anyone instructions that he should be taken there if he ever got seriously ill.

CONSULTING HIS LEAD DOCTOR

It was Sunday night when Bill Gay finally phoned the Acapulco Princess. Dr. Chaffin, Dr. Crane, Holmes and I were having dinner together when the call came in. Holmes explained the situation, and Gay told him that medical decisions should be in the hands of his brother-in-law, Dr. Thain, "Mr. Hughes' lead doctor."

Howard's "lead doctor" was not at his side and Holmes did not know how to go about finding Dr. Thain that evening. I suggested that maybe he should just try phoning his home in Logan, Utah. I picked up the telephone myself, and within moments, I had reached Dr. Thain's wife, Ruthie, who said Wilbur was headed for Miami for a meeting regarding a charity in which he had an interest. She said that he was due to fly down to Ecuador on Monday morning to look over the large beach condominium development that he was planning at Salinas.

I reached Dr. Thain himself just as he was checking into his hotel in Miami. I said, "Wilbur, your patient is in dire need of medical attention. He's in frightful shape. You have to do something. You have to come here now. Forget about the Ecuador trip. There's a Braniff flight out of Miami at 7:00 tomorrow morning that will get you into Acapulco at noon with one stopover."

"Quit playing doctor." Dr. Thain said disdainfully. "He's all right."

"No, he *isn't*," I replied desperately. "I've looked at him every day. You haven't laid eyes on him in two weeks. He is *not* all right!"

"I have to go down to build the condominiums in Ecuador," he argued.

He paused and finally asked to speak to "a real doctor." I put Dr. Crane on the phone to tell him of Howard's condition. When I got back on the phone, he had changed his mind, but he wanted me to get him an executive jet so that he didn't have to fly commercial. I told him to stand by while I located an aircraft in the Miami area that could get him to Acapulco quickly. In 10 minutes, I got him back on the phone and said, "Okay, Wilbur, you could be here at 7:00 o'clock in the morning. If you need a ride, I'll get the Summa secretary in Miami to pick you up."

I had called Bob Graf, the fixed-base operator in Ft. Lauderdale, and told him of our requirements. I knew that he had some LearJets and we could probably get Wilbur down there quicker on one of them than by his taking a commercial flight. Graf was the same man who had helped me get Howard out of Managua in December 1972 after the Nicaragua earthquake. I then called our secretary, Dorothy Culpepper, at the Summa office in Miami, and had her contact Ken Wright, the administrator for the Howard Hughes Medical Institute, and have him get her some glucose for intravenous feeding.

CALLING FOR HELP

Back in Acapulco, Howard's body was starting to implode. At one point on Sunday evening, his vision became blurred and I heard him say to George Francom, who was standing a few feet away, "I can't see you."

Dr. Larry Chaffin later explained to me that this was a sure sign of his kidneys beginning to fail.

According to Gordon Margulis, who was in his bedroom at the time, Howard woke up before midnight and started to inject himself with codeine. There were four men with Howard in the room—Gordon, George Francom, Dr. Crane, and Dr. Chaffin. It struck me as odd that Gordon was there, since he rarely, if ever, entered Howard's room. I wrote it off as his desire to see Howard one more time before he died.

I was just outside the bedroom, where I could hear Howard crying, whimpering, and begging.

"Please help me," he gasped weakly. "Help me, help me."

He was terribly feeble at that point, and I surmised hat he probably didn't have the strength to complete the task of injecting himself. I still recall how morbid the situation had become: Only one hour before he fell into the coma that would lead to his death, Howard was still seeking elusive happiness—an escape from the terrible pain that had been so much a part of his life.

I heard Howard cry out again, louder this time. His pleas were becoming more urgent. He had apparently stuck the syringe in his arm, but was too weak to push the plunger to complete the injection. The motion probably exhausted him, but he continued to try to depress the plunger with no success. The syringe just hung from his arm for a moment, and then it dropped on his bed.

I don't know what happened next. I just turned my head. His pathetic sounds were growing softer as, apparently, someone completed the job for him. I don't know who, if anyone, helped him, but I'm sure that it would not have been Larry Chaffin, as he would never have pushed the plunger, and I recalled that the aides had always refused to inject him.

Not long after midnight, Dr. Chaffin told me that Howard had slipped into a coma. By then, everyone else had gone to bed, so it was just the three of us. Larry said that he feared Howard could die before we could get him to the United States, and that it would be wise to have a responsible local Mexican doctor attending, or to get him into a local hospital. Larry had a long time friend in Acapulco, a retired California doctor, whom he called for a recommendation of a local doctor. We were referred to a Dr. Victor Montemayor, who agreed to make the house call right away.

After the doctor arrived, the oxygen tank ran empty, and I asked him where I might go in the middle of the night to get another one. Dr. Montemayor gave me the names and addresses of hospitals, and I left the Acapulco Princess at 3:30 am. I took a cab to the first hospital, which couldn't help me, and then to the next. I finally found a full oxygen bottle at the third hospital.

I got back to the Acapulco Princess at about 6:30 am, and we put the oxygen mask back on Howard. I could see that he had truly taken a turn for the worse. Dr. Montemayor and Dr. Larry Chaffin told me that they had agreed that there was no place that we could take him in Mexico, and Dr. Montemayor had strongly urged Larry to move him out to the United States at once.

After stopping for fuel at Key West, Dr. Thain arrived in Acapulco aboard Bob Graf's LearJet, and he reached the hotel about 7:00 am. At 7:30, I stopped by Howard's suite on my way to the airport to try to find an airplane to take Howard to Houston. Dr. Larry Chaffin was in Howard's bedroom with his patient, and Dr. Thain was in the outer office, where he seemed to be feeding documents through the paper shredder.

At the airport I discovered that, other than the LearJet that had just brought Dr. Thain in from Miami, there were two executive jets on the field, a JetStar and a Gulfstream II. Because the LearJet was quite small, and I knew that it would be uncomfortable to try to squeeze Howard into it for the flight to Houston, so I decided to try to find the owner of either the JetStar or the Gulfstream II. I made a few calls and managed to track down the hotels where they were staying, but both of them were out, so I settled on the LearJet. I identified myself and told the LearJet crew that we would need a jet to fly Howard Hughes to Houston that morning. They agreed, and I swore them to secrecy.

When I returned to the hotel at 9:00 am, Dr. Larry Chaffin was still in with Howard, but Dr. Thain—along with Chuck Waldron and Eric Bundy—appeared to be working at the paper shredder. I saw piles of papers everywhere, both typed documents and handwritten memos on paper from yellow legal pads. I didn't examine any of the pages being shredded, but I strongly believe that they included the detailed logs of Howard's "medication," that I had observed the aides keeping through the years that I was close to Howard.

As I watched Dr. Thain, Bundy and Waldron, an interesting thought struck me. Six months earlier, in late October 1975, I had received a call from Ken Wright, the administrator of the Howard Hughes Medical Institute, who was based at the Institute's headquarters in the Jackson Memorial Hospital in Miami. I recall having a sense that something sinister was going on. Bill Gay, Wright recounted, had been lobbying heavily to have his brother-in-law, Dr. Thain, named to the Institute board of directors. The board, which oversaw Institute activities, normally had three members—Bill Gay, Chester Davis and Raymond Holliday. However, Holliday's slot had been vacant since November 11, 1972, when Holliday resigned after the Hughes Tool Company went public. Apparently, the board could not act effectively with only two members. What I think this really meant was that Gay and Davis couldn't get along, and Gay needed a second vote to put Davis in his place. I believe that Gay thought he needed an ally on the board, and who better than a doctor who was his own brother-in-law?

Wright asked me whether I was aware of Gay's efforts to have Dr. Thain installed on the Howard Hughes Medical Institute board. I hadn't given it much thought and told him so. I also told him that it was a bad idea.

It occurred to me that morning that Gay's plan to bring Dr. Thain into the Howard Hughes Medical Institute might have explained the activity with the paper shredder. If the documents that I saw, but did not examine, were, in fact, records that linked him to Howard's daily activities and "medication," they would have prevented Dr. Thain from assuming the Howard Hughes Medical Institute post—if they had been made public. In the end, Dr. Thain would never get the appointment anyway.

A few minutes later, Wilbur wandered into my room looking for a cup of coffee. With a wheeze, he lowered his vast body into the only chair in the room and put his feet up on the table.

"You got any of that good Jack Real coffee?"

"No," I said. "How come you're not attending your patient?"

"Well," Dr. Thain told me, "He's going to die sometime today, so why should I worry about him?"

I thought this was a pretty callous attitude for a doctor attending a patient. In fact, it really frightened me.

FRIENDS FOR BREAKFAST

I returned to the airport at 11:00 am, where I discovered that our LearJet was being watched by three Mexican federal police officers, who I knew would delay our flight if they ascertained that we were trying to fly a critically ill man out of the country— especially if they found out who he was!

I had the aircraft moved to a corner of the field where it would be easier to load Howard and phoned the suite at the Acapulco Princess. I explained the situation and told them that it was urgent for them to get Howard to the airport immediately. John Holmes said that an ambulance had been called, and that they'd be moving Howard "any minute now." I could hear the grinding sound of the paper shredder in the background.

As I hung up the phone, the federales were still watching the LearJet and this was making me nervous. Finally, I decided that I had better do something other than standing around being nervous. I approached them and offered to buy them breakfast.

"Ustedes por favor comer conmiga en mi casa?" I asked in my broken, probably laughable, Spanish.

They were happy with my offer, however, and we all went to the little cantina at the edge of the tarmac. I positioned myself so that I could watch the LearJet through the window, and I situated them with their backs to the field. We ordered a hearty breakfast, and while we were waiting to be served, I excused myself to go to the bathroom and slipped over to the pay phone to call the Acapulco

Princess again. John Holmes reported that the ambulance was coming, and that they'd be moving Howard "any minute now."

As my three friends were enjoying their huevos rancheros, I watched nervously for any sign of the ambulance. I had just ordered them a second round of beer when I finally saw the ambulance pull up next to the LearJet, and a stretcher being unloaded. I watched Dr. Thain, Dr. Chaffin, and John Holmes getting into the LearJet, and I remember seeing the oxygen bottle that I had struggled to find being jostled aboard the aircraft.

The LearJet took off at 11:45 am. I said goodbye to the three federales, paid the bill and left.

Back at the hotel, everyone was packing to leave. George Francom, Gordon Margulis, Chuck Waldron, Dr. Norman Crane, and I all made reservations for the 4:00 pm flight to Los Angeles. Just as we were leaving the hotel, however, Kay Glenn called Waldron, and said that there was more shredding to be done. I don't know how much shredding they had done, or how much Glenn thought was still left to do, but Waldron went back.

GOING HOME

Before the LearJet had lifted off from Acapulco, the Howard Hughes Medical Institute had contacted Dr. Henry McIntosh, chairman of the Department of Internal Medicine at Methodist Hospital in Houston, to say that a seriously ill Howard Hughes was en route to his hospital. I imagine that this hospital was selected because of its affiliation with Baylor College of Medicine, which was a recipient of major research grants from the Howard Hughes Medical Institute.

The LearJet touched down in Houston at 1:50 pm Central Time on April 5, 1976. Dr. Thain, Dr. Chaffin, and John Holmes were aboard the aircraft, which was met by a team of doctors from Methodist Hospital.

Howard was already dead.

After a one hour drive from the airport, Howard's body was taken to the morgue at Methodist Hospital, where it was turned over to the coroner, who, in turn, called in the hospital's head pathologist. The autopsy was conducted the following morning. Dr. Chaffin monitored the entire autopsy, as did an IRS agent, because the tax collectors wanted to confirm that Howard was really dead.

The cause of death was listed officially as "chronic renal disease," which means that his kidneys had deteriorated over time to a point where they stopped functioning. Doctor Chaffin told me later that the autopsy revealed that his kidneys were smaller than large walnuts. He also said that Howard's kidney failure was brought on by the continual use of the Empirin compound containing codeine and phenasatine. The codeine secretes through the bowel and the phenasatine secretes through the kidney. This information was passed to Chaffin by the internists at Methodist Hospital that were brought in to supervise the autopsy at the request of the Houston coroner's office.

Howard's funeral took place on Wednesday, April 7, at Glenwood Cemetery, where he was buried in the family plot next to his parents. The services were attended by a small number of family members, including 85-year-old Annette Gano Lummis, his mother's younger sister, Howard's closest living relative, and her son, William R. "Will" Lummis, Howard's first cousin and the man who would become the administrator of his estate. Ironically, most of these relatives had not seen Howard in more than 40 years.

THOUGHTS ON HOWARD'S DEATH

There are many things in life you can never control. Other people's actions. The weather. Fate.

Yet there are things that happen that make you wonder. Would the outcome have changed if you had only done things differently? Howard's death was one of those events that has plagued me for more than 25 years. Was I the cause? Could I have been his salvation? Could I have done things differently?

As Howard continued to weaken in early 1976, it seemed to me that the men in his inner circle became less interested in the man, and increasingly anxious to take greater control of the empire. I was suspicious that Bill Gay, through Wilbur Thain, was devising a plan to get control of the multibillion dollar Howard Hughes Medical Institute. Such a blatant attempt to expand their influence disgusted me. I sincerely believed that it would be the end of the line for me if they had succeeded in pulling off their scheme. I really would have felt as though I had lost the battle *and* the war.

When I had told Howard that I'd never work for Wilbur Thain, I knew that the possibility of my leaving had upset Howard. Although I know deep down that his condition had progressed to a point where he was virtually in death's grasp, I cannot stop the persistent feeling that I expedited the onset of the inevitable.

Would he have eaten? Would that have bought him more time? I'll never know. But the emotional scars remain inside me today, and I often relive the last two weeks of Howard's life, wondering if something could have been done to save him.

CHAPTER 12

EPILOGUE

THE ELUSIVE WILL OF HOWARD HUGHES

In the weeks and months that followed Howard's death, the news media was consumed with speculation about the "Howard Hughes Will," the magic document that would tell who would inherit the billion-dollar estate of the world's richest man.

He was known to have written three wills. The one from 1925 was signed, but he destroyed it after his 1929 divorce from Ella Rice. The one written in 1929 was probably not signed, but we'll never know, because it was lost. The third one, which Nadine Henley originally typed in the 1940s, and which Howard continuously revised until 1950, was never signed. When he died, it was assumed by most people that a secret Howard Hughes will existed and that it had to be found. It became a Holy Grail.

In the weeks and months that had led up to Howard's death, the "Howard Hughes Will" had been a key subject of concern among those within his empire who were jockeying for power and wealth. All of the aides had been instructed, apparently by Nadine Henley, to get him to sign the old will, or to prepare a new one. Many people assumed that he had already done this, and that the Will was in a secret place. Obviously, there was a great deal of speculation about where that secret place was.

Howard last discussed his will with me in 1975. It was about four months before his death, and I think even Howard knew his time on Earth was short.

I had just completed one of my regular meetings with him in his darkened hotel suite at the Xanadu Hotel in the Bahamas. We had always talked about his favorite topics, and this time was no different. We covered everything from his desire to resume flying to buying more hotels, planes, and the like. He was alert, feisty and confident. He was, after all, Howard Hughes. This was, after all, Howard Hughes. On that day, we had discussed the renovation of the Lucayan Beach Hotel and how we would purchase it, as well as the Oceanus Bay Hotel, and the expansion into the beach property adjacent to the Lucayan Beach Hotel.

As I was getting up to leave, he ended the discussion by commenting on what a good conversation we'd just had. After a pause, he asked in an almost mocking tone, "Is there anything *else* you want to discuss?"

"No," I said, realizing that he had something in mind that he wanted to be asked about.

"Nothing you want to ask me?"

"No."

"Don't you want to ask me about my will?"

"No," I said, this time a bit more bluntly. "It's none of my business. It's between you and your lawyers. I don't want to know. I don't want to get involved."

"But everyone else is asking me," he said, obviously disappointed. "Everyone wants to know where it is."

"I don't want to know," I said again, realizing that, as his friend and confidant, he probably would have told me if I had just asked. I also realized that if I didn't know where it was, probably no one would ever find it. I felt that this would mean that Howard's heirs, and not the men who had been squandering his fortune for so many years as they manipulated him, would get a chance to fight over his estate.

Howard had always been his own man, but the drugs and his increasing fear of being seen in public, had made him more susceptible to being controlled, and I did not want those who strived to control him to have any idea where the Will was, or to know that I knew. Not having the burden of that knowledge was a victory for me. It was a small victory, but a sweet one nonetheless.

I don't think that I was in this Will, although in 1958, Howard told me that I was. He said that he was going to give me an old Sikorsky S-43 flying boat that he had in Houston, but I didn't think he was serious. In any case, I wouldn't have known what to do with it, and I doubt that he would have revised his Will to put this in it.

About two months after he gave the S-43 to me, he gave it to me again. I told him, "I don't think you even have a will. You told me two months ago you were giving it to me. You're not going to change that will just to put me in for that."

"No," he said. "I'll write a codicil. Do you know what a codicil is?"

"No."

"I'll just call up Raymond Cook [one of his attorneys] and have him make just a simple paragraph and add it to the Will and you may get the boat. You may not have to wait until I die. I may decide I'll give it to you in a year."

I am absolutely certain that Howard wrote and signed a will, and I am equally certain that it will never be found. The haggling over the Howard Hughes fortune would go on for years. Many forged wills showed up, some of them really amateurish and even comical, but some of them very clever and well-crafted fakes. Dozens of these were actually probated, but the one true will remains hidden—probably forever. I never let him tell me where it is, and I don't think he offered to tell anyone else.

CHASING THE WILL

About 10 days after Howard passed away, I received a phone call from Chester Davis, inviting me to meet with him at his suite in the Century Plaza Hotel in Los Angeles.

"Hi, *buddy*," he announced happily. "We're partners now."

"How do you figure that?"

"Well," he said, "I'm going to take over the company. I'll

become the administrator of the estate and you're going to be my man."

I was incredulous about being considered a "buddy" of Chester Davis. While we were in Freeport, Chester had agreed to work closely with me on a day-to-day basis after Howard had made my position clear to him, but it was a short-lived alliance. I felt that Chester had let me down. He was Howard's lawyer and he had an obligation to dutifully fulfill Howard's wishes. He talked a good game, but he was undeniably afraid of Bill Gay and the power he wielded. Soon after Howard had died, Bill Gay had manipulated the Summa board into naming him the president of the Summa Corporation.

Chester could have drawn up legal papers making the move official and paved the way for me to take control, but he faltered, dragging his heels as he looked for another option. Of course, I could see Chester's dilemma. He was being paid a king's ransom to handle Howard's legal affairs—often billing Howard more than $1 million a year for his services, and since Gay paid the bills, Chester's creative billing was never questioned. Why would Chester want to restructure the organization, especially knowing how carefully he'd be watched in the future?

Chester had never put anything about my promotion in writing. I pressed him, but he simply talked about how we would manage Howard's enterprises. That made it easy for Chester to be overly cautious and to move slowly. Six months passed very rapidly, and the chance to make the move official evaporated with Howard's death. I look back at those final days and wish I had told Howard about Chester's inaction.

If Chester had been merely inactive, however, Bill Gay had been openly, or I should say, covertly, antagonistic. In all of the work that I did during our years in Freeport to make a success of the Eastern Division, I never received anything but determined opposition from Bill Gay and his cronies in Encino. Although the reason for the move to Acapulco was never articulated, it seemed obvious to me that it was all part of Bill Gay's efforts to destroy the Eastern Division and to neutralize me as an obstacle on his road to the complete control of Howard's assets.

Rumors and facts about Howard Hughes were constantly interwoven by the news media. After Howard's death, when a tiny morsel of the truth surfaced, the media was quick to spread the news. Of course, sometimes the news was about me.

On August 21, 1977, *The Arizona Republic* would write that Howard's aides had reportedly thwarted Howard Hughes' attempt to put me in charge of his aviation companies. It was the closest I had come to getting the word out about my situation. Unfortunately, it had come more than a year after Howard's death, and its only relevance now is to confirm what I believe to be the truth about Gay and his associates. The article reportedly grew out of the "continuing battle over the control and taxation of the vast estate of Howard Hughes." Readers were told of a "palace revolt" by his inner circle of employees that "frustrated his efforts to reorganize the management of his affairs." The article suggested that before his death, "Hughes was planning to curb the power of Bill Gay, then executive vice president of the Summa Corporation, the Hughes holding company." The story, which was based on "sworn testimony and statements of persons familiar with Summa, cited testimony by Hughes aide George Francom. Francom was asked why the Hughes entourage moved from Freeport to Acapulco."

The article reported: "Some sources have said that Hughes told Real that he was concerned about the direction of his companies and wanted Real to become 'the man outside my door'—someone who would handle all business matters and advise him. Sources familiar with Summa affairs said that when Real tried to put Hughes' new plan into effect, the aides threatened to quit, and Summa directors refused to recognize Real's authority. Hughes then abandoned the Eastern Division plan. Gay, supported by Nadine Henley, senior vice president, has been the dominant figure in Summa's affairs for several years. The aides who lived with Hughes reported to Gay's subordinates and were hired by him or with his approval."

It was true, and I reminded my "buddy," Chester Davis, of this fact when he discussed my becoming his "man."

"What are you going to do with Bill Gay?" I asked. "He thinks that he owns the company now."

"I have a plan," Chester chuckled. "When I tell you what it is, you're going to be surprised at how easily I take care of him. We're going to sew up everything in Las Vegas. I hate those bastards anyway. We'll move the entire estate—the Nevada operation, Hughes AirWest Airline, the helicopter company, the entire Hughes Aircraft Company, to the Bahamas. We'll dispose of everything we've got. You're going to go back to the Bahamas, and set up the new operation. You've got a way with the 'natives' down there. All the operations and the estate will be run from the Bahamas. I want you to commit right now that you're my man. We'll have the cash and we're going to build an empire."

It didn't sound like he was asking my approval. He was giving me a job description.

"Chester," I said. "You have to find the Will."

"We'll find the Will," Chester said confidently, as if finding the Will would be as easy as scheduling an appointment with his dentist. "It'll take two, maybe three, more weeks to find the Will. But I have a plan. I want you to find out who the three closest friends to Howard Hughes are."

I told him that these would probably be Robert Gross, the former chairman of the board of Lockheed; Del Webb; and Sherman Fairchild, the founder of Fairchild Aviation and the inventor of the Duramold process that Howard had used in fabricating the Hughes Flying Boat. I explained that those men had been his three closest friends, but that all three were deceased.

"In that case," he said. "I want you to go to the executors of their estates, and find out whether there's a letter that Howard gave them to put away or hide under a rug somewhere or something. If you get that letter, it'll tell you where the Will is hidden, not put away, but hidden."

"I'm not going to the Bahamas," I told him, "but I'll give you a hand."

I knew that without Chester's help, Gay would surely try to fire me, so I figured that it wouldn't hurt to help Chester. The belongings of Bob Gross were stored at Lockheed's Rye Canyon Research Center, a facility that had reported to me from 1962 to

1964. I had no problem gaining access to and searching these premises, but there was no white envelope. I visited Mrs. Del Webb. She was most obliging, and I spent two days searching through Del's papers. I found no letter and no will, but as I was leaving the Webb home after my second visit, I was met by a group from Gay's office coming in. He'd obviously had the same brainstorm that Chester had.

I contacted the executor of the Sherman Fairchild estate, and when I told him what I was searching for, he inferred that I must be crazy. After several subsequent conversations, he convinced me that a search would yield no white envelope that would lead me to Howard's Will.

I had asked Chester what would happen to his plan to move the entire operation to the Bahamas if the Will could not be found. He responded by saying it would be more difficult, but not impossible. The events that followed showed that it was *both* difficult and impossible.

About a week after my meeting with Chester, Howard's cousin, Will Lummis, came to town and checked into the same suite at the Century Plaza Hotel that Chester had used in his meeting with me. Travelling with him was Mickey West, Howard's tax man, who was, like Will Lummis and the late Raymond Cook, an attorney from Howard's Houston law firm.

Lummis introduced himself and said that he was the court-appointed administrator of the Howard Hughes estate. He said that he was searching for Howard's Will on behalf of his mother, Annette Gano Lummis—who was Howard's closest living relative. His plan was to ask all of the men who had lived with Howard to search their memory for any clues as to where a will could be found.

He called a meeting at his suite which was attended by the six aides, Howard Eckersley, George Francom, John Holmes, Levar Myler, Jim Rickard and Chuck Waldron, as well as myself and the four doctors, Dr. Thain, Dr. Crane, Dr. Clark, Dr. Chaffin. Gordon Margulis, Mell Stewart, Eric Bundy, and Alan Stroud, the office managers, did not attend. They may have not been invited.

I had never before met Will Lummis, but my enduring

impression of him was formed early that day. He impressed me then and continued to impress me for the next 15 years. Here was a man looking desperately for a will that, if found, would probably leave nothing to him or to his family.

What impressed me was that he was just a straightforward man who wanted to dispose of the matter. He didn't want the money. He just wanted to find the Will and get it over with.

By the fall of 1976, as Will Lummis was moving quickly to assert himself in the role of the estate administrator, Chester's attitude toward me became very hostile and we seldom saw one another anymore. From his attitude, I assumed he had brought Gay into his scheme.

Eventually, I joined forces with Will Lummis, while Chester teamed with Gay. They never found the Will, so they started calling it "The Lost Will." Chester Davis died in 1983 while the case was going on, and Bill Gay continued in his efforts to become the sole trustee of the Howard Hughes Medical Institute, which is, today, an endowment worth $13 billion, one of the largest endowments in the United States.

In court, Gay explained that he and Howard were inseparable, and that they were two close friends, sharing their lives and close personal feelings. He didn't mention that he had seen or spoken with Howard no more than once or twice in the last 16 years of Howard's life. Ultimately, the Delaware Supreme Court ruled against him in January 1984. The Institute wound up with nine trustees. Bill Gay was one, but not the *only* one.

CARRYING ON

I paid little attention to the proceedings involving the attempts to probate the so-called "Lost Will" of Howard Hughes. I'd had my chance to be told where it was, and I had passed on it. It really didn't concern me. If I was in it, my "prize" was an S-43 that I didn't need or want.

While I continued to be employed by the Summa Corporation, I never had any sort of employment relationship or any other relationship with the Howard Hughes Medical Institute. My official job title at Summa was senior vice president, and my primary responsibilities were those that I'd had with the company before I went to London in 1973 to be with Howard. These included the aviation activities, with the exception of Hughes AirWest, which was sold in 1980. Mainly, I was to be concerned with running the Hughes Helicopter Company, but in the months immediately after Howard's death, I spent a great deal of time disposing of all the aircraft that he had purchased through the years, and which were stored at various locations around the world. I also looked after the Xanadu Hotel in the Bahamas, and the various airport activities that the company had.

I never read, received or signed the employment contract that I was supposed to have been given in September 1975. However, I would see it again at a distance in April 1976. The day after I got back to Los Angeles following Howard's death, I met Nadine Henley in the hallway at the corporate office in Encino. I hadn't seen her since that day in Miami when I had walked away with Gay holding my contract.

"My dear, I've got your contract," she purred. "It's here waiting for you. You never came and got it. Come and get it."

"Nadine, I don't want it. You keep it for awhile."

She looked at me as though I was kind of a strange person.

Six months later, she approached me again. Levar Myler was with her this time.

"My dear," she said. "I've got something I need you to sign."

"Is it that contract?"

"No, we decided not to give you a contract. Bill Gay doesn't want you to have one, but we're going to give you a real sweetheart gift. You're going to get $25,000, providing you leave right now, never write a thing, and never mention Howard Hughes again. He's gone from your memory. Sign your name right here. You leave Summa this week and you get the $25,000."

I looked at her. I took the pen in hand a few times, and finally I said, "Nadine, you must think I'm the dummy of all dummies."

"Levar, let's get out of here," she sniffed. "This guy is not rational."

Shortly thereafter, Will Lummis fired all the aides. Then he terminated Chester Davis, Bill Gay and, finally, Nadine.

HUGHES AIRWEST

When Howard passed away, Hughes AirWest was owned 100 percent by the Hughes estate, 22 percent held directly, and 78 percent indirectly through Summa. Having earned, after tax, $3.64 million in 1976 and $9.4 million in 1977, the airline's encouraging trend and rising results from operations ended abruptly in 1978, the year of airline industry deregulation. Many of us remember those days only too well.

Although it began 1978 with good earnings, leftover momentum from 1977, deregulation placed Hughes AirWest's management in the unfamiliar environment of cutthroat competition. They were totally unprepared for "peanut fares," skyrocketing fuel costs, interest outlays, and highly inflationary labor costs. After-tax earnings for the whole of 1978 nosedived to $5.3 million, wiping out the good earnings experienced early in the year. These events led to the decision in early 1979 to try to sell the airline. However, since other airlines were experiencing similar dismal results at the time, there was no market for Hughes AirWest. Late that year, the airline suffered a 60-day strike, 60 days with all the fixed costs and expenses and no income, so the year-end picture was painted in the red ink of a $26 million loss. In the meantime, the Hughes estate was committed, under the terms of its bank credit lines, to keeping the airline afloat.

Meanwhile, however, changes had been occurring in the newly deregulated industry. As smaller airlines failed, the larger, stronger airlines absorbed them, assuming that "market share" would be the key to future profitability, to say nothing of ultimate survival. In early 1980, Republic Airlines, a regional carrier that had recently extended its system by its acquisition of Southern Airways, decided that Hughes AirWest would be a good "fit." Fearing that rival

Northwest Airlines also had its sights on Hughes AirWest, Republic moved quickly. Despite the fact that Hughes AirWest lost $15 million during the first nine months of 1980, Republic paid the Hughes Estate and Summa $24 million in cash, plus $14.5 million in 13 percent, convertible, subordinated debentures. As a bonus, this released the estate from its obligation to put an additional $50 million into the operating capital of the airline, an obligation in effect assumed by Republic.

The total value initially realized by the estate and Summa was $88.5 million. Ultimately, from the $14.5 million, 13 percent debentures, the Hughes estate and Summa realized a total of $25.62 million (sales proceeds in connection with the later sale of Republic made to Northwest Airlines, plus principal payments and interest payments made in the meantime). Total realizations over time would total $99.62 million. Not bad for an airline that was broke.

HUGHES HELICOPTERS

When Will Lummis took over the job of running the Hughes estate and the Summa Corporation, he ran into nothing but trouble. All of the companies were teetering on the brink of disaster, but he went in and straightened out each one individually. Bill Rankin was assigned as the chief financial officer, and former Nevada Gaming Control Board chairman Philip Hannifin was brought in to run the hotel and casino operations. To sort out the Hughes aviation interests, Will Lummis turned to me.

When *Forbes* Magazine published an article that discussed how well Will Lummis was running the Howard Hughes estate, it was mentioned that my control of the Summa aviation interests included the Hughes Helicopters division. This was the Culver City-based entity that had built the OH-6, and which had been the Aircraft Division of the Hughes Tool Company until 1972 when the parent company went public. This reference greatly disturbed Thomas Stuelpnagel, who was then the president of Hughes Helicopters.

Stuelpnagel decided to go up to Summa headquarters in Las

Vegas to express his displeasure to Will Lummis personally. Stuelpnagel said that Jack Real's involvement brought disfavor on the company because of my association with the Lockheed Cheyenne program in the 1960s. Stuelpnagel complained that the article would be interpreted by his fellow members of the prestigious aviation fraternity, Conquistadors del Cielo, as a criticism of him.

Lummis suggested that I resign from having Stuelpnagel report to me. When I had accepted this elimination of my management assignment with the helicopter company, Will assured me that there would be enough to keep me busy without my being directly involved in this financially troubled division. Soon after, Bill Rankin told me that Will Lummis had full confidence in me and that he did not think that Stuelpnagel would be in his job for long.

By the late summer of 1979, the Summa Corporation board of directors was making plans to sell or close Hughes Helicopters, or put it into bankruptcy under Chapter 11. However, Will suggested that they give it one more shot, and to try letting Jack Real turn it around. Earlier in the year, Will had asked me to write him a memo detailing the problems at the helicopter company and telling him whether the difficulties plaguing the division could be rectified. I submitted my findings within a month. It was obvious that the company was in trouble. They hadn't made a net operating profit for years. They made some gross profit, but they had bank loans, so they never made any real money.

On Thursday, September 27, 1979, Will called me into his office to tell me that the board had decided to send me in to save Hughes Helicopters. I respectfully declined their generous offer, and I gave him the names of three potential replacements.

"That company hasn't made any money in 17 years." I told Will Lummis. "Anybody who could turn that company around would be a miracle worker. I'm not a miracle worker. I'm 65 years old. I'm ready to retire, not ready to start a new career."

"You're going to take it," he said. "I expect you to turn it around."

I took over immediately. I was back in the helicopter business, which is where I had been with Lockheed when I had left to join Howard in 1971. Ironically, the primary helicopter project at Hughes Helicopters at the time was the AH-64 Apache, which was being developed for much of the same US Army requirements as the long-ago-cancelled Lockheed AH-56 Cheyenne, to which I had devoted many years of my life a decade earlier.

Will Lummis later hired Peat, Marwick & Mitchell, an independent management consulting firm, to do an outside assessment of the condition of the company. When their study was finished, it agreed completely with the analysis that I had done for Will before he put me in charge. Will later said that he could have saved $250,000 if he had used mine.

The same day that he put me in charge, Will Lummis told Stuelpnagel that he was making a change. Jack Real was going to be the president of the company. Tom was going to be the chairman of the board, and his only responsibility would be commercial derivatives of the existing Hughes helicopters. He would have nothing to do with the US Army, the US Marine Corps or with any other military work.

The next day, Stuelpnagel called me to arrange a meeting, off campus, to discuss this turn of events.

"Well, I guess we're working together," he began. "What do you think about the arrangement?"

"It's Will's company," I said. "If he wants to do it, he can do anything he wants. I just wish him the best of luck."

It was obvious that Tom didn't want me, but I didn't want him either. I had enough to do without having to put up with his pettiness.

I asked him, "Doesn't it bother you that the company hasn't made any money in years?"

He just scowled.

The following day, Friday, September 28, Stuelpnagel made contact with a retired US Army general, and over the weekend, the two of them proceeded to telephone a dozen high-ranking officers and civilians at the Pentagon to tell them what they thought of what Will Lummis was doing. The two of them were like a pair of gossiping school girls.

"Have you heard what Lummis is doing to Hughes Helicopters? Well, he brought in a ringer." They whispered to the Army brass. "You remember Jack Real? Mr. Cheyenne? Well, Lummis now has Mr. Cheyenne running the company. You know what that means. You had better stop this quick, or else the Apache is going to be as big a disaster as the Cheyenne was."

At 6:00 am on Monday morning, Will Lummis received a phone call from the assistant secretary of the Army, Dr. Percy A. Pierre.

"Mr. Lummis, we've heard from Mr. Stuelpnagel that you're thinking of making some changes that involve the Army's Apache program," Pierre said. "We'd like to have you come back to Washington and talk to us about it."

Will said okay, and called me.

"Get yourself a clean shirt," he said. "We're going to Washington on the JetStar."

The next morning, before we headed out to the airport, Will went into Tom Stuelpnagel's office, and in the shortest words, he said, "You're fired. I want you out today."

For the meeting at the Pentagon, we were joined by Carl Perry, who had been the Hughes Helicopter Company's Washington representative for years.

Dr. Pierre chaired the meeting, at which we were surrounded by about a dozen generals, colonels, and civilians.

The opening question was not a question but a statement: "We hear that you're thinking of making some changes."

Will's reply was not an answer but a statement: "I'm not 'thinking' of making any changes, I've made them. The new man running this company is Jack Real. He runs everything, commercial, military, foreign, the whole works. Give him six weeks. See if he can straighten the program out. I think he can. I think it's a good step."

The meeting was adjourned after five minutes, and Carl Perry suggested that we go over to Capitol Hill and meet with some of the key congressional people. This was a mistake. Everyone we visited seemed to ask the same question: "You're not still putting out a bunch of lies about the Apache program?"

After we had spoken to several staff assistants, Will said, "Let's get the hell out of this town."

Turning to me, he added, "I don't want you back here until you straighten that company out. You have a big job."

The following morning, I was back in my office in Culver City when two gentlemen from the Office of Management and Budget (OMB) arrived unannounced.

"What are you here for?" I asked.

"The AH-64 Apache program is being cancelled, and we're here to determine whether the program cancellation should be 'for cause' or 'for convenience of the government.'"

I pleaded with them not to complete their work.

"We just finished a meeting yesterday at the Pentagon," I told them. "The Army brass agreed to give us time. I'm going to ask the same thing of you. Give us six weeks to straighten the AH-64 program out."

They agreed to defer their investigation.

The following day, I called key members of the company together to tell them of our need to complete the design of the low horizontal tail plane and to quickly test the changes on the static ship and then on the aerodynamic flight test vehicle. I could see the problem with the Apache as it existed. The tail was in the wrong place. The tail was up on top of the vertical fin instead of on the bottom. This meant that when the helicopter landed, it had to have an 18-degree nose up altitude. The pilot would have to look to the right and to the left, because it was pointed up and he couldn't look forward. The aerodynamicists could see what was wrong with it. It was a classic engineering problem, but Tom Stuelpnagel couldn't see it and he refused to try to fix it unless the Army paid extra.

I closed by telling them that the aircraft with the changes would fly on October 30. At that, one engineer asked, "What year?"

I asked him to leave the room, and announced that if anybody else thought we could not meet the schedule, they too could leave the meeting. Nobody else left.

We worked the engineers overtime, and put sections of the shop on a 24-hour, seven-day-a-week schedule. I worked seven days a week myself. I felt that I had to show my interest on weekends. I would deliver parts to our base at Palomar, California, about 35 miles north of San Diego, in the Beech Queen Air. I didn't know what they were all for or where they went, but I was there with them every Saturday and every Sunday.

Throughout those 30 days, I worked closely with General Ed Browne, the Army's man on the Apache program. In essence, he was our customer for the AH-64. He and Tom Stuelpnagel had never hit it off very well. Stuelpnagel felt that his AH-64 program manager, John Kerr, was responsible, and that he should interface with the General. Stuelpnagel had a grandiose plan and he was the president of the company. He couldn't be bothered, and he had told General Browne not to bother him. If he needed anything, he was to see John Kerr. That was an insult to General Browne, who knew that Hughes Helicopters wouldn't exist without the Apache program. I treated the General like he was my customer and we developed a wonderful working relationship.

I had said that we would fly the Apache within 30 days, which was to be before 6:00 pm on October 30, 1979. I picked the hour because, by our own rules, we would not fly after sundown. When it came down to the wire, General Browne and I both set our watches back two hours just to be safe, but the Apache lifted off just as the sun set on October 30, 1979.

A couple of months later, I was at a social event where I ran into General Ronald Keith, a four-star general who had been at our Pentagon meeting in September. He told me that they'd had a pre-meeting about a half hour before Will Lummis and I had arrived. The other participants wanted to know how bad "Mr. Cheyenne" really was.

"I was on the AH-56 Cheyenne program," Keith had told them. "Let me tell you, it was the toughest requirement anyone had to meet. Everything that was in the specifications, such as 220-knot level flight, rolls and loops, and maintenance man-hours-per-flight-hour, all had to be met. And they were met. We wrote that spec. Who met it? Jack Real did. Did he miss a point? He didn't miss any points. So why are we condemning the guy who executed the program points that we laid out to be met?

"That's why you got away with the five-minute meeting when you got in there," General Keith smiled. "I was on before you."

I would serve as the AH-64 program manager, as well as president of the Hughes Helicopter Company, during my first two years at the company. In mid-1981, Norm Hirsh, a very able man who was the assistant program manager, became the program manager. The following year, the decision was made to move the Apache assembly operation to Mesa, Arizona, and a brand-new 570,000-square-foot assembly and delivery center was dedicated in December. The city of Mesa gave us all the land we wanted for $10,000 an acre, and they even built an underpass on McDowell Road for us.

The reason that I wanted to move out of Southern California was that I felt it was too dangerous to conduct flight test operations over a heavily-populated area, especially where we had a great deal of air traffic. In the process of looking for a new site, I met Arizona Governor Bruce Babbit, who was a wonderful, challenging guy. After our initial meeting, he would call me almost every night to ask whether I had made up my mind yet to come to Arizona. I think the pressure that he put on us was a good effort, and we eventually moved to Arizona. It was a big change, though. I remember taking the Summa board of directors down on a JetStar to see the site. There was no road, just cactus. Some of them didn't want to get out of the JetStar. They said, "Who would ever put an expensive plant in that dirty desert where you can't see the end of it?"

Will Lummis agreed with me, and we got started. We couldn't have made a better choice. Mesa proved to be a perfect place to set up a manufacturing and test center, and the first production AH-64 was delivered to the Army from Mesa on September 1, 1983.

Of course, the Apache was not the only project with which I was involved during my time at the Hughes Helicopter Company. I sold the Hughes Model 300 to be built by Schweizer Aircraft

Company in Elmira, New York, a well-known manufacturer of gliders and agricultural aircraft. Our selling price was, $132,000, but our costs were running as high as $180,000 to build the machine. When we put the program up for sale, we received extremely attractive offers from companies in Canada, Belgium, and Portugal. However, since the US Army intended to continue to operate the aircraft as the TH-55, and we were unable to reassure the Army that a foreign owner would guarantee an adequate supply of spare parts, we licensed Schweizer. Their relationship with us and with the Army was excellent, and they were able to sell the machine for $132,000 at a nice profit. Meanwhile, the popular Model 500 went through many iterations, with the Model 500E being designated as the "official helicopter" of the 1984 Olympics.

COMING FULL CIRCLE

In August 1983, Will Lummis called me to a meeting down at the Bel Air Hotel in Los Angeles. He thought he was going to surprise me.

"You probably don't know why you're here," he told me.

"Let me guess. You're going to tell me that you're going to sell the helicopter company."

He was a little startled, but not really surprised. He asked me what I thought of the idea.

"I'm all for you," I told him. "I think it's the best thing you could do. How much do you want for the company?"

Without batting an eye, he said, "$500 million."

When we made the announcement of our intention to sell the company, which had been reorganized as Hughes Helicopters, Inc. in 1981, we had six interested parties. The winner was the McDonnell Douglas Corporation of St. Louis. They bid $488 million. Back in 1979, when I took over, the estate was ready to just put the company into bankruptcy. Nothing satisfies the ego better than turning around a company like this when you are 65 years old.

This was a great period for Will. He had been a great boss. He never bored me, and he was great to be with. He gave me everything I needed, and, even though he knew he was going to have to sell the company, he wanted it to be in top shape when he sold it. The turnaround of the helicopter company had been a major triumph for Will Lummis, and it was described by his estate attorney, Bill Miller, as "Lummis' home run."

It was also a great day for me, because I would be asked by McDonnell Douglas Corporation to stay on as president and to manage the company that would become the McDonnell Douglas Helicopter Company.

After the bid was accepted, we met to close on January 4, 1984 at the courthouse in Wilmington, Delaware. I represented the Hughes Helicopter Company, and Bob Little, their executive vice president, represented McDonnell Douglas Corporation.

Ironically, on the same day, across the street in another government building, under the proceedings of Chancellor Grover C. Brown, they were settling the Howard Hughes Medical Institute case, which had been going on for eight years. Bill Gay had been seeking for all that time to become the single trustee of the board of directors. On that day, the Delaware court ruled that the company would have nine trustees. Everybody that was on the board became a trustee, including Bill Gay and Will Lummis. This ruling forever ended Bill Gay's chance of becoming the single trustee. It was another big day for Will Lummis.

I rested easier when Gay was neutralized to the point of having very little to do with the Howard Hughes Medical Institute. It remains one of the least appreciated and one of the most enduring legacies left by Howard Hughes.

By this time, most of our helicopter operations had relocated to Mesa, Arizona, although we were still building parts in Culver City. Shortly after we became a part of McDonnell Douglas, I ran into Arizona Senator Barry Goldwater in his office in Washington. He chided me, saying that we should move our entire operation to Arizona. I told him that this was our plan, and he asked, "Why don't you do it now?"

I put together a plan for adding more acreage and another big facility in Arizona, and placed it before the full McDonnell Douglas board. At the board meeting in the St. Louis headquarters, I said jokingly, "Gentlemen, I'd like to purposefully move this board item as quickly as we can because there's a man waiting at his office in Washington for our decision regarding going ahead with the program. It's Barry Goldwater."

Goldwater was a key member of the Senate Armed Services Committee. They wanted his vote in the Senate, so this hastened their vote. The expansion helped turn the Mesa facility into one of the best helicopter production centers in the world. This is a tribute to Bob Morrison, from the former Hughes staff, who did the planning, and Mike McCormick from St. Louis. It was a team effort, and they did it wonderfully.

I stayed on as the president of the McDonnell Douglas Helicopter Company for two years, and then served as the chairman of the board of the helicopter company for most of a third year. I spent much of my last year in Culver City winding down operations there and planning the future of the Model 500 program.

After the 1988 Farnborough Air Show in London, I retired from the McDonnell Douglas Helicopter Company. In the meantime, I joined the boards of directors of Midway Airlines of Chicago and Evergreen International Aviation of McMinnville, Oregon. I first met Evergreen Chairman Del Smith in 1983, when I sold him some Model 500 helicopters. I was impressed with his honesty. He was a winner, the type of person I like to work with. After my wife died in 1994, he asked me to come to work for him as president of the aviation museum that he was planning. He was generous to a fault with me. He has true generosity in his heart to those he likes and respects.

Coincidently, in 1992, just two years before I went to work for Del, he had acquired the Hughes Flying Boat, which is now the centerpiece of the museum in McMinnville that I am helping him build. In 1980, four years after Howard died, Summa had sold the Hughes Flying Boat to the Aero Club of Southern California and Aero Exhibits, Inc., to be put under a big dome at a site leased from the Wrather Corporation across Long Beach

Harbor. In 1988, the Walt Disney Company acquired the Wrather Corporation, and with it, the lease on the Hughes Flying Boat. Jack Wrather was the motion picture producer who produced television series such as "The Lone Ranger" and "Lassie," and who was married to actress Bonita Granville. When they died, Disney announced plans to convert the complex to a major sea park and to not renew the lease on the Hughes Flying Boat.

There were five companies that wanted to buy the Hughes Flying Boat, including one that wanted to turn it into a Las Vegas casino, but the best proposal came from Del Smith and his son, Michael King Smith. Mike did most of the work and it was an exceptional proposal. The other proposals were also good, but Will Lummis and the board of directors of the Aero Club of Southern California were most impressed with Mike's. Tragically, Mike Smith died in a car crash in 1995 before we broke ground for the museum he proposed. To commemorate Mike's contributions, his father renamed the museum for him, calling it the Michael King Smith Evergreen Aviation Educational Institute.

My life had come full circle. After six decades in the aviation business, and two decades with Howard Hughes, I was now Chairman of the Board of the aviation museum and learning center that will be the permanent tribute to Howard's contributions to the history of aviation. For me, there is no better place.

THE END

APPENDICES

APPENDIX A

EXTRACTS FROM COURT DOCUMENTS ALLEDGING A CONSPIRACY BY THE SO-CALLED 'PALACE GUARD'.

After the death of Howard Hughes the administrators of his estate filed a legal action against various individuals regarding the estate. The individuals were called the 'Palace Guard'. The following extracts are from documents file in Case A 185995, Dept. I, Docket J, in the Eighth District Court of the State of Nevada in and for the County of Clark. These extracts retain the original page and line references.

The defendants named in the action were Hughes executives, Bill Gay, Chester Davis, Nadine Henley, and Kay Glenn. Also named were Hughes' attending physician, Dr. Wilbur Thain, and Hughes' aides, Levar Myler, John Holmes, Chuck Waldron, Howard Eckersley, and Jim Rickard.

Others named in the documents but not named as defendants were physicians, Homer Clark, Norman Crane, Verne Mason, Lawrence Chaffin, Raymond FowLer (expert witness for the estate). Hughes' aides whose names appear in the court documents but were not defendants are, George Francom, Gordon Margulis, and Mel Stewart.

EXTRACTS:

2-1.   The administrators of the Hughes estate "seek to recover damages for an extraordinary scheme perpetrated upon Hughes and his companies by the "Palace Guard" which surrounded Hughes for the last 10 years of his life. These individuals, all of whom owed Hughes and his companies the highest fiduciary duties known to the law as his executives, physicians, attorneys, and personal aides, are charged with having seized control of Hughes' empire and having enriched themselves at Hughes' expense. They are alleged to have done so, in large measure, by taking advantage of Hughes' drug addiction, seclusion and mental incompetence to run Hughes' enterprises—ostensibly in his name, but in fact for their own personal benefit—and by manipulating and controlling a virtually helpless Hughes.

2-13.   This scheme is alleged to have begun in Nevada while Hughes was secluded in the Desert Inn here in Las Vegas in the period 1966-70 and to have continued until Hughes' death 1976 and beyond. Not only was the conspiracy formed here, but substantial acts in furtherance of the conspiracy were committed here and the object of the conspiracy—Hughes' fortune—was largely centered here [in Nevada].

3-7.   And when the evidence is viewed as a whole, it points directly to the conclusion that the defendants . . . did conspire to gain control of Hughes' empire and to use it for their own advantage.

30.   The Estate further [alleges] that important acts in furtherance of the conspiracy took place in Nevada including:

    1.   The unlawful supply of drugs to Hughes,
    2.   The procurement of Nevada gaming licenses,
    3.   The procurement of a proxy purporting to grant to Davis and Gay substantial powers over Hughes' Nevada properties, and
    4.   Removal of Robert Maheu from the Hughes Organization.

13-1.   If Howard Hughes was fully competent to manage his affairs, unaffected by any improper influences of others, and simply elected to confer upon these defendants the enormous rewards which they reaped, we would not be here today. But that is hardly the case.

13-6.   The administrators of the Estate stated "that these defendants, acting in concert, cruelly took advantage of Hughes' physical and mental disabilities, his drug addiction, his eccentricities and, ultimately, his mental incompetence to help themselves to Hughes'wealth.

13-23.   Hughes arrived in Las Vegas in November 1966. He was accompanied by four personal aides. They went directly to the ninth floor of the Desert Inn Hotel, which Hughes did not leave until November 1970, when he left Nevada for good.

13-29.   When Hughes arrived in Las Vegas, he already suffered from severe mental and physical disabilities. They are of enormous significance here because they contributed to his isolation and provided the opportunity and the means for Gay, Davis and the others to take control of his assets and to [use] them for their own benefit, unbeknownst to the outside world.

14-3.   By 1966 Hughes had been a drug addict for many years. And throughout the four years in Nevada, Dr. Norman Crane supplied Hughes with codeine and valium.

14-14.   Hughes regularly was under the influence of codeine, valium and other drugs throughout the Desert Inn period. He injected himself with codeine using syringes kept in a small metal box in the refrigerator in the aides' quarters outside his room.

15-10.   Throughout the Desert Inn period, Hughes' behavior suggested severe mental problems as well. He was totally nude almost all of the time, only occasionally wearing a pajama top. He demanded that the windows be draped or closed and indicated no awareness of or concern with what the date or time was.

15-17.   Hughes required the aides to perform a series of bizarre rituals, many of which related to his unnatural fear of contamination by germs.

15-24.   This fear of germ contamination was particularly anomalous when contrasted with his lack of personal hygiene and his use of an unsterilized syringe and needle to self-inject himself with large amounts of codeine.

15-31.   Davis, Gay and Henley Marshall were well aware of Hughes' mental condition. In actions reminiscent of Captain Queeg and *The Caine Mutiny* Gay and Henley Marshall referred to Hughes' mental problems in "code".

16-10.   In 1968 Gay approached Maheu twice about having Hughes committed.

16-21.   Nor was any of this a surprise to Chester Davis. When he was told by Jack Real of Hughes' fear that Bill Gay would attempt to have him declared incompetent for the purpose of assuming control of the Hughes enterprises, Davis' reaction was, "Well, he (Hughes) may be right."

16-26.   Hughes' physical condition also was appalling when he came to Nevada. He never brushed his teeth and had a foul breath odor. He seldom took a bath or shower. His hair was approximately shoulder length and his beard went down to approximately his chest. His eating habits were very poor. He was seriously underweight. He spent most of his time in bed, often staring blankly ahead, especially after taking large amounts of drugs. He often slept for lengthy periods, sometimes as long as 24 hours at a stretch. He suffered from chronic and severe constipation, often going two weeks without a bowel movement and requiring frequent enemas. When he did go to the bathroom, he often spent long periods of time there—as much as 12 hours.

18-6.   Hughes was isolated on the ninth floor of the Desert Inn from virtually any contact with the outside world. He was attended at all times by aides, who worked rotating shifts and were stationed in a room adjoining Hughes' bedroom. Hughes never left his suite and, other than his aides and personal physicians, saw no one during his entire four years in Las Vegas except for an [accidental] contact with a room service waiter.

18-15.   Nor did Hughes speak regularly to anyone by telephone, other than Bob Maheu and Jack Real, a former business associate. He gave virtually all his messages to the outside world to his aides. Similarly, virtually all incoming messages, whether written or y telephone, were received first by the aides. Although they were Hughes' "eyes and ears"virtually all were former drivers and message clerks with no business or secretarial experience.

18-27.   The aides were the gates through which all contact between Hughes and the outside world passed. And Gay, with his principal assistants—Kay Glenn and Nadine Henley Marshal—controlled the aides. Gay set the aides' salaries and bonuses, and Gay—not Hughes—apparently controlled their continued employment. Each aide knew that if he were 'on the (Bill Gay) team" and the "boss" (Hughes) wanted him dismissed, that the person simply would go "out of sight" and remain on the Hughes payroll at Bill Gay's direction.

19-4.   The aides reported regularly to Gay, Glenn and Henley Marshall on Hughes's daily activities, including his drug usage, his physical and mental condition, and his communications. They provided Gay and Glenn with copies of, or access to, daily logs they kept of the same information.

19-14.   And they did so despite the fact that Hughes announced
         shortly after his arrival in Las Vegas "that he wanted a
         complete severance from the 'Hollywood crowd' and
         identified specifically Nadine Henley and Kay Glenn and
         Bill Gay."

20-1.   But Gay and his colleagues did not stop with merely
         spying on Hughes. Gay used his power over the aides to
         direct them not to deliver to Hughes messages which
         Gay did not want Hughes to receive and not to transmit
         Hughes' messages to others which Gay did not want
         transmitted. Aides who refused to follow these procedures
         were severely criticized by Gay, Glenn, or Henley
         Marshall, as well as by other aides.

21-17.   By 1970 Robert Maheu had become a major force in
         the Hughes organization. Gay plainly was concerned
         with Maheu's rising power. During 1970, he began
         to try to cut him off from Hughes. Gay, directly and
         through Glenn and Henley Marshall, directed the
         aides to withhold Maheu's messages from Hughes. As
         a result, Maheu's messages piled up without being
         delivered. Maheu himself was told that even his "urgen
         messages" to Hughes (e.g., concerning the appeal from
         the $145,000,000 default judgment against Hughes
         in the TWA case) were not delivered on Gay's
         instructions.

21-20.   During the year, however Maheu nevertheless gained
         another prerogative. He obtained full authority to take
         over control of the defense of the TWA case from Davis.
         22-1 On or about November 12, 1970, Maheu fired
         Davis as counsel and directed that Davis' name not appear
         on future briefs. This set the stage for a power struggle
         which culminated with Davis and Gay seizing control of
         Hughes' empire.

22-6.   Two days after Maheu fired Davis, Davis and Gay obtained a proxy giving them nearly unlimited control over Hughes' Nevada operations. The proxy, purportedly executed by Hughes in Nevada, purported to appoint a majority of Gay, Davis and Raymond Holliday as Hughes' attorneys in his name to exercise all of his rights over his Nevada property . . . .

22-16   At the time the proxy was obtained, Hughes was seriously weakened from the second in a series of bouts with anemia, complicated in November 1970 by pneumonia (during the period 1968 through 1969, Hughes was so anemic that he required a series of frequent blood transfusions).

22-24.   Dr. Crane later described Hughes as having "nearly died" from the 1970 bout with pneumonia.

22-27.   Despite his critical illness, the amounts of codeine and valium made available to and apparently used by Hughes during the weeks shortly before the proxy was obtained soared to among the highest levels of his life.

23-2.   The November 14, 1970 proxy is a curious document indeed. It gave Gay and Davis, acting together, absolute power—certainly a strange act from one who has expressed his dislike for Gay and who had authorized Maheu to fire Davis just a few months earlier. It purportedly was executed when Hughes was critically ill and under the influence of drugs.

23-8.   There is specific evidence that Hughes in later years was forced to approve employment contracts for members of the palace guard by his doctor's threat that he would cut off Hughes' codeine if the contracts were not approved. Given Hughes'serious illness, his mental weakness, his drug addiction and the use to which that was put on another occasion, his seclusion with aides loyal to Gay, and his prior expressions of lack of confidence in Gay and Davis, one may readily infer that the proxy [to fire Bob Maheu] was procured by undue influence.

23-18.   Moreover, the motive for the use of such influence is plain. Chester Davis used the proxy to get rid of Bob Maheu, lest Maheu get rid of Davis. And Gay too was threatened by Maheu's rise to power.

23-23.   The proxy gave Davis and Gay the power to get rid of Maheu. But another obstacle first had to be overcome. Hughes lay critically ill and under the influence of drugs on the ninth floor of the Desert Inn. Firing Maheu inevitably would cause a confrontation. If Hughes were in Nevada, he could be forced to testify in any litigation over the validity of the proxy. Any court appearance or, indeed, any effort to avoid an appearance on health grounds, might disclose Hughes' addiction and other disabilities for all to see and would cast doubt on the validity of the proxy. Indeed, it could well lead to an inquiry into his sanity. The proxy therefore could not safely be used until Hughes was out of Nevada. And so Levar Myler, one of the aides, took the signed document and put it in his safe deposit box at a bank in Las Vegas.

24-12.   On November 25, 1970, Hughes flew from Las Vegas to the Bahamas. He apparently had been convinced by the aides that it was necessary to leave to avoid a confrontation with Maheu. The Court may infer that he was convinced as well that codeine would be more easily obtainable in the Bahamas.

24-19.   With Hughes out of the way, Gay and Davis acted. On December 3, 1970—within days after Hughes' departure from Nevada—Maheu was fired. Gay and Davis came to

Nevada to establish physical control over Hughes' Nevada operations. They ensconced themselves in executive suites at the Hughes owned Sands Hotel and from there directed the changeover of control of the casinos.

24-27.   Maheu struck back, filing an action in this court challenging his removal. But the damage had been done— Hughes was beyond the reach of the court's subpoenas. With Davis in Nevada personally directing the litigation, Hughes' condition was concealed from the court.

25-3.   Davis invoked Hughes's physician-patient privilege preventing Dr. Feikes from testifying about Hughes' condition. Dr. Clark submitted an affidavit falsely attesting to Hughes' good health. And Davis and Gay prevailed.

30-31.   Hughes' health remained poor from the time he left the Desert Inn until he arrived in London. He continued taking large doses of codeine. His isolation, his peculiar rituals, his long periods of sleep, his chronic problems with constipation, and his poor diet all continued at the various hotels in which he was secluded.

31-6.   Then, in August 1973, Hughes fractured his hip while going from his bedroom to the bathroom. He was x-rayed by Dr. William Young in London in connection with the fracture. Dr. Young described his condition as being in a state of malnutrition comparable to that of prisoners of war in Japanese prison camps during World War II.

31-16.   After the fracture, Hughes never walked again. For the rest of his life, he was bedridden and emaciated, with a body weight of approximately 100 pounds although he was originally 6' 4" tall. He had increasingly long periods of unconsciousness, up to a day or more . . . . He was totally out of touch with the outside world and his business affairs. The aides continued and, indeed, encouraged his isolation.

31-29. Hughes' mental condition suffered from a parallel decline. According to plaintiff's expert, Dr. Raymond Fowler, Hughes was mentally incompetent by August 1973:

32-1. "Hughes . . . consumed (codeine and valium) in sufficient quantities to cloud his consciousness, reduce his mental acuity and profoundly decrease his ability to make rational decisions and judgments. It is difficult to overstate the degree to which a large intake of these drugs would reduce the thinking and reasoning capacity of an individual such as Hughes who was elderly, isolated, ill, extremely regressed and suffering from a mental disorder."

32-7. "In any mental hospital in the United States, a mental patient who showed behavior as aberrant and as regressed as Hughes would be classified as psychotic. The most likely diagnosis for such an individual would be chronic undifferentiated schizophrenia, a diagnosis which reflects a profound mental illness and mental incompetence of a chronic and regressive nature . . . ."

32-11. "Hughes' condition in these last years of his life resemble that of a chronic psychotic patient in the very worst mental hospitals. He was incapable of caring for himself or of surviving without the assistance of attendants. He was continuously drugged and his consciousness clouded. He was ill, emaciated, bedridden and incapable of normal mental and physical activity. He could not have made informed and rational judgments involving complex business and legal affairs; nor could he have given competent assistance to those representing him."

33-7.   In April 1974, [Dr.] Crane refused to continue supplying drugs to Hughes. Terrified at the risk that his illegal activities would be discovered by tougher narcotics enforcement efforts, he wrote Hughes a lengthy memorandum telling Hughes that he was afraid to continue and that Hughes either would have to be taken off drugs or find another doctor "to do what I can't justify doing any more."

33-14. With Crane reluctant to supply Hughes' drugs, [Bill] Gay and [Kay] Glenn made substantial efforts to continue the supply. Almost contemporaneously with Crane's refusal to write further prescriptions, Gay and Glenn expressed their concern with respect to the drug situation in a conversation with Dr. Chaffin. Subsequently, they tried to convince Dr. Chaffin to write a letter for all Hughes' doctors stating that Hughes' continued use of drugs was medically justified, but Dr. Chaffin apparently refused.

32-4.   The reason for Gay's and Glenn's efforts to find a drug source for Hughes may readily be inferred. As we [the administrators of the Hughes estate] demonstrate below, the threat that drugs would be withheld was the means by which Hughes was controlled. So the problem of a drug source was a grave one indeed.

34-9.   The answer came in the form of Wilbur Thain—Gay's brother-in-law and a relatively unknown physician from Logan, Utah.

34-13. When Crane refused to continue supplying drugs to Hughes, it was unanimously agreed by the doctors, including Thain, that Hughes should be taken off drugs. According to Crane, Hughes could have easily been "detoxified". Nevertheless, Thain took over as Hughes'

drug supplier in August 1974 and was Hughes' drug
connection until Hughes death.

34-8.   [Immediately after] Thain's appointment as chief drug
supplier, his influence and importance increased
dramatically.

35-17. On October 22, 1974, Hughes apparently offered Thain
the job heading the HHMI Medical Governing Board.
Thain's notes of the event recorded both the offer and
Thain's contemporaneous agreement to maintain Hughes'
codeine supply.

35-27. On November 8, 1974, Thain and Hughes had a further
conversation that was recorded in Thain's notes. This time
the connection between Thain's supply of drugs and his
promotions and contracts was even more explicit: Thain
demanded that he have firm decision on his employment
contract by January 1 and at the same time set a January
1 cutoff date for Hughes supply of codeine. The message
could not be clearer—Hughes would continue to get his
codeine only if Thain got his contract.

36-10. From November 1974 until the contracts were obtained
in September 1975, there are frequent notations in
Thain's diary regarding discussions of drugs and contracts.
In some conversations, Hughes is recorded as balking at
a contract, but Thain is insistent.

36-17. Thain used his position as the "feeder of the fish" [a
reference to his role as drug supplier] to secure contracts
later for other co-conspirators as well.

37-19. The manner in which Hughes' purported approval of
the contracts was obtained was clear to both Thain and
Hughes. Shortly after the contracts had been approved

by the Summa board of directors in September 1975, Thain recorded the following: "Meeting with HRH. First since he approved contracts . . . Discussion primarily about supply problems—seems to be a problem which totally absorbs his attention and energies. [Discussion] became quite heated as he continues to attack B.G. [Bill Gay]-feel this is *primarily to emphasize his displeasure with me for forcing the contracts.* (emphasis added).

37-38.   Thus, Thain and his control of Hughes' drugs, which "totally absorb[ed]" Hughes attention, "forced" Hughes into contracts.

38-4.   The evidence therefore shows that Thain mercilessly manipulated Hughes, forcing him to give employment contracts to most of the defendants, not to mention himself, as the price of the drugs to which Hughes was addicted.

39-24.   [Chester Davis was well aware that Hughes was addicted to drugs and of his mental condition. In June, 1971, Dr. Chaffin told Davis and Gay in a conversation in a car in a vacant lot that "Howard's primary problem was drugs; if he stopped the use of drugs, he could easily be rehabilitated and return to his normal way of doing business."

39-28.   During a walk with Davis at the Xanadu Hotel in Freeport, Nassau, in early February 1974, Jack Real told Davis that he "thought [Davis] should be aware that [Hughes] was a 'dope addict.'" Real began to explain to Davis the severe nature of Hughes' disabilities, but Davis began swearing at him in a loud voice, told him that Hughes was probably taking a lot of "aspirins" and "that he not want to hear any more about it, because it was none of his business."

40-23.   Real, who had been a close business confidante of Hughes in the 1950's, joined the Hughes organization in May 1971. Between 1973 and 1975, he again became very close to Hughes and, indeed, was virtually the only person other than Hughes' aides and physicians to have personal contact with him after 1970. Hughes apparently suggested that he wanted Real to have substantial power in running Hughes' businesses.

41-3.   Thereafter, Myler, Holmes, Waldron, Eckersley and Rickard engaged in a series of successful actions designed to isolate Real from Hughes. They literally locked Real out by changing the locks to the aides' office—which led to Hughes room—without giving Real a key. They held messages from Hughes to Real and from Real to Hughes. When Hughes asked for Real to visit him, the aides falsely told him that Real was unavailable.

41-12.   There is no doubt as to who directed the aides' actions. When [George] Francom [one of the aides] balked at the directions to cut off Real, and delivered messages to Hughes, he was criticized by Gay, Glenn, and Henley for "being a Real man." Glenn told [Francom] there were two sides, the Gay side and the Real side, in February 1976 Hughes was moved from the Bahamas to Mexico. His condition took a sharp turn for the worse. He refused to eat for the last several weeks in March and the beginning of April. By April, he was incoherent and comatose.

41-24.   Hughes was attended in his last days by Drs. Crane and Chaffin. They placed urgent calls to Gay, Glenn and Davis and requested that Thain come to Acapulco at once. On the morning of April 5, 1976, Dr. Thain finally arrived. Before examining Hughes, however, he shredded documents. Finally, the determination was made to fly Hughes to Houston. By then is too late. He died en route.

88-2.   It was essential to the conspiracy that on impenetrable wall be built around Hughes, entirely separating him from the outside world. This wall served two purposes. It prevented outsiders from looking in, and thus learning the true facts of Hughes' pathetic condition—that he had become a mere figurehead in whose name the conspirators acted on their own behalf. Second, it prevented Hughes from looking out, and establishing relations with others who might challenge the conspirators' influence with Hughes, and hence jeopardize the firm control which they wielded over his empire.

88-13.   The conspirators acted as the guards and the gatekeepers— power which they wrongfully exercised to serve their own illicit ends.

88-21.   All communications between Hughes and the outside world first were filtered through the aides, who determined which to deliver, which to delay, and which to withhold, as their instruction from Gay, Glenn, and Henley regulated, with precision, the activities of the aides. Their dominance was understandable: Gay hired them and could fire them—and could keep them on the payroll even if they were dismissed by Hughes himself.

89-22   The conspirators abused their power over Hughes in another, equally significant respect. Hughes, in his isolation, was as dependent as a child, since he could do virtually nothing for himself. Yet the conspirators failed to take the most elementary measures to protect Hughes' failing mental and physical health from further deterioration.

END OF TRANSCRIPT

APPENDIX B:

DR. LAWRENCE CHAFFIN'S NOTES REGARDING THE INJURIES SUSTAINED BY HOWARD HUGHES IN THE XF-11 CRASH ON JULY 7, 1946

Right ribs 1-2-3—involving first costochondral junction. Left clavicle. 7th cervical vertebra, involving right transverse process and right articular facets between 6 & 7, with slight anterior displacement of 6 on 7. Hemothorax left. Hemorrhage into superior mediastinum. Hemorrhage around the esophagus, causing esophageal obstruction for four days. Subcutaneous emphysema right and left chest walls. Marked shift of mediastinum to the right. Heart in right chest by X-ray. Contusion of heart.

Burns left chest wall, left ear, left buttocks, left hand.

Multiple lacerations, bruises and abrasions.

Blood Transfusions:

> July 7, 1946 = 500 cc
> July 8, 1946 = 500 cc
> July 8, 1946 = 500 cc
> July 13, 1946 = 500 cc
> July 18, 1946 = 500 cc
> Chest Taps—Left
> July 17, 1946 = 1300 cc
> > very bloody
> July 24, 1946 = 1100 cc
> > less bloody
> August 1, 1946 = 1300 cc
> > less bloody

His general conditions improved rather rapidly during the second and third days. To ease the pain, Dr. Mason prescribed morphine.

APPENDIX C:

HUGHES HELICOPTER DIVISION PROFITABILITY 1954-1973

Dated 12/14/73

With the exception of 1954, 1955, and 1956, when extensive contracting to your own Hughes Aircraft Company resulted in modest profits, the Helicopter Division has suffered heavy losses each year. A record of the operating performance only (not including Hughes Flying Boat and other aviation costs) follows:

YEAR	PROFIT (LOSS) IN $1000
1954	$ 2,669
1955	379
1956	520
1957	(564)
1958	(1,541)
1959	(963)
1960	(2,166)
1961	(3,340)
1962	(3,103)
1963	(3,278)
1964	(4,896)
1965	(1,172)
1966	(7,661)
1967	(25,576)
1968	(36,768)
1969	(15,259)
1970	(7,721)
1971	(10,024)
1972	(10,337)
1973	(Thru November) (4,356)
TOTAL	$ (135,207)

APPENDIX D:

HOWARD HUGHES' FLIGHT LOG FOR JULY 17, 1973

To: Kay Glenn
From: Marian Grazier

Listed below are the headings that appear on Mr. Hughes' Pilot
Log sheets:

Date: 7-17-73

Description of Aircraft Flown
    Make and Model   DH-125-400
    Identification No.   G-AYOJ
    Make of Engine   Rolls Royce Viper
    Number of Engines   2
    Type of Engine   Jet Engine
    Total Horsepower   3500# Thrust (T.O.)

From (City and Field)   Hatfield (London) 18:28
To (City and Field)   Hatfield (London) 20:47

Remarks   Went to Stansted & made seven (7)
                       landing and T.O. before returning to
                       Hatfield
Instrument Time   Total Time 2hr : 19min
    Actual
    Link   0
    Hood

Time—Under H.P. Classification
Land Planes (HERE HE CHECKED LAND PLANES)
Sea Planes

Footnote on Pilot Log sheet shown:

Type of Engine: R-Reciprocating, J-Jet, T-Turbine
Horsepower shown as "Meto" Power
* Indicates Night Flying Time

You will note theses sheets do not provide for takeoff time or landing time, merely total time.

APPENDIX E:

HOWARD HUGHES' FLIGHT LOG FOR JULY 27, 1973

To: Kay Glenn
From: Marian Grazier

Listed below are the headings that appear on Mr. Hughes' Pilot
Log sheets:

Date: 7-27-73

Description of Aircraft Flown
  Make and Model   DH-125-400
  Identification No.   G-AYOJ
  Make of Engine   Rolls Royce Viper
  Number of Engines   2
  Type of Engine   Jet Engine
  Total Horsepower   3500# Thrust (T.O.)

From (City and Field)   Hatfield (London) 17:30
To (City and Field)   Hatfield (London) 20:20

Remarks Total Time   2:50 (2hr 50min) See Below

Instrument Time
  Actual
  Link   0
  Hood

Time—Under H.P. Classification
Land Planes (HERE HE CHECKED LAND PLANES)
Sea Planes

Footnote on Pilot Log sheet shown:
  Type of Engine: R-Reciprocating, J-Jet, T-Turbine

Horsepower shown as "Meto" Power
* Indicates Night Flying Time

You will note theses sheets do not provide for takeoff time or landing time, merely total time.

T.O.	HATFIELD	17:30	T.O.	STANSTED	19:38
LAND	WOODFORD	18:10	LAND	"	9:44
T.O.	WOODFORD	18:20	T.O.	"	19:48
LAND	STANSTED	18:48	LAND	"	19:53
T.O.	STANSTED	19:00	T.O.	"	19:57
LAND	"	19:10	LAND	"	20:03
T.O.	"	19:18	T.O.	"	20:06
LAND	"	19:23	LAND	HATFIELD	20:20
T.O.	"	19:27			
LAND	"	19:33			

APPENDIX F:

LOCKHEED MARKET ACTION, SEPTEMBER 1973
(Before and After the Acquisition of Lockheed)

Date	Tues 9/11	Wed 9/12	Thur 9/13	Fri 9/14	Mon 9/17	Tues 9/18	Wed 9/19	Thur 9/20	Fri 9/21
Open	6	6 3/8	6 5/8	6 3/4	6 7/8	6 3/8	7 1/8	7 3/8	6 3/4
Close	6	6 1/2	6 3/4	6 7/8	7 3/8	7 1/4	7 1/4	6 7/8	6 3/4
High	6	6 1/2	6 3/4	6 7/8	7 3/8	7 3/8	7 1/4	7 3/8	6 7/8
Low	5 7/8	6 3/8	6 5/8	6 3/4	6 3/4	7 1/4	7 1/8	6 3/4	6 3/4
Vol.	4600	17000	13100	7800	30400	12000	12005	10800	5000
Dow Jones	885.76	881.32	880.57	886.36	892.98	891.26	910.37	920.45	927.9

-----------------|------------------
                BEFORE   AFTER

APPENDIX G:

LIST OF MESSAGES:
JACK G. REAL TO HOWARD R. HUGHES, JUNE 1975
THROUGH MARCH 1976

This record shows how alert Howard Hughes was in a window of our life together from June 1, 1975 to his death. We discussed these messages after he read them and gave me directions. This list proves that Howard Hughes was still active in the year before he died.

6/1/75	Hotel air conditioner
6/2/75	Dupont 240
6/2/75	Lucayan Hotel
6/3/75	General Somoza
6/4/75	Prime Minister Meeting
6/5/75	JetStar II
6/6/75	Homestead Airport
6/8/75	HK-1, IRS
6/10/75	Hangars
6/11/75	G-1 Aircraft
6/16/75	Montreal Trust Meeting
6/16/75	4-Bladed prop. vs. 3-Bladed prop.
6/17/75	Fort Lauderdale 240
6/17/75	Lucayan
6/17/75	Montreal Trust
6/17/75	Convair
6/17/75	Propellers
6/18/75	JetStar II
6/18/75	Propeller Characteristics
6/19/75	Lucayan
6/20/75	G-1 #086
6/20/75	Lucayan
6/21/75	Freeport Airport
6/23/75	Aircraft

6/23/75	Trailers
6/24/75	"Other" Lucayan Property
6/24/75	Lucayan
6/25/75	Trailers
6/26/75	Las Vegas Terminal
6/26/75	Improvements to Freeport Airport
6/27/75	Lucayan Development
6/28/75	G-BAZB
6/28/75	JetStar Serial 5118
6/30/75	Lucayan
6/30/75	Freeport Airport
6/30/75	G-I
6/30/75	Engines—Dart and others
7/1/75	Allison—T56 Engine
7/1/75	Motor Home—Freeport
7/2/75	Grumman Aircraft Availability
7/2/75	DH-125 Aircraft
7/2/75	Aircraft Location
7/3/75	HAC Satellite Display
7/7/75	JetStars II
7/8/75	Freeport—Lockheed—Hughes
7/8/75	JetStars II
7/9/75	Fort Lauderdale 240
7/10/75	DH-125 vs Falcon Aircraft
7/12/75	University of Michigan
7/12/75	Available 240 Aircraft
7/13/75	Port Authority
7/13/75	Freeport Airport
7/14/75	Freeport Airport
7/15/75	G-I #086
7/16/75	Freeport Airport
7/16/75	Convair 240
7/16/75	Lockheed Bahamas
7/18/75	Rolls-Royce RB211 Status
7/20/75	North American
7/20/75	Engine Reliability
7/20/75	Convair 240

7/21/75	Engine Reliability—T56 Engine
7/21/75	North American
7/24/75	Wrather 240
7/24/75	Las Vegas Terminal
7/24/75	Pending visit to Nassau with CCD
7/24/75	Lucayan
7/26/75	Status of Las Vegas Airport
7/27/75	United States Airlines
7/28/75	Las Vegas Terminal
8/1/75	Cargo Passenger Airlines
8/2/75	Beta Controls—Turbo Props
8/6/75	Lucayan Property
8/8/75	"House" Aircraft
8/10/75	Freeport Airport Land
8/11/75	Lockheed Developments
8/12/75	DC-9-10 and BAC 111
8/13/75	Las Vegas Terminal
8/14/75	Las Vegas Terminal
8/18/75	Tom Morrow—death
8/18/75	Freeport Airport
8/20/75	DH-125, G-BAZB
8/25/75	Lucayan Property
8/26/75	Lucayan Property
8/26/75	Lockheed—Bahamas—Hughes
8/27/75	Kings Inn and Bermuda
8/28/75	Trip to Iran
8/29/75	National Airlines
9/1/75	Fort Lauderdale 240
9/2/75	Oceanus Bay Hotel
9/2/75	Airport Facilities
9/3/75	Lucayan Property
9/4/75	National Airlines
9/5/75	Freeport Airport
9/7/75	Las Vegas Air Terminal
9/10/75	Trailers
9/15/75	Asphalt—Freeport Airport
9/18/75	Airport—Freeport

9/19/75	Freeport
9/20/75	"We Fly"
9/21/75	PBY Aircraft
9/22/75	PBY and Fort Lauderdale
9/23/75	Lucayan Beach
9/24/75	Freeport Airport Lease
9/26/75	Freeport and Oceanus
9/27/75	Freeport and Oceanus
9/27/75	Proposed meeting with P.M.
9/28/75	Status of Convair
10/1/75	Freeport Airport
10/2/75	Freeport Airport
10/2/75	G-I #198
10/2/75	Hangars—Freeport
10/8/75	Lucayan Beach Hotel
10/9/75	Lucayan Beach Hotel
10/10/75	"Prime" Minister
10/12/75	Las Vegas Terminal
10/12/75	Lucayan Beach Hotel
10/13/75	Lucayan Beach Hotel
10/13/75	National Airlines
10/19/75	Lucayan Areas
10/19/75	Las Vegas Airport
10/19/75	P.M. Meeting
10/25/75	DH-125 (G-BAZB)
10/30/75	Lucayan Beach Property
10/31/75	Lucayan Beach Property
11/5/75	Great Harbour Cay
11/6/75	Great Harbour Cay
11/7/75	Great Harbour Cay
11/9/75	Grand Bahamas
11/14/75	Kendall Nottage
11/15/75	Las Vegas Terminal
11/16/75	Las Vegas Terminal
11/20/75	Asphalt Plant
11/20/75	G-I #086 Hangar

11/26/75	Ecuador
11/28/75	Airline Merger
11/30/75	National Airlines
12/1/75	Las Vegas Terminal
12/2/75	JetStar Fan Engines
12/3/75	Lucayan Beach
12/5/75	Casino Operations
12/10/75	Birthday Flight
12/11/75	Lucayan Beach Hotel
12/14/75	Convair 240
12/15/75	Las Vegas Terminal
12/30/75	Opalocka Airport
12/31/75	Aircraft—Summa
1/4/76	Great Harbour Cay
1/12/76	Opalocka Airport
1/16/76	Las Vegas Terminal
2/7/76	Trip—Plans
2/8/76	Lucayan Beach Complex
2/8/76	Location—move
2/9/76	BAC 111
2/10/76	Princess Hotels
2/15/76	Movement of Aircraft
2/18/76	Ecuador
2/19/76	General Somoza
2/20/76	Air conditioning
2/21/76	Hughes AirWest Civil Aeronautics Board Approval Vancouver/Acapulco
2/22/76	Acapulco Airport
2/25/76	DH-125-600 for C.C.D.
3/1/76	Hangar—Acapulco
3/3/76	Pritzker
3/5/76	Meeting with Summer—Princess Hotels
3/7/76	Aleman
3/10/76	Somoza Letter
3/15/76	Somoza

Note:

No messages were submitted from 3/21/76 until Howard Hughes' death on 4/5/76, as he was not receiving messages during this time.

INDEX

A

Printed in the United States
42246LVS00002B/335